W9-CGZ-763

Dark Days

Also by Roger Reeves

King Me

Best Barbarian

Dark Days

Fugitive Essays

Roger Reeves

Graywolf Press

Copyright © 2023 by Roger Reeves

This publication is made possible, in part, by the voters of Minnesota through a Minnesota State Arts Board Operating Support grant, thanks to a legislative appropriation from the arts and cultural heritage fund. Significant support has also been provided by the National Endowment for the Arts, the McKnight Foundation, the Amazon Literary Partnership, and other generous contributions from foundations, corporations, and individuals. To these organizations and individuals we offer our heartfelt thanks.

Published by Graywolf Press
212 Third Avenue North, Suite 485
Minneapolis, Minnesota 55401

All rights reserved.

www.graywolfpress.org

Published in the United States of America
Printed in Canada

ISBN 978-1-64445-241-7 (cloth)
ISBN 978-1-64445-242-4 (ebook)

2 4 6 8 9 7 5 3 1
First Graywolf Printing, 2023

Library of Congress Control Number: 2022946112

Jacket design: Kyle G. Hunter
Jacket photo: Julio Jimenez

For Naima,
because you must
live here for now.

Geography is fate.

—Ralph Ellison riffing on axiom of Heraclitus

Contents

Dark Days

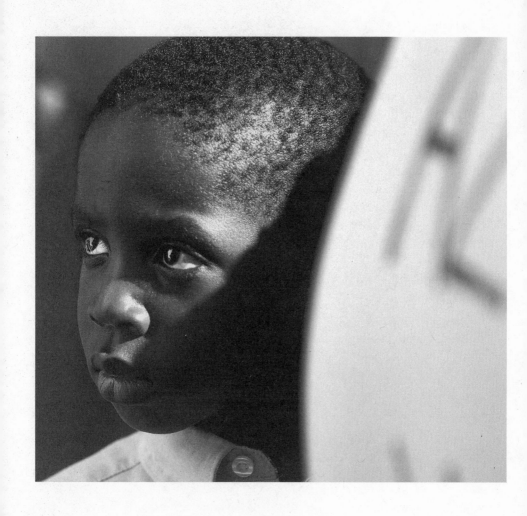

Our Angel of History

History rarely has an angel. A few dogs, some demons, and then the rest of us. But if there were an angel of history, of the historic moment of the worldwide pandemic, of the uprisings that flashed and burned across the United States of America in the summer of 2020, he lived in the photograph at the top my stairs. Every day, when the world had been sent to its sickbed and silence, I stood on the landing at the top of the steps of my house and stared at a photograph of a young Black boy at a political rally for then presidential candidate Barack Obama in 2008 in Phoenix, Arizona. Photographer Julio Jimenez caught the boy in a shadow that cuts across his face, moving from the back of his head to his chin. The shadow, which looks to be made by a white sign that bears the letters "AZ," rises vertically on his face to the top of his lip. The boy stares expectantly outward, upward, his face stoic, giving nothing away. It's a rather serious expression for what appears to be a six- or seven-year-old boy. Who taught him that—to look askance at the bearbaiting and circus of political rallies?

Whatever is being said, the boy is concentrating into it, appears to be trying to look and listen beneath it. If I were to name the picture, I might call him, the photo *The Listener*. He listens to every hesitation, every stutter, to the twist of syntax and metaphor, but what he makes of it we don't know. The boy is the epitome of silence. His gaze, his expression, is teaching me how to listen. He's looking askance at what is being made in front of him, which is how I look at and into this moment, this epoch in history. The gnashing of teeth, the crying, the hand-wringing, the dying, the killing, the speaking truth to power. I'm looking into this epoch, into the dark of it, past the light and what the light hides, looking past its slick and not-so-slick branding, past its corporate commercials and neoliberal political support for Black life, past the selfies and solidarity statements, past the loquaciousness and gregariousness of our age, which is where our freedom allegedly springs from but feels more and more like unpaid labor, like the opposite of freedom. I'm looking past our epoch's various forms of sentimentality, including our various forms of magic and magically marginalized peoples. I'm looking at what it takes, who must die to "get the bag" and "the cake" and "the scrilla." Become a boss. I want to hold in question the romantic reenchantment of the human and humanity, the disingenuous cry for universalism.

Like the boy in the photograph, I'm holding on to the leg and arm of something, maybe history. If it's history, it is not the nationalist history regurgitated in textbooks or even the revisionist history of projects that would recenter the American empire in the exterminated and deracinated people that the founding fathers sought to genocide into oblivion. No, it's the vernacular histories of the fugitive, the runaway— of nowhere. The vernacular histories of the hush harbor, of men and women who went underground, histories and practices that disappear and reappear with its practitioners. I stare, I read, I critique and think from these zones of nowhere, from the territories of the invisible, and I do it from the crowd, like the boy in the photo, *The Listener*, from among my people who are called by various names, very few of them accurate.

The staring boy is our Angel of History, except he is staring simultaneously into the present and the future. Unlike critic and philosopher Walter Benjamin's Angel of History, which is blown into the future with his back to it, blown into the future by the catastrophe and violence of the past, our Angel is unmoving, still, and nothing is shrouded from him except maybe the past. If anything, History has yet to account for all of him, all of his years, his many desires. The shadow that cuts him across the face is a symbolic marker of that obscuring, of the yet-to-be-accounted-for.

The boy stands on the precipice of a complex, momentous, and sublime moment of history. He stands at the threshold of the election of the first Black president of the United States of America in 2008 and an economic downturn that will be called the Great Recession that was, in actuality, a depression. The country, unwilling to name our financial failure for fear it might sully and tarnish the gilded dream of ourselves. The doddery and foolishness of shame. The boy seems to be staring into a militant and radical turn on the political right that will manifest in an attempted coup at the Capitol of the United States in 2021. The boy's cautious disposition anticipates the reinvigorated assault on Black life in America—the killing of Trayvon Martin, Sandra Bland, Eric Garner, Michael Brown, Korryn Gaines, Ahmaud Arbery, George Floyd to name a few of the many that would die because Black death—beneath the knee of the police or private citizen—makes the American silver shine, is the soil, seed, and water that feeds our hungry nation. Not yet has the presidential candidate and first Black president, Barack Obama, won the Nobel Peace Prize, and in his acceptance of the award given a speech about the justness of war. The boy stares into that irony, into that hubris and delusion. He stares into the nation and its mirage of justice. Most of the children and young adults who will participate in the Uprisings in the summer of 2020 after the murder of George Floyd have not yet taken their first American or world history class. Some are in the first grade, still learning to spell "was" and "said," as in it was said, "God gave Noah the rainbow sign, no more water, the fire next time." And that's what the boy is staring into: the fire next time, which looks an awful lot like the fire last time, a fire still burning in city council meetings, in state senate chambers where politicians decry the teaching of American history and inequality. In this way, the politicians of the twenty-first century remind us of our Puritan and Calvinist forebears of the eighteenth century who called for the banning of incendiary literature, called for the burning of books and ideas and people. Oh, the fire, the fire this time—what will we do with it and who will bear it and who will be consumed by it?

Like the boy, our Angel of History, I am staring at what we have become in our dark days, in this fire. I am listening into our silence. I am celebrating that, sometimes, there is nothing more accurate, more useful than silence. Remember, before the walls of Jericho were shouted down, the Israelites had first to march seven times around them not yet shouting but marching, preparing the ground for the shouting, for the tearing down of the walls. The tearing down of the kingdoms of this world—the jailhouses and prisons, the senate chambers and immigration detention centers, the corporations and the financialization of our lives—begins with some quiet. In the quiet, in the silence, we can be like the boy in that photo: seeing below and beyond the easy rhetoric, the mirage of miracles that are nothing but air. The peace we fight and search for begins and ends with being still.

Through the Smoke, Through the Veil, Through the Wind

Sometimes, I make promises to myself that cannot be kept. Yet, I make them out of some hard-to-articulate principle but one that is quite clear in my mind, clear to me as I descended through the night sky into Charleston, South Carolina, the land below me fields that my foremothers and forefathers planted, harvested, chopped, and picked whatever would come from its soil either as sharecroppers or enslaved peoples. The promise I made to myself while descending into the dark of Charleston to visit the McLeod Plantation to give a poetry reading in June of 2019—not to be overwhelmed.

I was there to trouble history, not to be troubled by it. Or, if troubled by history, not be made an incomprehensible mess by it. If there was any disturbance to be done, any razing, it would be of the former plantation owners moldering in their graves and afterlives by putting my Black body where they never intended it to be—giving a poetry reading on the grounds beneath a canopy of trees, a cotton field that refuses to bear cotton behind me, the white clapboard cabins the former enslaved bunked in to my left, the Georgian-style plantation house with its large white columns and wraparound porch in front of me.

Disturb, disturb the bones, terror, and trauma of history. Or at least that's what my host, Katherine, thought we were there to do and said as much when we were sitting in rocking chairs on the gray-painted veranda of the big house earlier that Sunday afternoon awaiting our tour of the grounds—the ginhouse, the dairy building, the cabins, the carriage house. She remarked how disturbed the last owner, Mr. McLeod, would have been to have a White woman and a Black man leisurely sitting on his porch on a Sunday afternoon. In front of me, I saw it— the whole scene, all of the former owners of the plantation, standing there, silently staring at us, angry at our consorting in this fashion, on a Sunday, the Lord's Day, no less. It made me smile, and I rocked a little harder in my chair, leaning farther back in it as if trying to relax into the thought of it, into the perturbance and all those angry faces in their bonnets and long white linen Regency dresses and one-tail frock coats and ruffle-collared dress shirts and riding boots and whalebone corsets and petticoats and deep, deep chagrins and rage, rage in their small eyes, all of them watching us.

But then the wind. The wind began to pick up and drove the dirt from the once cotton field into my eyes, and the clouds gathering overhead seemed to be trembling toward rain, and our guide, Shawn Halifax, came out of the big house and ushered us into the interior of it, as if to say we will start here.

I don't remember much about the plantation house other than the second floor was off-limits, and the first floor had these large rooms that smelled like the old, colonial homes that I had entered and visited as a child growing up in southern New Jersey. Like South Carolina, New Jersey is one of the original thirteen colonies, and, often, the towns and boroughs are older than the nation itself, so one gets used to going into old homes that are now libraries and historic monuments to observe some obscure bit of early American history on field trips in grade school. Or to visit a friend's family who now lives in one-half of an old house originally built in the eighteenth century. Or the local library in Mount Holly, New Jersey, once the Langstaff family mansion, now a library with a hedgerow labyrinth behind it that my sister and I would wander in during the summer after checking out books. The books in plastic bags banging at our sides, we ran through the tall, green-bush corridors of the maze. The traffic outside the labyrinth inaudible inside it; so inaudible that you felt as if you might truly disappear and possibly never be found. Even the birds, the sound of the birds in the trees that overhung the labyrinth seemed never to make it down into its corridors, which unnerved my sister. I would always have to backtrack to find her, hiding somewhere in the labyrinth, refusing to move.

We moved through the big house, and I kept drifting, drifting back to New Jersey, where I thought of a friend's house in my hometown, the house formerly owned by Quakers through the eighteenth and nineteenth centuries, a house that once harbored the Underground Railroad in its basement. The smell of it was the smell of the McLeod Plantation. I know it's the wood, humidity in the air, and age of the house, but I couldn't help but think of termites gnawing at the bones and boards of the house and the Black people walking on top of those old bones or huddled beneath them, underneath the work of the termites. Something about the big house seemed like smoke, or it existed as smoke, as something disappearing, something that was not there though whenever I stepped in it was firmly and treacherously there. While touring the house, I kept looking out of the windows to see where we were in relationship to the cotton field, to the clapboard cabins, to the ginhouse.

Because it was the ginhouse that I had been meaning to get back to, the brick and chicken wire, the darkness, the old beams holding it all up at the bottom of that short hill. Though I was receiving my official tour on the Sunday of my reading, I had been to the plantation the day before, walking the grounds with Katherine, my host, who thought I might want my own time at the plantation and the unmarked graveyard across the street. She was right. I wanted my own time there, to map and mark my own course across the grounds, to wander and see and touch and stay. Stay with whatever and whoever might call me. And, it was the ginhouse that called me, and no matter where I wandered, I always returned to it, to this small detail among the brick and chicken wire and darkness. A child's fingerprint. A child's fingerprint in the brick.

At the McLeod Plantation during slavery, children who were not yet old enough to work the fields or in the carriage house with the horses or in the plantation house as servants were put to work turning over hot bricks to dry after they had come out of the kiln or pulling the bricks out of their molds before they went into the kiln. I imagine the children, in their potato-sack and burlap-bag clothing (if any clothing at all) clambering and climbing over, up, and down rows of bricks sitting in the sun, the bricks hot against the tips of their fingers, the children moving, moving over the bricks and the heat from them burning the pads of their feet, their wrists and fingertips. Or did they fashion themselves a glove, some sort of mitt to help stanch and rebuff the heat?

I shouldn't do that. The evidence—their fingerprints in the brick—shows they used their bare hands. And, with my bare hands, I wanted to lay my finger in the gash, in that indentation left in the brick, but should I? All weekend, I returned to the same brick and stared—the ginhouse that once held all of the harvested cotton from the plantation reduced to this one brick for me. You might think my hesitation unnecessary, even overly cautious, but hear me out. My hemming and hawing at touching the brick had less to do with the preservation of the physical structure of the ginhouse, less to do with whether the oils of my hand, my finger, would bring about the rotting or degradation of the brick as material. My hemming and hawing had everything to do with the limits of empathy, catharsis, historical reckoning, and the ease by which we think we salve the open wounds of history and the ongoing catastrophe of racism and discrimination in America with personal epiphany and gesture, with tears and the gnashing of teeth. And besides, I had made the promise to myself not to be overwhelmed.

If I allowed myself to be overwhelmed, what would I be missing? What might my focusing on my own tears and heaving, my inconsolability obscure? How might I miss seeing the child whose hand had to turn this brick, this child who was not supposed to be seen or remembered; or, if remembered, remembered in the way that chattel or property is remembered, as another line in a ledger, useful or as useless as a shovel or hairbrush, as something outside of history? How might my focusing on my inconsolability replace this child's absence in this neat body swapping, which brings me back to my hemming and hawing, my desire to touch the brick, the fingerprint in it. What would sliding my finger into the indentation erase, overwrite, make opaque? What is gained in putting my hand into this lacuna of history?

The child does not move closer to me if I touch the brick. Their ambitions, their love or disdain for corn, for syrup, for the night sky or the feel of their mother touching their brow are lost in the flotsam of history, of genocide. It is unrecoverable. As an American, I must reckon with this absence without seeking to escape it through the catharsis of weeping, through merely placing my finger into this hollow in the brick. Because my finger does not address what allowed the brick to be made, does not address that this brick (which is a synecdoche for a certain sort of structural inequality and labor and death) still holds up a ginhouse, still holds up the fraudulent and disingenuous storehouses of American wealth. Our collective fingers pushed into the fingerprint of the child, our photographing of it, our placing our head against this wailing wall, our wailing does not tear down the walls of this house.

Nothing easy. Nothing without work. Which is what I was at McLeod to do—work, to trouble history, which is quite un-American. We Americans like to leave our history like we like to leave our garbage—thrown down a chute to disappear into some invisible darkness or left at the curb to be carried off by men and women who wave at our children from behind beatific smiles while standing precariously close to a blade crushing and cutting our sweltering and stinking waste, the trash truck's maul churning, churning our garbage, compacting it as it moves off and out into the distance. And we go back into the house; we move on. "Move on" is what this country wants Black folks to do. Touch the old wounds, the old brick, cry a little if you must, and shut up about it.

But the old wounds are not so old. They have not been closed or dressed. In fact, some of the old wounds, most of the old wounds, are opened and opened again with the reinvention and renovation of the old lash. Though our children are no longer on plantations, turning over hot bricks, they are still being deracinated and forced to bear unspeakable acts that call back to and echo the disciplinary technologies of slavery. In Arkansas, a White schoolteacher recently forced her Black kindergarten student to clean a feces-stained and -drenched toilet with his bare hands. As historian Cedric Robinson notes in *Black Marxism: The Making of the Black Radical Tradition*, slave breakers and masters often forced enslaved people to drink urine and eat excrement as ways of subduing and subjugating them. I do not recount these horrors to be salacious or to muck about in spectacle but to exemplify that the disciplinary acts that have been used historically to make slaves have been recalibrated and reinstituted in our public schools, which are responsible for making citizens. What is that teacher making in that moment? What is she teaching us about the nation and what we love and whose children must be subdued and who does the subduing?

The Black child in Arkansas in 2021, the children on the McLeod Plantation in the eighteenth and nineteenth centuries turning over hot bricks, centuries apart, face, faced annihilation, and here I am bringing my mouth and hand to it. Something in me wants to touch all of this despite what I know or think I know about the irreconcilability of touching the brick, despite my potential touch making nothing happen, despite my oath not to be overwhelmed, not to put my body in the way of history and its lacuna.

Despite my oath, I touch the bricks. I touch the fingerprint. I photograph it, but I know I've done nothing in the touching. I've reconciled nothing. There's no relief in the touching, only the sense that I've transgressed my oath to myself, but the transgression seems necessary because I affirm that yes, I'm alive. I am more than a mind, more than a reckoning, more than a lofty principle that evacuates and voids the body of its sentience. I touch the fingerprint because I am trying get beyond the imposed limits of my Black life. Which is to say I'm trying to get to life and that more abundantly. A life beyond what history can imagine. A life beyond the gates and brick and lash, where the velocity of the dead's ambition is in the wind—is the wind.

The tour of the plantation, my memory of it, is slipping from me. I remember standing at the carriage house with Shawn and Katherine discussing what we would do if it rained and the poetry reading could not be held outdoors at the edge of the cotton field. However, I don't remember anything about the carriage house, its function, its history, the significance of it in the everyday life of the plantation. I was still distracted not only by the child's fingerprint in the brick but also by the story of the plantation and enslaved folks who resided in the small white clapboard cabins at the edge of it at the end of the Civil War.

Here's the story as it was told to me. The Union Army established a camp at the far edge of James Island on the beach, now known as Folly Beach. Word, somehow, made it to the enslaved folks on the McLeod Plantation that if they could reach the Union Army stationed on the beach then they would be free. But they had to journey tens of miles of woods and wetlands infested with Confederate troops and encampments to get there. A group of enslaved Black folks ranging in age from ten months to eighty struck out into the forest and swamp at the edge of the plantation at night. Somehow, they made it undetected through the woods, to the beach, to this New World or at least their version of it.

Since hearing of their flight, their journey out of slavery through the pines and stinging insects, into the marshes and wetlands, I imagined or tried to, at least, imagine what that flight must have felt like, moving off a plantation that you possibly had never left before, walking toward the Atlantic, then coming upon that big body of water. A body of water that you possibly crossed a few years before in the hold of a ship in shackles. Now, ironically, you must walk back toward it to gain your freedom. And, if you hadn't crossed it before, surely you had heard of it, maybe learned of it, learned of this torturous trip across this abyss. Or, maybe you hadn't. Maybe the water lapping against the shore and rolling out to more water was to be your first glimpse of freedom. To see out onto the water, out onto its largeness must have felt like an apocalypse and simultaneously an act of creation. I can't help but think of moments like this as radical imagining. These folks walking off that plantation had to imagine into several abysses. The abyss of the woods, the abyss of the water, the possibility of capture, disappearance, liberation. Abyss, abyss, abyss. Moving out into those many abysses required what the old parishioners in the Pentecostal church I grew up in called "stepping out on faith," which is a kind of art and artistic practice. "Stepping out on faith" is the practice of inhabiting the invisible, moving off feeling and sound, negotiating the future not by sight but by touch even if what must be touched has not yet arrived. This might not make sense, but you might have to expand what you know of sense—what it is to feel, what it is to come to something, to come to something like freedom—to touch what can and cannot be felt. This feeling for the future is a matter of art, the art of self-making, of fashion and fashioning a life in bondage and out. This is not a matter of the king having no clothes on, strutting down the street in his birthday suit, as much as it is a matter of the people leaving the king's story altogether, taking to the woods with what they can carry in their hands and building their own thing, their own sound, their own story, sewing their own clothes. The "it" here is freedom—the making and inhabiting of it. Allow the king to wear whatever suit—real or imagined—he wants, without a gawking or judgmental eye because the People are no longer concerned with the Kingdom. They have left for the future, stepping out into the abyss.

"Stepping out on faith," stepping out into the abyss of escape is about occupying a nonexistent form and turning that into fact. In the case of the enslaved on the McLeod Plantation, the fact was freedom; the form—that it existed. In the middle of the catastrophe of slavery. I can't help but think of Frederick Douglass who wrote in *Narrative of the Life of Frederick Douglass*, his first slave narrative, that after fighting back and whipping the slave breaker Edward Covey, "however long I might remain a slave in form, the day had passed forever when I could be a slave in fact." Douglass understood that freedom did not exist in some amorphous future but could be occupied in the middle of his enslavement. Occupying that freedom required a willingness to do the unthinkable, the ungovernable—to step into the sublime—to fight. I would caution us not to sequester fighting to only the realm of pugilism and combat. Fighting can take a whole host of forms. And running away, stealing away, which is a type of silence, is one.

Where was I?

Shawn, Katherine, and I were somewhere in one of the white, clapboard slave cabins that line the drive that dead-ends at the big house. The cabins, in their quietness and vacancy, reminded me of mourners, their heads bowed as if to offer a counterargument to the line of trees arching over them leading toward the picturesque plantation house with its stately columns. It's as if in the cabins' hush they are whispering, "Don't be fooled by this constructed beauty. What lies ahead, that big house, isn't beauty. It is actually the absence of beauty." Or the quietness, their curated dilapidation is saying something about what it takes to build a big house, a plantation—amnesia, moral decrepitude, and death.

Regardless, I was somewhere inside a cabin. An outline of a cross was high on what I would call the front wall of the cabin, a wall where a potbellied stove might have stood. Stenciled along the other walls were passages from the King James Version of the Bible, but the sun had faded the passages so that they were difficult to read. I squinted and tried. Shawn explained to Katherine and me that this particular cabin used to be a church; that, in fact, the descendants of those enslaved on the plantation had lived in the cabins—the slave cabins—into the 1990s. I was—and am—stunned by this fact—and shouldn't be. That Black folks lived, married, loved, raised children, prayed, worried in these cabins in some form or fashion through the Civil War into the twentieth century and Jim Crow and past Jim Crow and Civil Rights and the Berlin Wall falling. They lived in these cabins during the assassinations of Patrice Lumumba, Malcolm X, and Martin Luther King. They lived in these cabins well into the first Bush administration, the LA Riots, the first Gulf War, the beginning of the tech boom. These cabins not much bigger than two walk-in closets at best. These cabins with no electricity or running water. These cabins Black folks rented— rented! in hopes of buying—from the descendants of their former masters, working the same land as sharecroppers that they once worked as enslaved. They had to pay for the pleasure of this.

I was overwhelmed but trying not to show it. I was trying to make it through the tour without breaking down there in the dark heat of that cabin, but the day, the heat, the history started to press against me; was moving inside me, fraying me, and it wanted out. Or, at least, wanted me to register it, touch it, without some hard-to-articulate principle guiding me through the flotsam and jetsam of it. And, I wondered if it was time to relinquish the promise that I made myself—not to be overwhelmed—while taxiing on that dark runway, whether it was a worthwhile promise at all. Should the promise be scrapped? Or, had it offered me a reprieve, a moment to sit in the complexity and largeness of something like three hundred years of Black people forced to work and love and make do on a piece of land? Had my promise allowed me to contend with the ongoingness of that catastrophe, an ongoingness that was still there in the cabins?

Yes, laudable to want to face history without centering the self, to allow the past its full body without obscuring it with my own, but my body couldn't be ignored because my body was sign of the ongoing and uninterrupted phenomenon of Black folks trying to make life in and despite America—sign in the sense that we never stopped making family, never stopped making song and sound and moaned and thought and read and ran even when we were told not to. We compelled ourselves toward life and that more abundantly despite the plantation and prisons, slave patrols and vagrancy laws, Black Codes and cabaret licenses and redlining and apartheid and the police and the counterinsurgency intelligence programs and the FBI surveilling our writers, artists, and movement makers; and the Tuskegee experiment and sterilization programs aimed at Black women and their uteruses and reproductive rights and Moynihan Reports and bombings of Black churches and the bombings of private Black citizens by city governments and restricted covenants and telling us we can't wear our hair how we want and the disbelief, the constant disbelief of our inability to breathe.

I was able to make it out, make it outside the cabins without breaking down. The clouds overhead roiled and pitched, covering everything in gray. I looked out onto the cotton field for a moment of relief, for something else other than the heaviness of that dark. The wind slunk across the field, tossing up wisps of dirt. And my mind, like my eyes, drifted into the woods just beyond the edge of the field, and I was thinking again of those enslaved folks journeying away from the plantation out to the shoreline at the end of James Island. Had they looked back at what they were leaving—the cabins, the field of cotton, the plantation house? Or had they run into the pines concerned only with what was out in front of them? Did any of the children whose fingerprints were in the bricks of the ginhouse go with them? I imagined some looked back and some didn't. But if they left at night, what would they have to look back upon? Then, I remembered—no, not remembered, I was not there so I can't remember—more so realized—realized in a way that feels closer to memory than epiphany—I realized that some had to leave something behind—a child, a mother, a favorite tree, a memory—something that could no longer be touched. I wasn't overwhelmed with this thought as much as I was full with it, standing there in the door of that cabin, looking out into that cotton field that refused to bear cotton.

I thought I had made it through the gauntlet of history and terrible feelings and come out on the other side a little weary, ruffled, and singed but nevertheless whole. The white chairs for the poetry reading sat in neat rows beneath the canopy of trees next to the cotton field. The sky had decided to hold on to its rain, and I was turning my mind toward what poems I would read that would be in conversation with the landscape and the history of the plantation. Maybe a poem about Emmett Till's body coming to rest next to a dead horse in Money, Mississippi. Or a poem about running through Austin, Texas, being followed by a White man who decided to yell "nigger" at me.

But history was not through with me. And neither was the tour. Shawn motioned for me to follow him to the back of the cabins. We stepped through the unevenness of the underbrush and stood there in this little copse of trees, our feet entangled in some sort of creeping vine, kudzu perhaps. Around us, the ground undulated in what looked like little burial mounds, the underbrush overgrowing the mounds completely. I asked what this was. It felt as if Shawn had brought me to something that was not on the official tour. It felt as if we had stepped into a broom closet or crawled into an attic, into the rafters of some great hall and were touching the bones of something, the bones of God perhaps, the bones of something that was never to be touched.

When the city decided to turn the plantation into a historical site, according to Shawn, they emptied the cabins. Tossed everything out. Mattresses, clothes collected by the church for charity, hymnals, Bibles—anything left in the cabins by the descendants of those that once sharecropped, worked, and were enslaved on this land was beneath our feet. It was all beneath our feet.

I don't remember if I turned away from Shawn, but I do remember crying, walking out of the trees, walking back toward the cotton field and watching the wind blowing over it. Everything was present, too present—the child's fingerprint in the brick, the big house, the enslaved running away from the plantation to the edge of the world, the old church in the cabins, the little death mounds of discarded clothes. I wanted to bear it all without being overwhelmed, without crying, but I couldn't. It was silly of me to think I could.

My tears were not merely my version of a belated elegy for the folks that lived and worked and died on this plantation. I was in awe at Black folks' imperishability. That despite the several-hundred-years' attempt to alienate and divorce Black people from their bodies, from creating loving and meaningful bonds with each other, despite the nation's many attempts to extinguish Black folks' desires for freedom, for touch, for intimacy, for nearness, Black people consistently and constantly slipped that yoke, troubled their trouble until it yielded something else. In the middle of disaster, we made the unimaginable—joy. Political will. Mutual aid societies. Churches. Women's leagues. College funds. Clubs from Nowhere. Fraternal orders. Panthers. Deacons for Defense. Washing machines. Vacuums. The blues. Jazz. Rock and roll. The Stanky Leg. Funk. Dat Dere. And Dis Here. If there's anything worth doing in America, it was because some Negro got near it and touched it—put their shoulder, mouth, and mind to it.

We troubled history even as history troubled us, even as history wanted to keep us outside of it. This, this, this was all in front of me, touching me, moving through me. It was in the wind and beneath the wind moving over the cotton field that refused to bear cotton.

There beneath the umbrellaing oaks, I wept and watched the wind warp and bend across and over the nonexistent rows of cotton as if the wind were remembering the bodies that once stooped over in this field, separating husk from white, shoving it all down in a croker sack before drifting to the next boll and repeating. It was as if the memory of the workers was still there in the thick marsh air. Or was it their presence, the spirit of the formerly enslaved, the trace of their physical selves, tethered to the land, to the landscape, even after their deaths? Or was it the motion of their work haunting the present? What was making itself known? I couldn't tell. All I could do was feel full and cry and watch the wind work over the dirt, the dirt lifting into plumes of what I was sure was memory shattering in the air as the wind raised it, raised it from the earth.

What was I facing? What was I witnessing? And who was I, not known for visions, to see what it was that I was seeing? I had a sudden impulse to record the wind—not the sound of it but its motion, the dirt kicking up in the field. I wanted to make a short film, wanted others to see the wind moving over the shoulders, hands, backs, and faces of the formerly enslaved, wanted others to feel and see this history, in these almost invisible gestures made by the wind. In this way, I wanted companions, coconspirators, a record of this history because the wind was acting as history, making known the lives of men, women, and children who may have been no more than a line in a ledger; the wind remembering the arch and curve of their backs, the angle of their bending; the wind acted as an archive of the dead's ambitions—was the dead's ambitions. Something about witnessing the wind in this field felt liberating. The air moving, moved because of the dead. I was beyond science and scientific explanation of the wind—the uneven heating of the earth by the sun and the earth's rotation causing air to move. The wind was under the auspices of a different science, a science that bears its fact and truth not through observable data only but through movement felt along the skin, the dead's presence still in a field long after they are no longer in the field. The dead walking and working in the air, walking with me, wanting me to know they were still there, are still here—alive and living. Working. Working after death, working the day beyond their coerced labor. Working life into me, into us despite the trials and tribulations at every city council and school board meeting and legislative session, despite the surveillance of our communities by the police, despite . . . despite . . . despite . . . The dead are in the field toiling with us.

But then came doubt: Would this be enough? Would a film about wind carry, would it matter to Black folks who are facing voter disenfranchisement in Georgia, police brutality in Texas and Minnesota and all over this vast land, gentrification in Charleston along the Gullah Riviera? Would looking out into a field, looking out on what might or might not be moving, would that matter? What is the place of opacity in art that seeks to plumb the long and difficult history of the erasure of Black folks in this country? Born in 1980 and therefore a grandchild of the Black Arts and Power Movements, a child reared on vinyl records of Malcolm X's and Martin Luther King's speeches playing on a console that sat beneath the large glass picture window, a place of honor, in my grandmother's living room, I worry about the efficacy of what might be called abstraction, making a film that does not explicitly answer the call of what Black Power scholar and artist Larry Neal defined as one of the central concerns of Black art and artists—"to speak to the spiritual and cultural needs of Black people."

But the field is—it is speaking to the spiritual and cultural needs of Black people, but it's not doing so explicitly but implicitly, imaginatively one might say; another might say spiritually. The field's refusal to bear cotton is not merely symbolic. The field is offering us a type of vision, a pronouncement of the future. It is as if the earth is comprehending our history, reading the history of the land and oppression that has transpired upon it, and has decided to quit, to go on strike. The earth, there, is reading the gentrification of the Gullah and the Sea Islands off the coast of Georgia and South Carolina, reading the problem of runoff water from development projects in the area, and it is saying "no more." It is as if the cotton field in Charleston anticipated the Coronavirus pandemic, the world shutting down, and now is asking us: what should we refuse, what should we break, what should no longer work? How ironic is it that the crop that ushered America into the world economy will no longer grow in this American field. It is as if the field anticipates America slipping from the pedestal of world power. I can't help but think of Martin Luther King's fear that he was "integrating [his] people into a burning house" because of the United States' commitment to injustice, violence, and oppression not just at home but abroad as well. Maybe, this field is also articulating the burning-house-ness of America. An America in decline. A fallow America.

There is something in this field, in watching the wind move in it. And being moved by it. It is offering us a type of imagining, a way of seeing, of knowing that reminds me of the poetic (the poem, the lyric)—something tied to the past yet free of it simultaneously. A renouncement that is also an enactment. An ending that is also a beginning. Just like the lyric poem, the field does not submit itself to narrative and its attendant discourses of time, which is unfortunately how we've come to understand change, particularly political change. Everyone wants a narrative—beginning, middle, and triumphant end. Some happy future that derives from this ignominious present. But what if history is a lyric? What if the freedom you seek can't be narrated in some linear or teleological fashion? What if this field, the watching of it offers us the space—both literal and meditative—to steal away, plan, study? What if in the watching, our minds drift, and we find some answer to how to get medicine to our sick family? What if we drift and the field brings us back to some incident of pain, of sorrow that we have yet to reckon with? What if our freedom, some instantiation of it, some idea of it, is in watching wind move over a field?

And, there in the wind, in the dirt, the memory of the dead moving off into the pines behind the field. There is no definitive narrative to escaping, to freedom. It is—only is.

A Little Brown Liquor

1

"If you play with dirt, it will get in your eyes," my grandmother used to say to me after I let her screen door slam shut, and she'd look me up and down, tallying the grass stains on the knees and legs of my jeans. The "dirt" that could possibly find its way into my eyes was not just the rocks, grass, and busted-up cement in the parking lot behind the grocery store I played in as a child, but "dirt" also referred to some of the neighborhood children who stole candy, doughnuts, and quarter waters from the grocery store, whose parents sometimes sat on their verandas at dusk and drunk and cussed and sometimes fought each other, the night ending with blue lights running along the metal siding of everyone's house as the police dipped their heads beneath the threshold of my friends' houses, pulling out a drunk uncle or father yelling something back into the house. I was raised to eschew dirt of all kinds—especially the dirt of the body, carnal dirt—that of worldly or secular music, the music of Michael Jackson and the Beastie Boys, the type of dirt that might get up inside you and start to moving you in ways that caused you to turn your face from God's, turn it toward flesh and its sweat and the rhythm of your body dancing next to another and then touching that body and feeling that in the touching you've grasped something you've never had before, a brush of silence and collision of want and belonging, what you might call holy and it all in the dark of some club, gymnasium, cafeteria, or your homeboy's living room, Luther Vandross's voice now lifting above the smoke, steam, and the liquor, which you were also supposed to eschew, but Lord, the liquor, got you in your body, got you right, and Luther's pushing you toward the soft part of night, which is like a mouth, and there is a mouth on the other side of the darkness, on the other side of you, and it, too, wants you, though it confessed earlier that "we shouldn't be doing this,

I don't want to do this guy I'm seeing dirty," but Lord we're here in the dirtiest part of the night, which is also the clearest and the cleanest, if you let the liquor tell it, and the liquor is telling it, and Lord we're listening. We're listening to the possibilities of dirt and what might be arriving, which feels like a future. And, Lord, the future gets closer with your hands on her hips, your thumbs rubbing along the exposed bulge of her bones. And you notice a brown smudge on the breast of your white shirt, but it doesn't matter now. Everything is smudged or rubbing something, exposing the dirt of it, which is to say it's life. No one is eschewing anything tonight. Dearly Beloved, I'm here to play with dirt. I'm going to let it get all up in my eyes. In fact, I hope it gets all up in my ears, my mouth, in my blood, on my tongue. And yours too. Not just dirt—but the grime, funk, and get-down of it. The mischievous, rebellious, opaque, smart, signifying dirt of us, our rebellious bodies and mouths and language at the end of it. In fact, I want the ringworm and tetters. I hope to be so low, so in the dirt, I might come up talking like a flower, maybe even a worm. Maybe, freedom itself.

2

Dearly Beloved, Black life is a constant improvisation on what it means to be human, which is to say dirty. In the parlance of Outkast in "Skew It on the Bar-B," a changing of the rules. From old school to new school and back again. A simultaneity. Bad and boujee. Being in time and out of time—yet being on time. In other words, timeless but hella present. As a practitioner of this sort of living, I am constantly astounded at the discourse Black folks have created to transmit, signify, and inhabit the hoodoo, heteroglossia, and hauntings of our improvisational and luxuriant lives. We've created a sonic landscape in which we can ironize, cry, and celebrate Black life in the space of one line of verse. Louis Armstrong's "(What Did I Do to Be So) Black and Blue?," for instance. In Armstrong's singing you can hear both a smile and a wince of pain and simultaneously a little laugh as the term *blue* in the chorus takes on a plethora of meaning. It's a shifting blue—a blue of both midnight and the river that calls you a little too close, a blue that Langston Hughes writes about in "Suicide's Note" when he declares the face of the river asked for a kiss. Armstrong's blue is this blue of loneliness and a blue of dawn, of possibility, a blue of Jimmy Rushing when he declares he's "goin' to Chicago" and "sorry but I can't take you, / There's nothing in Chicago that a monkey woman can do!" While it might seem Rushing is singing this song forlornly to a lover, it's a devious, sort of tongue-in-cheek confession in which leaving his lover offers the possibility of new territory, new horizons, the avant-garde. Yet and still, in Rushing's singing, we hear some ambiguity, a tinge of sadness. Black life needs and creates the linguistic and epistemological flexibility that can articulate and allow these simultaneities—getting up to be getting down, riding dirty as a way of riding clean, with an ounce in the sock, on D's and Vogues, the paint job candy-coated or suicide-wrist red. We've created a discourse that accommodates the irony of once being property, the irony of objects that can and do resist, objects that speak, moan, and make love all while dancing to Outkast or Ornette Coleman or Sister Rosetta Tharpe or that sister from around the way who sings only when she gets a little brown liquor in her, a Red Solo cup in one hand, a lit and burning-down cigarette in the other.

3

Dearly Beloved, when I think of a discourse that can lean into, luxuriate, juke, jump, and eagle rock in the multitudinous ways Black Americans must live their wide and sometimes contentious Black American lives, I think of the American South, cities like Shreveport, Macon, Port Arthur, where folks angle "over-sized automobiles / Into the ditches," just before walking up to somebody's grandmother's house to play Spades and bullshit into the blue of the morning. In particular, I think of our long-standing signifying practice, a practice inaugurated and convened anytime we had to confront the limitations, shackles, and laws of this country, laws that would keep us in involuntary servitude, leave us emotionally and culturally deracinated and bereft. Our linguistic signifying practice is a twin of our fugitivity, our running away from plantations. Often, they are conjoined and uneasily separated. Henry "Box" Brown is an exemplar of this practice, an enslaved man who climbed into a wooden shipping crate in 1849 and mailed himself out of slavery in Virginia to freedom by way of Philadelphia. In the stealing of himself out of bondage, Brown problematizes the notion that he is chattel because he animates the question "How can property steal property?"

4

"How can property steal property?" Originally, I thought Brown uttered this question in response to a reporter asking him about his infamous escape to freedom, wanting him to divulge all of the spectacular and gory details. Subversively undercutting the reporter's query, Brown offers this ironic quip, questioning not just his fleeing to freedom, a sort of linguistic impossibility, but also the fiction and fabric of the terror of slavery—the making chattel of Africans, of people. I never was able to find a source that linked the quip to Brown. I consulted my mentor from graduate school in whose class I thought I had learned this some twelve years ago. No dice. My mentor did not remember uttering the phrase, nor did he remember anyone else in the class uttering the phrase. Perhaps, he suggested, it was something said when riffing upon the legal and linguistic conundrum of designating people as chattel and objects, one of those pearls cast out into the ether of the classroom only to exist there in that fecund space beneath the halogen lights and anxiety of feeling as if one has not read enough. Maybe, then, I've come out of the depths and abyss with this phrase, out of the hole of the earth. Dearly Beloved, what is most important about this misapprehension, misrecollection is that it's Henry "Box" Brown's fugitivity, his daring something like freedom, that inspired the quip, created the possibility for this blue question, this blue feeling.

5

"How can property steal property?" This question animates the ironic dynamic of not only Black life in America but also the linguistic expanse of Black life, the dirt and the divinity of it. In the syntactical construction of the question, in its ironizing of the term *property*, I also hear pleasure—the pleasure of eloquence, of rhetoric, of trouble that I associate with the luxuriant abjection of Black life. It is the making of a delicacy out of offal, out of the discarded, the guts, the marginal, the impolite; Black life revels in the possibility of the awful, in the din as an opportunity for discourse. Rather than eschewing or trying to gussy up the absurdity of designating *human* flesh property, this question— "How can property steal property?"—dwells in the absurdity of it all. For instance, I begin to think of other sorts of property—a shovel, a cow, a book—acting with agency. Imagine a cow jumping over a fence and running down a dirt road, itself stealing away, or a cow trying to steal another cow, or a cow stealing a shovel from his owner's barn or a book from his owner's shelf. You get the idea, the absurdity of it all. This question creates this sort of ripple effect, this visual and linguistic possibility. It is at once playful and simultaneously deadly serious. This simultaneity is the luxurious abundance of Black southern speech and the Black American linguistic tradition. Its ironies are like Russian nesting dolls. One doll contains another. One ironic gesture contains another, each gesture a wider smile, a sharper knife. And more blood on the soil.

6

The playfulness in Black speech is the pleasure of getting free while cakewalking the master's discourse—liberation through inhabiting the anarchic possibility of mimicry but with a dip in the hip and letting the backbone slip. What the philosopher and rhetorician Judith Butler might call "subversive repetition." What we in the Black community might call "signifying" or "cakewalking," a mucking up and mucking about in the master's musty clothes while making them fresh—wearing a fitted or porkpie hat off-center, letting it lean, cut across the forehead, the brim pointing toward the sky as if to say "I'm so fly my hat can only point heavenward." Cakewalking repurposes the master's music and march. Enslaved people mimicked their White masters' "walk" or walking but with hyperbole, with a variation, a variation that troubled beauty, troubled European convention and aesthetics. This sort of walking and dancing became so popular that White folks emulated it, not realizing that this Black dance tradition they were now mimicking was one that actually mocked them, their waltzes, their better-than-thou airs, their humanity. This sort of signifying and ironizing of Whiteness is the subversive practice of southern Black discourse. This is the *dirty* in the term *Dirty South*. This signifying, playing in and wallowing in abjection. A refusal to wipe clean or sanitize the long history of living on the land that our foremothers and forefathers slaved, worked, sharecropped, bought, bonded, and bled upon. It's a being that decenters a White sensibility, a White gaze, decenters the notion that dirt, in its basicness, in its vulgarity, must be eschewed, wiped clean after the abjection of working in a field. In the southern vernacular tradition—from spirituals to field hollers to blues to jazz to rock to hip-hop—grime, dirt, the rough, the ugly, are all essential, welcomed, played with; it has its own eloquence—the eloquence of the moan, the bark, the holler, the growl. This eloquent vulgarity marks the inception of the improvisatory nature of Black life existing and emanating despite the casualness of the daily violence that Black life encounters.

Through its de-creation and rabble, this vulgarity (here I am using the term to mean "of the everyday") creates an illegibility, an opacity, that allows for its emancipatory possibilities to go undetected. It's Muhammad Ali's rope-a-dope. Look over there, while over here I'm doing the actual work of getting free. Black folks have used these sorts of disguises, feints, and ruses throughout our long history of subjection in America. Whether it be with the loudness of our voices, with drums that helped enslaved folks communicate with one another without the master's or White folks' knowledge during slave revolts, or through the hushing of our voices in the subversive zones of Black study known as hush harbors, Black folks have deployed the subversive nature of sound to articulate Black life—its pleasures, its indeterminacies, its pain. Again, an improvisation on what it means to be human.

7

Dearly Beloved, in our playing in the dirt and dirtiness of the intellectual life of Black folks, I would have you turn your attention and your Bibles to the signifying, cakewalking pleasure-practice of Zora Neale Hurston, the hoodoo-ist of the hoodoo of the Black vernacular, a Negro-ologist who annotated and sometimes annoyed the Niggerati, an anthropologist and folklorist who collected the bones of our knowledge often left in the dust and the dark of our exile on these North American shores. And, she could write a mean short story as well. Short stories that plumb the depth of Black vernacular language and thinking, stories that explore the difficulties and conflicts of Black life in America. Take "Drenched in Light," for example, a story published in 1924 that critiques the consumption of Black people—our bodies, our aesthetic and intellectual labor—by White elites during the Harlem Renaissance. Hurston plays the trickster by dislocating and displacing the story, thus wrapping the wolf of her critique in the lamb's wool of a Black southern setting. The terror now over there, the White people those other Whites. Not us. "Drenched in Light" is set in Florida, somewhere on the road between Sanford and Orlando rather than on 125th Street in Harlem. Rather than the characters being Black artists and writers of the Renaissance, they're a grandmother and her grandchild, who has a flare for the performative but in actuality is just a child. If you do not have the story readily available, let me turn to it for you. Isis, the eleven-year-old protagonist, is ogled and fetishized by a traveling White couple in a car while dancing on the road with her grandmother's new red tablecloth wrapped around her shoulders. While Harry, the man in the car, is nonplussed by Isis's dancing and spirited ways, Helen, the woman in the car, is infatuated and asks Isis's grandmother, Grandma Patts, if she can take Isis back to the hotel where they are staying to dance for them. Grandma Patts agrees. In the last moments of the story, Helen articulates her desire to consume and transubstantiate something of Isis's existence. "She put her arms about the red draped figure at her side," writes Hurston in the last paragraph, and "drew it close until she felt the warm puffs of the child's breath against her side. She looked hungrily ahead of her and spoke into space rather than to anyone in the car." The last sentences of the story come from Helen's mouth and speak to her desire to consume Isis: "I want a little of her sunshine to soak into my soul," she says. "I need it."

Hurston's critique of Helen is subtle. It's in the transformation of pronouns. In the first sentence quoted above, the draped figure, which is Isis, is called "it" not "she." Here Hurston emphasizes Helen's objectification of Isis. Isis becomes no more than something delectable, a thing to "soak in," a prop in Helen's spiritual catharsis, in her delight. In *thingifying* Isis via Helen's desire, Hurston is able to create a powerful link between Helen's objectification and the fungibility of Black bodies during slavery and after. The specter of slavery, its hauntings and vestiges, suffuses the last scene, in which Isis is taken from her grandmother to perform and labor for White folks. This scene harkens back to Black children sold and given away during slavery, separating them from biological family for profit. The subtlety of Hurston's syntax—the transforming of Isis into a figure, from she to it—symbolizes the routinized and banal terror embedded in the lives of African Americans—how easy it is to transform Black people into objects for consumption, chattel. The grammar allows this transaction with very little fanfare. Hurston is signifying once again, making visible the terror of something like English, the grammars of it—that the violence of anti-Black racism is supported and harbored in the syntactical structures of the language, in the transactional nature of pronouns and naming.

But there's a wrinkle—Grandma Patts allows Isis to go to the hotel with Helen and Harry. Here is where Hurston performs the hoodoo of haunting the story with allegory, calling back and critiquing the patronage system of the Harlem Renaissance. Grandma Patts's allowing Isis to go with Harry and Helen to the hotel for more ogling and potential violation is the racial calculus Black artists and writers maneuvered in allowing their work to be championed by and their economic livelihoods contingent upon White benefactors during the Renaissance. Like many of her Black compatriots, Hurston, too, relied on the kindness of rich White socialites like Charlotte Osgood Mason and Carl Van Vechten for financial stability. This dependence often brought these writers and artists into infantilizing and custodial relationships with their patrons. Having to participate in this process, Hurston had to be careful in her critique of it, hence her loud-talking. Loud-talking is the subterfuge of playing the dozens out in the open but implicitly so. It takes the form of calling out, making fun of, or critiquing a person or, in this case, a system without explicitly naming them or the system, but the person or system called or critiqued feels the sting of the call-out. And, if done well enough, the mocked or critiqued party identify themselves as in, "Are you talking about me?" And, of course, the response by the one offering the critique is, "Did I say your name?" Or in the vernacular: hit dog will holler. Because Hurston was in the delicate position of herself being supported by Charlotte Mason's patronage, she had to opaquely and subversively render her critique, disguise it through the improvisatory act of dislocation.

Hurston's improvising Florida for Harlem also links the struggles of Black folks of the South to the artists and writers of the Harlem Renaissance, two groups of people who seem to occupy different social and economic positions. While they may live in separate rooms in the house of America, nevertheless they sleep and eat under the same roof. The infantilization of Black artists at the turn of the twentieth century is an extension of the ongoing infantilizing of Black people by the nation. Blackness and Black people must be managed and maneuvered toward success, toward citizenship under the guidance of beneficent White patrons or, in the case of citizenship, the State. At the turn of the twentieth century, Black folks were still wrestling with the vestiges of Reconstruction and the bewilderment of federal and state governments as to what to do with all of these free Black folks running around the United States. Do they know how to clean themselves? Do they know how to make homes, how to care for their children, how to be citizens? These sorts of misguided and frankly racist questions flooded the minds of legislators, causing them to create social programs whose purpose was to teach Black people how to live with their newly gained freedom and not soil the hands of the nation with their alienness, their potential ignorance and filth. Hurston experienced this as a southerner from Florida and writer in Harlem, and "Drenched in Light" illustrates the complicated relationship Black people have with their former captors and masters and the nation.

This sort of signifying and critique performed by Hurston is an expression of a Black vernacular dialectical tradition, one that we normally associate with Black vernacular speech. Because there isn't any dialogue or traditionally understood Black speech in the last paragraph of "Drenched in Light," I see it as deploying the form, consciousness, and dynamic process of Black vernacular speech without its sonic manifestation. In using this nontraditional example, I hope to extend what we've come to think of as Black vernacular tradition, extend it to a way of thinking, imagining, and revealing. Black vernacular speech is not merely athletic, something purely physical, something that happens in the mouth and with the tongue; it is of the mind, thinkerly, an intellectual tradition. The sound, the syntax of the Black vernacular speech can be deployed when addressing something like the syntax and grammar of our collective subjection and routinized terror in America, addressing this terror in what might seem like the master's language and grammar. The sound is philosophical; the linguistic possibilities, epistemological. Black sound, the Black vernacular tradition is an art of subtlety, of seeing a wince in a smile, parsing and procuring moments of pleasure in the middle of catastrophe.

8

Dearly Beloved, this signifying tradition of playing with dirt and letting it get all in your eyes is jumping like kangaroos not only in Hurston but in the work of the dirtiest of the dirty, the coldest of the cold—them brothers Outkast. And, the dirt is most bouncy, most fecund in the picturesque lyrics of 'Kast's "SpottieOttieDopalicious." Like a Deana Lawson photograph that captures the tattooed vulnerability and sensuality of shirtless Black men sitting on couches while holding a stack of hundred-dollar bills or a recently born baby, Outkast plays in and with the tropes of the southern tradition of the club, its eros and duende, its timelessness and ephemerality, while ironizing and signifying on the proletariat narratives of Charles Dickens and simultaneously calling back to Jean Toomer's "Karintha" from *Cane*. This last sentence was busy, some might say dirty, but that's because of the simultaneities of Outkast's citational and lyric practice. I'm just getting down where they're at. While the drum kit gives us that 1-2-kick, 1-2-1-kick that involves the snare drum, hi-hat, and bass drum talking back and forth to one another (a beat sequence that has become synonymous with hip-hop), the horns have fallen out, and what we get is André 3000, one half of the duo that makes up Outkast, setting up his short story (Victorian novel, perhaps) in verse. "As the plot thickens," rhymes André, "it gives me / the dickens, reminiscent of Charles / A lil' discotheque nestled in the / ghettos of Niggaville, USA / Via Atlanta, Georgia." Already, in the first four lines of the first verse of the song, allusion, irony, funk, grime, and the dynamic process of signifying collide, creating a sonic landscape that is at once old school (in several variations of the term) and new school, myth and reality, in time and yet out of time. In other words, an always that is also particular.

In those last four lines, André marks the aesthetic and intellectual territory of the verse. His lyric is both a song and an antisong. It is both epic (and I mean this in the classical Greek sense, with its battles and nationalisms) and a novel. The diction and syntax feel old school, Victorian. For example, the use of the term *dickens*, which refers to the devil, is not common in our contemporary parlance. And beginning his lyric with a subordinating conjunction ("As the plot thickens") does not bring to mind contemporary notions of sentence-making. It calls back to a previous sound, a previous grammar, but it's all situated over a funk-influenced, late twentieth-century hip-hop beat—new school. The song touches several old schools (seventeenth-century English literature and drama, Victorian England, funk) all while doing it in the nouveau genre of hip-hop, reminding us of what novelist and essayist Ralph Ellison said of the dynamic process of the Black vernacular—"the styles and techniques of the past are adjusted to the needs of the present."

And what are the needs of the present, the needs of André at the beginning of his verse? Answer: time, attention, rest, relief, and your willingness to slow down, to allow the song to wind up slowly, something closer to R&B or a slow drag between partners after all the fast songs had us in a tizzy, pulling us apart, and all we wanted to do is get closer, allowing nothing—not even the night's dark finger—to slip in between each other's hips; hence, the call to Charles Dickens, another layer of signification. When André announces, "As the plot thickens, it gives me / the dickens, reminiscent of Charles," he alerts the listener that a yarn is to be spun so hold my mule, and hold yours too. Prepare yourself for a story. Pause. The sensuous winding of the beat, its slow knock, confirms that despite the fanfare of the trumpet, this song takes its time unraveling before you. And, like a good storyteller, André provides a setting: "lil' discotheque nestled in the / ghettos of Niggaville, USA." "Niggaville, USA" signifies on Dickens's own stories and settings, which were often set in the liminal zones between common British citizenry and the elite—the streets. André, however, locates his story firmly in the commons, in the nightclub, "where young men and / young women go to experience / they first little taste of the night / life." André also places the story firmly in the domain of pleasure.

But the pleasure here is fraught, tenuous, and hard-won. This pleasure requires the DJ to sweat "out all the / problems and troubles of the day." As André notes, the problems of the day had been so overwhelming that he doesn't even make it to the door of the club because he was so "engulfed in the Ol' E'" (i.e., drunk). Ironically, sweat becomes the restitution and metaphor to address the problems and trials of the day. Relief comes through stressing the body more, through making the body funkier, dirtier. Relief from trouble requires troubling the body. "Work, work, work, work, work, / work," says R&B singer Rihanna. Labor is the antidote to the travails of Black life. But this labor is not that of capitalism and hourly wage work, but the labor of pleasure, of choosing your pleasure and working for it after having to work against it for most of the day; this, the labor of getting closer to the griminess of ecstasy, of dirt. An ironic labor, for sure, playing in the abjection of the body, in the funk of the flesh. The irony does not end at one's own body, but it involves sharing that abjection with another, not through Christian confession but through dancing, through melding one's body with another, creating community. There, there is transcendence.

Ecstasy in the eros of the other. André expresses this ecstatic possibility in the latter part of his verse, when he describes meeting his SpottieOttieDopalicious angel on the dance floor:

> While the DJ sweating out all the problems and troubles
> of the day
> While this fine bow-legged girl fine as all outdoors

Lulls lukewarm lullabies in your left ear
Competing with "set it off" in your right
But it all blends perfectly, let the liquor tell it
"Hey, hey look baby, they playin' our song"

In this "fine bow-legged girl fine as all outdoors," we glimpse a cor-roboration of the notion that the erotic is a laboring that leads toward ecstasy. Big Boi, the other half of the brothers 'Kast, also partakes of this sort of thinking in his verse when he describes his love interest as moving like a "brown stallion horse / with skates on / Smooth like a hot comb on nappy-ass hair." Farther along in the same verse, Big Boi asserts that he "was almost paralyzed" when he walked up to her: "Her neck was smelling sweeter than a plate of yams with extra syrup / Eyes beaming like four carats apiece just blinding a nigga." Though there is a bit of the sublime in the "blinding," what these moments elucidate is that in the South the angels who bring relief smell like yams and lull lukewarm lullabies in your ear. These are Black angels. And one aspect of their divinity, certainly not all of it, is in their ability to bring heaven to a little discotheque in Atlanta, interrupting the problems and troubles of the day as well as the problems and troubles that will eventually enter the discotheque. As both Big Boi and André attest to in their verses, these SpottieOttieDopalicious angels only pause "the trap," briefly delay three brothers getting hauled off in an ambulance after a knife fight, two other brothers busting shots, and one brother taking off his shirt and declaring, "Now, who else / want to fuck with Hollywood / Court?" And "it all blends perfectly" not just because the liquor is telling it, but because these women help these brothers to be present in something other than trouble; they teach them of ecstasy—that it's achieved through a reveling in, a working of, the body.

But more than angels, these women are also folk heroes in the southern tradition of Karintha from Jean Toomer's *Cane*. Like Toomer in his description of Karintha—"She who carries beauty, perfect as dusk when the sun goes down"—Outkast evoke the agrarian past in their description of the grace of their respective angels. This remixing of the southern past extends and complicates the long history Black folks have with the land in America—from working the tobacco rows in North Carolina to the cane fields in Florida to sharecropping cotton and peanuts post-Emancipation in South Carolina. Outkast's evoca-tion of the outdoors also creates a subversive history that counters the

New Critical works of scholars and poets John Crowe Ransom, Allen Tate, and Robert Penn Warren. Like the New Critics, Outkast play with irony and paradox, but they are not interested in a nostalgic relationship to the Old South, to the land and its political order, or in creating a closed system of reading and thinking. Instead, they bring the outdoors in. The metaphor system is wide open—surreal, as in "a brown stallion horse with / skates on." Outkast bring together multiple traditions, eschewing nothing, adjusting the past for the needs of the present, which might be another way of saying, "those brothers are dirty."

9

Dearly Beloved, this dirtiness, this melding, is the difficulty of beauty, of making beauty for and of a people who are constantly improvising their humanity, always troubling beauty and troubling trouble for beauty. This troubling, the grit of pleasure—wrestling with the devil for his light, wrestling with the light for its bedevilment.

Beyond the Report of Beauty

The dead dance and yelp far beyond their dying. This, the irony of our digital age—the dead undead in the afterlife, dancing. The image of them easily obtained with a few strokes in a search bar—"Michael Williams dancing." There, on the screen: the scar across Michael's face, his dark skin, gold chains bouncing against his chest, his arms striking the air as if beating a large invisible drum. I watched this video every day, multiple times a day, in my hovel of a studio apartment in Cambridge after his death. Michael, dead, yet released from his death each time I clicked the YouTube video's link. His body full of motion and vibrantly so. Maybe it's not ironic. The dead have always done this—moved, danced—in the phantasmagoria of memory. But now we can touch them with pixelated accuracy, where the blue of Michael's shirt becomes midnight blue, and the red a gutbucket red. In this digital age, detail that would have become a casualty of time refuses to lose its luster, refuses to slip into the fog and sublimity of an aging mind, of a bygone world, of history.

So for weeks after his death on September 6, 2021, Michael K. Williams, native son of Brooklyn, dances in a park in Brooklyn on my screen. Michael, the actor known for playing Omar Little on *The Wire* and Montrose Freeman in *Lovecraft Country,* known for groundbreaking roles that complicated American representations of Black masculinity and sexuality, known for holding his dark body unashamedly up and against our eyes, for the scar that ran down the center of his head over the right side of his face, continuing over the bridge of his nose and down along his cheek, a scar given to him in a fight at a club, a scar that defies the patinaed beauty of Hollywood. In the video— recorded in October of 2020, well into the pandemic—his arms wash the sky in front of him as if they have transformed into the limbs of some dark tree. He bows, spins, bounces, jumps, beseeches, hops, and tosses himself into the heat and thump of the house music playing in the background. The driving bottom of the beat lifts him into ecstasy, causing him to clutch his head, to yip and growl in pleasure. I watch and watch and watch Michael not only because I am looking for something to hold onto, for some memento that defies and counters the tragedy of his death, an overdose. But also because he's beautiful and loved to dance, and his darkness, his dark skin, reminds me of the hue of my own skin, my own beauty, my love of dancing, and the necessity of reveling in what one loves, even if it has taken you years to love it. The necessity of loving the way your skin moves against the skin of others or disappears when a lover puts her body on top of yours. The disappearing not a relief because my skin could no longer be seen but gratitude for the way she could see me enough to want my body beneath hers and know that as love, as the feeling she wanted.

Watching Michael dance, getting caught up in spirit, reminds me of my time wrestling with a deathless God on the floor of Full Gospel Church of God, the Pentecostal church I grew up attending. The church was nomadic, housed in homes of parishioners or the pastor, or in storefronts and strip malls up and down the Delaware River in southern New Jersey. In the summer of 1997, services convened in a storefront that shared its parking lot with a barbershop. Everything in the sanctuary—from the crosses on the Christian flags in the corner of the pulpit to the folding chairs to the long heavy curtains that covered the large plate-glass window—was burgundy or red. In that bloody sanctuary, when I was seventeen, I tarried, wept, and called out to the Christian God for relief, for salvation. My back arched and bucked against the cloth-seated folding chairs. Eventually, I found myself on the floor, my mouth stumbling over itself, stumbling after God.

The saints—the congregants of the church—implored me to call harder, to chase this God who would come closer only if I showed myself worthy of His touch; they gathered about me praying, crying, and beating bottoms of tambourines until the metal zills latched to the wooden frame of the tambourine broke off and fell about me. This God would cease his fleeing from me if I would humble myself there on the floor, becoming something for him to walk or lie upon. Clean, white as snow. Fear had driven me down onto the floor of the church. Fear of going to hell for wanting to bring my mouth to the lips of K or J who sat by me in school or at Clementon Amusement Park, the press of their backs against my chest. I feared what my life would be after submitting to those desires. Where would I reside after going underground in a casket and my flesh became the road the maggots traveled and churned to milk?

My tongue tumbled through the dark of my mouth calling "JesusJesusJesus," moving so quickly it sounded like a child's feet shuffling in fallen leaves—as if my words were the brown, red, and yellow murmur and cry of the leaves. I wanted to drive those feelings from me. I wanted relief from having to worry about living and what my life would come to after the living was done.

"Running away is easy / It's the living that's hard," sings Samuel Herring on the band BADBADNOTGOOD's "Time Moves Slow." I knew this at seventeen—the jumble of my desires to touch, to be touched, to run away from all of it. As a young Christian raised by a mother who was devoted to the denial of the flesh, a mother who never drank an ounce of liquor or wine, who upon rising fell immediately to her knees in prayer, I was taught to eschew the carnal, which included anything corporeal. If I was found dancing, I was severely punished. Any mention of desire for another was met with a disapproving face. To live in my house was to live with your body shepherded and locked away from itself—except when it would rebel. And there'd you be, at the park or on a rollercoaster at Six Flags pressing your body into another, a lock of their hair brushing against the side of your face, and for the rest of that day and for many days after you felt only that—the lock of that hair against your face. I wanted to be free of my rebellious body, to be possessed by the same spirit that kept my mother calling "JesusJesusJesus" throughout the day. I wanted to be down onto the floor of that church so that I could come up possessed, with the language of God on my tongue.

But what possessed Michael in the video I was watching? What sent him up-rocking, winding his hips, grabbing his head, yelping in ecstasy—if ecstasy is what he felt? A neon yellow bike lies discarded on the ground behind him. Maybe he heard the music wafting out of the speakers (somewhere off-screen), leapt from its seat, and started dancing. In the precision of his footwork, you can see the professional he once was—he choreographed for pop stars like Crystal Waters and danced on tour with George Michael and Madonna. His dancing is improvised but it contains the *sprezzatura* of a man who knows how to turn grit and grind into fine art, into a delicacy. His voice mirrors his dancing. His yelping moves in many directions at once—toward ecstasy, maybe—but not the ecstasy of the erotic; rather, it is the hard-worked-for ecstasy of a body that understands the weight of itself. A body not relieved of its flesh, its age, its mortality.

In the video Michael sports a thick white beard, which startles me a bit, because it conveys his age in a way his dancing and even his roles as an actor did not. Maybe the beard is another sign of the pandemic, of the isolation, of the weariness of having to sit in an apartment alone and pass the days watching the seasons announce themselves on trees, the leaves the only thing allowed to go unmasked in the streets. The dancing seems to convey all of Michael's fifty-three years, his wrestling with addiction, his vulnerability that always seemed just below the plane of his face, his aches and wants. In the video, the moaning and yelping calls to and out beyond limitation. In his arms reaching out to some unseen thing, unseen desire, it seems as if Michael is trying to call something to him, a something else. A something else that only a moan locates: a desire expressed without the locutions and grammars of language. Some din that replaces discourse.

Michael's grunting coupled with his dancing reaches out beyond ecstasy, reaches out to grace, to the desire for it, reaches out to the community who's there dancing with him in the form of a woman who wears a black surgical mask over her mouth and a long black sweater, her dancing sometimes mirroring his. Sometimes she takes the lead, her footwork mimicked by Michael. At other times they work together but contrapuntally so, her moving in and Williams moving out. Folks like to call this collective, improvised art-making "call and response." But that's not quite it. At a conference on Black poetry at Princeton University in 2019, the scholar, poet, and critic Fred Moten called it "Black sociality." I've come to think of Black sociality as a type of social work or working the social, a making of society that affirms the luxuriance and fecund materiality of Black life in America. The term "call and response" positions Michael's dancing as merely technique, as an apolitical, facile motion of brute force rather than as what it is—world-building, an epistemological and ontological intervention that disrupts the ongoing catastrophe of racism and gentrification. Michael K. Williams and the Woman in Black build a world in the middle of gentrifying Brooklyn, in what I facetiously call Season Three of the pandemic: a period when the vaccine was on the horizon and an inept attempt at a coup took place on the white steps of the United States Capitol Building.

Michael and the Woman in Black risk stepping out into the end of the world, stepping into their potential deaths to build a zone of autonomy, one that contradicts gentrification. It is a zone full of speculation, a zone of what-if, "ontological and lustrous," even science-fictional. If Octavia Butler were a choreographer and designed this social dance, it might be called "Parable of the Dancers." It's as if Michael and the Woman in Black have escaped from Kurt Vonnegut's short story "Harrison Bergeron." Like Harrison, the main character, who throws off his government-issued and mandated impairments, Michael and the Woman in Black cast off their metaphoric chains, shackles, and masks and dance defiantly in the street, overthrowing the sequestering of beauty, the corralling of Black life. Unruly and unbothered, they dance and dance and dance despite the handicappers who might come with their blue lights, batons, dogs, and heavy faces. Handicappers who fear their beauty.

If you listen closely to the video, you can hear a woman's voice, off-camera, chanting "Still Brooklyn, still Brooklyn, still Brooklyn" and "Welcome Home." Michael seems to dance harder, dance toward her chanting, as if she were calling him back into the borough after a long journey, saying, "This is where you belong, where you will *always* belong." Her voice, the tether between who he was, who he is, and who he will be. But this exchange occurs improvisationally. The dance, then, becomes a co-performance between him and his community. Together, they make a *polis*, a zone of autonomy, something akin to a State, a State that is constantly under revision, augmentation, and subject to debate, unlike most of the political states we suffer under today. The "state" that Michael and the Woman in Black dance and chant into being is not based on the exclusionary politics of citizenship and statehood—federal and state governments deciding who is foreign, domestic, or alien, who and what should live and who and what should die. Rather, they articulate a vision of a hierarchy-less future, one built on the need for an improvisational and flexible politics. A politics that calls everyone in, thus erasing the fiction of who and what is centered and who and what suffers at the margins.

By dancing, Michael and the Woman in Black resist their disappearance. They slip the yoke and dodge the arrows of gentrification that are aimed at shutting down these social acts of community. In Prospect Heights, for instance, the latest round of gentrifiers, these covered wagon White settlers, complained of the inordinately loud music coming from a Crown Heights bar called Ode to Babel, a fixture of social life in the community. Owned by two Black women, Ode to Babel caters to the Black Diaspora. Jamaicans, Trinidadians, Puerto Ricans, Guyanese, and all manner of Black Americans (from Up South to the Dirty Dirty) sit in the concrete backyard on wooden benches, their glasses and elbows touching, while inside the bar, "the DJ sweat[s] out all of the problems and troubles of the day." And if you want to chase some of those problems with a shot of Barbancourt or Flor de Caña, all the better. Sometimes, the sweating and the funk spill out onto the sidewalk in front of the bar. Unable to stomach these rowdy Negroes, several alabaster-complexioned neighbors complained to the community board, hoping to block the owners of the bar from renewing their liquor license. The local Black community rallied behind the owners, attended the next board meeting, and reminded their White neighbors that the area where they decided to lay their weary heads is a historically Black one: alive, vibrantly so, and not in the bulldozed past. In other words, mind your manners. Know how to act when you're coming into somebody else's house. Nobody's walking into your house and turning down your funky little stereo or telling you how to make your French-pressed latte. So don't tell us how to make ours.

This problem does not stop at the boundaries and bridges of Brooklyn. It's an everywhere problem: San Francisco, Austin, Oakland, Cambridge, Atlanta, Chicago, Puerto Rico . . . If I were to borrow or playfully signify on W. E. B. Du Bois's famous pronouncement in the first paragraph of *The Souls of Black Folk* ("the problem of the Twentieth Century is the problem of the color line"), I might say: the problem of the twenty-first century is the problem of the American empire, the cyclical and savage nature of it.

Here's the cycle. Those that have been colonized and subjugated, their resources stolen from them, migrate to a metropole (some place that explicitly and implicitly supported the pilfering). When they arrive, they set up enclaves and communities on the edges, in the bottoms, in the crevices, in the nowhere and abysses on the margins—where bourgeois and high society refuse to reside. Here the marginalized make life, building, improvising, and continuing the traditions and practices they brought with them. Those hoods and zones of nowhere, neglected by civil society and social programs, become havens to the children of the well-off to experiment artistically and socially, a dynamic that eventually attracts social services, dollars, and commercial development previously denied to these communities. These former zones of nowhere experience "urban renewal," which begins the grift again. The once-colonized are subjected yet again to the whims and wishes of the colonizer, forced out of their homes through rising taxes, their communities bilked of the few resources they've squirreled away, their homegrown culture seized and repurposed. A park where musicians gathered on Sundays to play bomba and plena into the evening is now a dog park where French bulldogs struggle to breathe through their inbred noses, and the music that once carried over the catalpas and maples and ginkgos now only alive somewhere in the trunks of the trees these purebred dogs pee against.

None of this process is new; it is all pornographically and gratuitously known. Gentrifiers such as universities study and decry the effects of gentrification. They create think tanks around gentrification, hold conferences on it, pay professors to write paper after paper about it—and continue to gentrify. Ironic, yes. And vampiric.

"Still Brooklyn, still Brooklyn, still Brooklyn" acts as a poetics of resistance. The chant affirms belonging: despite the gentrification of the neighborhood, it is still a Brooklyn of the Black Diaspora, a Brooklyn of the global south, a Brooklyn that is ongoing, alive, and moving beyond the catastrophe of its disappearance.

Michael's dancing stills Brooklyn, holds it in place, calms and quiets it, even as he is juking and jigging the future into being. Michael ecstatically dances in the streets because we, Black folk, want to dance ecstatically in the street. We are alive in the middle of a pandemic, despite it all.

Michael dances, raising and lowering his arms as if gently placing a top sheet on a newly made bed, and I wonder if I'm glimpsing his death. If Roland Barthes is correct, that photography embalms its subjects, stripping them of subjectivity and turning them into objects, then film and video act spectrally, embalming and simultaneously animating the objects, the dead subjects, in the confines of the frame. Video allows us to watch ghosts move in the afterlife, turning them into facsimiles of a deathless God. The dead—the ghosts—are made into objects that are beyond mortality. However, the movement of the ghosts in film and video is like that of the panther stalking in the prison house of his cage at the zoo: though his stalking accentuates the aliveness of his body, his life is confined, pent-up. This, the pornography of the medium: we watch the dead move behind the veil, but the ghosts are unaware they are in the prison of the afterlife.

Over and over, the ghost of Michael who is not yet a ghost spins and rocks on the chalked sidewalk there in Brooklyn. When he throws his body backward, was he denouncing, resisting, naming, or merely locating his death? *My death, my death, my death here!* Or was it the opposite? Rather than an announcement of his death, maybe Michael was calling out to his life—*my life, my life, my life here!* Maybe his dancing was a sort of tarrying, like what I had done on the floor of the Pentecostal church, a calling for power, deliverance, relief; an abiding in the body, in its divinity, in its sweat and exhaustion, in wanting to get outside of it while moving firmly in it.

"Come on, come on, come on now, Lord, I can't tarry," the saints would sing and moan above the organ walking the bass line and tom-tom drum thumping the bottom of what was called "shouting music" in Full Gospel Church of God. The saints' heads would tip toward the ceiling, singing out into the small expanse of the storefront church: during a shouting song, you might hear a grunt or yelp that sounded a lot like what Michael belted out as he walked in circles over the pavement in Brooklyn. A shouting full of its own logic. A logic that has not been codified or known until the shout bursts forth from the lungs and throat of the shouter.

Dancing would follow the shouting. The old folks in the church called it "getting happy." The quick foot movements, the shuffling steps acted as way of articulating the unsayable, embodying the ephemeral, the opacity of desire. The getting happy isn't like European partner dances or even the modern dance glimpsed in nightclubs and music videos. There's nothing choreographed about it. Asymmetry, improvisation, the punctum of desire orchestrate and dictate the dancing. As singular as desire is—or at least the manifestation of desire—so is the dance.

You should have seen Sister M get happy when the spirit got to moving inside her during Sunday service at Full Gospel Church of God. Sitting in the second or third row left of the pulpit, her face wincing in pain from various ailments that sent her in and out of the doors of doctors' offices throughout the week, Sister M squirmed on the padded seat of her folding chair, her body never comfortable despite an extra cushion she brought from home. To cool herself, she waved a small paper fan that depicted a brown-haired, blue-eyed Jesus sitting on a rock. She spent most of the service like this—fan-waving, fidgeting—until the music leapt out from the pulpit and lifted every saint in Full Gospel Church of God to their feet. When the organ started that bluesy walking that found its way out of juke joints and into holy tabernacles of Black churches, Sister M's eyes would close, and despite the pain, a tambourine would start flying against her wrist. She'd try to hold herself in her chair, but it was no use. Once the feeling got going there was no stopping it. Sister M would stand and start this beautiful running-in-place, almost side-to-side, her knees pulled up, the hem of her long skirt in her hand.

I didn't know it then, but I would learn—after taking dance classes in Atlanta during college—that the sort of step where the knees come up and the hands go down belonged to several West African traditions of dance. As a boy, I didn't know anything about the ring shout in the antebellum South, a tradition of worship and praise in which Black people formed a circle and danced ecstatically during religious ceremonies. In it, they could often be seen lifting and stomping their feet—getting happy—like Sister M, like Michael, like me at church, my hand waving above my head as if trying to signal the Christian God, *Lord, here am I. Come by here.*

Under the tutelage of my first college writing mentor, I learned that enslaved West Africans brought their traditions of praise and worship with them in the holds of slave ships to the United States, secretly and not-so-secretly grafting them onto Christian forms of praise their white masters foisted upon them. I knew nothing of these traditions while tarrying in the Pentecostal church all those years ago while parishioners beat their wrists and cuffs with tambourines pushing their praise, possession, and bodies higher. I knew none of this while watching Sister M dance, her feet moving so rapidly it looked as if she were levitating above the burgundy carpet. Despite the arthritis, body aches, and what may well have been fibromyalgia, Sister M never stumbled or wavered, her head shaking back and forth as if answering questions, as if saying "no, no, no" to the pain in her body.

Like the dancing disease in Ishmael Reed's *Mumbo Jumbo*, the church sometimes broke open into a chorus of getting happy. Arms reached out and up, feet tore at the floor, bodies turned and turned in circles like Michael; the church shattered into a glorious tumble of tongues. You could feel the weight of longing—longing to be outside of diabetes, high blood pressure, insulin shots, short paychecks, breast cancer, sick husbands and hospitalized wives, won't-do-right bosses, wayward children who took to the avenue with an ounce of this or that in a sock, in a pipe, in a glove box.

Was that struggle in Michael's dance as well, the struggle to free himself from addiction? He had been open and forthright in discussing his bouts with substance abuse throughout his life. Was his dancing a plea to the body, as if the body—already beleaguered with its own wounds, worries, and struggles—had to be the conduit for the alleviation of its struggles? I can't answer these questions for Michael, but in Full Gospel Church of God, the body was the conduit toward relief and release. While the church's teachings asked believers to mortify the flesh, Full Gospel Church of God's version of God required the body to become a beautiful thing, a dancing thing. Maybe the God of Full Gospel was a different God altogether from the one in the King James version of the Bible. The King James God called for a "joyful noise" and a stifling of bodily desire. The God of the Pentecostal church called for the grunt, the shout, the moan.

The only way out was in and through the flesh, lifting it higher. Higher as in taking its measure, luxuriating in its finitude, its exhaustion, its absolute presence. It must be done through the beat—the tambourine, the bass drum, the tom-toms—and the syncopated crash of the hi-hats and cymbals. Through repetition. In Full Gospel Church of God, the saints clambered toward ascension through dance, yes, but repetition catapulted and catalyzed the ascension, was the meta- and subtext of it. Repetition prepared and activated the soil for the saints to grow their desires. Repetition was a type of devotion. A call. A prayer. *If I dance in this one spot over and over again, my mouth calling after Jesus, then God, beauty, relief might visit me, might know I am serious— devoted. Lord, I only ask you to take the difficulty that doesn't allow you to be seen in me.* Like the Woman in Black pushing Michael, Michael grimacing, trying to reach where her dancing is pushing him. Going into the gut as if that is where God and all the beauty that one possesses resides. That is why Michael must grunt.

Yes, his grunting says. *Here am I.*

Here am I in Full Gospel Church of God, thrown down in memory, watching one of the saints tip her head backward, her eyes closed, singing just one word: Yes. Sometimes, she holds that yes for a whole measure, her voice trembling because she's at the edge of herself and wants more. And can almost touch it.

On Ecstasy

Freedom. It's how I come to art. It's what makes me stay. This metaphysical striving. This opaque and sometimes sublime longing. I hear it in the corners and alcoves of American music and poetry—sometimes in far-flung and estranged places. Some of these far-flung and estranged freedoms calling to each other. In Pharoah Sanders's "Love Is Everywhere," for instance, I hear a desire for freedom through his constant chanting of love's omnipresence, Sanders making his voice ragged in his reaching and gesturing toward everywhere that love might reside. Sometimes, overcome with the ecstasy of the declaration that "love is everywhere," Sanders sheds and refuses language, embraces pure sound, his melismatic runs tipping over into glossolalia. His chanting, his calling corroborated by his horn and his backing band reaching to something beyond pleasure. Sanders is making a gospel, one that sends me trembling because of the way it seems to find the bits of love and freedom that are locked away inside me and loosens them, brings them up out of the abyss of me. And, I find myself dancing. It has happened more than once while listening to Sanders's "Love Is Everywhere." I'm spinning about the dining room, my arms reaching toward the horn coming out of the speakers, my arms reaching toward Sanders's voice, which is pushing me toward ecstasy, toward freedom. This ecstasy and freedom that I hear in Sanders's voice, in his chanting and glossolalia is akin to what I hear in the third section of T. S. Eliot's "Little Gidding," the last poem in *Four Quartets*: a desire for freedom through ecstasy. And not just ecstasy as a solipsistic romp of pleasure but ecstasy as world-changing, transfiguring, liberating. Eliot writes:

> There are three conditions which often look alike
> Yet differ completely, flourish in the same hedgerow:
> Attachment to self and to things and to persons,
>   detachment

From self and from things and from persons; and, growing
    between them, indifference
Which resembles the others as death resembles life,
Being between two lives—unflowering, between
The live and the dead nettle. This is the use of memory:
For liberation—not less of love but expanding
Of love beyond desire, and so liberation
From the future as well as the past. Thus, love of a country
Begins as an attachment to our own field of action
And comes to find that action of little importance
Though never indifferent. History may be servitude,
History may be freedom. See, now they vanish,
The faces and places, with the self which, as it could,
    loved them,
To be renewed, transfigured, in another pattern.

So ecstasy through memory, through expanding love beyond desire, beyond the past, beyond the future, so liberation. Eliot's articulation of the use of memory expresses and opens up a maximal idea of freedom. A freedom not constrained by nationalism or patriotism. Eliot's articulation also expands the field of the poem, or the possibility of the poetic in articulating a not-yet-achieved thing or way of being. This articulation of the use of memory challenges and extends William Wordsworth's well-cited definition of poetry as a rearticulation of memory in *Lyrical Ballads*: "poetry is the spontaneous overflow of powerful feelings; it takes its origin from emotion recollected in tranquillity." For Eliot, memory (and subsequently the poem) can do more than represent emotions and reproduce kindred feeling. I read Eliot's characterizing of memory as akin to ecstasy. Ecstatically inhabited, memory can produce a way of being that is beyond desire and affect. In gesturing toward something beyond desire and affect, Eliot points to a *beyond*, which is a critique and reimagining of the future.

This beyond is unlike the future in that it does not uncritically carry or reconvene the past as the future tends to. Often, the future traffics in the "losses of the past," carrying them forward without subversion of the traumatic ends. Here, we can think of William Faulkner's famous koan: "The past is never dead. It's not even past." According to this logic, the past becomes both the seedbed and grave of the future.

The future is nothing more than the already achieved and archived past, a past apt to be heralded back into existence via nostalgia—as in the Trumpian carrion call "Make America Great Again," that "Again" the sound of death, the last breaths of a dying democracy, nation.

What Eliot calls for is an ecstasy that subverts and rearticulates the imagination and memory—and with them the old order, the "older pattern" of politics, intimacy, progress, and liberation. A liberation that is not deferred but instantiated wherever and whenever. Even, say, in the middle of a protest. This notion of liberation puts Eliot in a strange company, one might even say a queer company.

What I came to sense is that Eliot's articulation of memory and ecstasy is ontologically Black and queer. Yes, I'm putting Eliot's Modernist poem in conversation with scholars, philosophers, and poets like Fred Moten, Judith Butler, Essex Hemphill, José Esteban Muñoz, and Aliyyah I. Abdur-Rahman. I suggest this neither to shock nor to reify any patriarchal notion of lineage that seeks to trace an idea back to its source. On the contrary, I do it as a means of disarticulating the smooth sequestering of ideas to culture, race, or historic moment only, or what Abdur-Rahman calls the "logics of teleological progression." In other words, I'm playing along, one might say as an ensemble, with Eliot, improvising over the chord changes, aligning this meditation ontologically and epistemologically with what Eliot and these Black and queer scholars, artists, and philosophers cajole us toward in their wonderings, wanderings, poems, and essays: a beyond, an inhabitation that allows us to "feel beyond the quagmire of the present."

Those words just quoted are not from Eliot's *Four Quartets* (though they sound as if they could be), but from Muñoz, the late Latinx queer theorist. They articulate Muñoz's notion of the queer ecstatic in *Cruising Utopia: The Then and There of Queer Futurity*. Echoes are everywhere. Similar notions of escaping the "quagmire" of the teleological reverberate in Abdur-Rahman's articulation of a Black ecstatic in "The Black Ecstatic": "As an affective and aesthetic practice, the black ecstatic eschews both the heroism of black pasts and the promise of liberated black futures in order to proffer new relational and representational modes in the ongoing catastrophe that constitutes black life in modernity." We hear a similar disinclination to aggrandize the past as heroic in Eliot's "Little Gidding," a stanza after the one quoted earlier: "We cannot revive old factions / We cannot restore old policies / Or follow an antique drum." The ecstatic—Muñoz's queer ecstatic, Abdur-Rahman's Black ecstatic, Eliot's transfiguring ecstatic—requires disentangling the past (as nostalgia) from futurity, and vice versa.

This is, of course, easier said than done. Often the past is nostalgically carried forward as an apotheosis, as the cure that will allay or remediate a present ailment or condition. Hence the fascistic turn by governments during moments of economic and social upheaval. Mussolini, Hitler, and Donald Trump all called back to a prelapsarian period in their respective country's history as a way of pointing to an Edenic future. A fool's journey. A purse made to look full only because of the hot air blowing in it, nary a gold coin in its pocket. The future attached to some opaque and possibly fictitious—surely mythological—past. Muñoz, Eliot, and Abdur-Rahman push us to consider how the logics of such attachments reinscribe that which we sought to escape, bogging down the present in "old," inefficacious "factions" and "policies."

So, ecstasy. Ecstasy as inhabiting a beyond that liberates us from the future and the past through nonattachment. Ecstasy as that which can detach us from the teleological, from the old patterns of the past that delimit the potential for a new pattern, a maximal freedom. Ecstasy "not less of love but expanding / Of love beyond desire, and so liberation." Eliot's notion of the expansion of love beyond desire finds its echo, its diasporic kin in Abdur-Rahman's extension of ecstasy beyond pleasure. As she writes: "Ecstasy is not mere pleasure, or inevitability or even necessarily sexual. Ecstasy exceeds pleasure and sex. More important, it resists the logics of teleological progression by opening an immediate space of relational joy for black and brown people, for whom the future is both yet to come and already past." Abdur-Rahman's dislocation of ecstasy allows for a productive defamiliarization. No longer tied to notions of progress, either in the form of satiation and resolution or some purifying end that will fix or heal past and current wounds and historical traumas, ecstasy can be experienced and inhabited *in the wound, in the tumult*, bearing out and extending that Black vernacular adage that states, "There's a blessing in the storm."

Ecstasy, then, is a theft, one in which one steals oneself back from catastrophe, neutralizing and overwhelming something like slavery, segregation, surveillance, and American apartheid in the middle of these disasters, declaring in the face of terror something like joy. In

Scenes of Subjection: Terror, Slavery, and Self-Making in Nineteenth-Century America, literary critic Saidiya Hartman explores this complicated relationship between Black folks, pleasure, joy, subjection, terror, and the banality of that terror in the coffle, the marching of enslaved Black people to market in order to sell them, an internal Middle Passage, and stepping-it-up-lively for the master during forced dances on the plantation. In both situations, enslaved Africans were told to dance joyfully, cavort for their master, or, in the case of the coffle, for the purchasing parties. Generally, dancing is thought of as an act of pleasure, or at the very least as an act that has the potential for pleasure. It is a counterintuitive task to dance in a lively, expressive, or joyful manner if one is being compelled by a whip or a master's surveilling eye—when the end result, as in the case of the coffle, is to be sold away from friends, family, and children. In the case of slave dances on the plantation, the master gave no consideration to the fatigue of the enslaved or whether they felt like dancing in the first place. They danced until the master tired. The "pleasure," the dancing of the enslaved, was the pleasure of the master. Their dancing *belonged* to him just as their bodies did in the cruel economy of slavery.

Yet, Hartman also suggests that we consider whether there might have been fleeting moments of pleasure stolen from these everyday demands of oppression. A subversion and corroboration occurring simultaneously. Property stealing property. A stealing away while being stolen. Hartman writes:

> Pleasure was fraught with these contending investments in the body. As Toby Jones noted, the Saturday night dances permitted by the master were refashioned and used for their own ends by the enslaved: "The fun was on Saturday night when massa 'lowed us to dance. There was a lot of banjo pickin' and tin pan beatin' and dancin' and everybody talk bout when they lived in Africa and done what they wanted." Within the confines of surveillance and nonautonomy, the resistance to subjugation proceeded by stealth: one acted furtively, secretly, and imperceptibly, and the enslaved seized any and every opportunity to slip off the yoke.

Pleasure was not deferred until some later moment outside of the master's gaze but was stolen within it. Ecstasy can be opened in the middle

of ongoing catastrophe. Memory and artifice, storytelling, also participate in the furtive disruption of subjugation and inhabiting pleasure. To
dismiss Jones's testimony of Black folks discussing their lives before enslavement as mere nostalgia would be a gross misreading. As Noel Leo
Erskine notes in *Plantation Church: How African American Religion
Was Born in Caribbean Slavery*, "Enslaved people remembered Africa,
and the memory of Africa became a controlling metaphor and organizing principle for Africans in the New World as they countered
the hegemonic conditions imposed on them by their masters. . . . The
memory of ancestors and a sense that their spirits accompanied them
to plantations in the New World served as sites of a new consciousness." Memory, in the space of the plantation dance, subverts domination; and thus, allows for "another pattern," to bring back Eliot—a new
one that appropriates and contests the pattern of injustice and oppression that the master seeks to perpetuate. A subversion appearing as
corroboration. Ecstasy and joy do not have to be delayed until some
amorphous future. Ecstasy now. Ecstasy whenever.

Inhabiting ecstasy in the middle and muddle of abjection is not
only an aesthetic act but also a political one. Ecstasy as protest. Ecstasy
as a type of protest aesthetic. Insisting upon itself in the middle of the
wound, the ecstatic subverts and opposes the disciplining and oppressive act. Here, I am thinking about Civil Rights rallies and our current political moment under the Trump regime and its wake. Many
citizens—those who have fought for their citizenship over decades and
centuries—feel aggrieved and overwhelmed by this regime's assault
on civil liberties, civility, and rights. Often their response takes the
form of marches, rallies, die-ins, and sit-ins. I understand the impetus for these sorts of protests. And yet it cannot be denied that such
protests and their attendant calls for change are subject to the grace
offered by others. Redress of pain still lies outside the agency of the
pained—with political entities like Congress, the president, or the judi-
cial branch. Pleasure, agency, and liberation are again deferred to some
amorphous time in the future.

Yet what if we practiced a type of protest that deploys ecstasy in
the middle of struggle—even in the middle of the grief of protesting
police brutality? What if ecstasy were practiced publicly, employed as
a liberating force, reminding both ourselves and those who would strip
away our agency through legislation, executive order, and police baton

that our joy and our bodies are our own? Again, consider the Civil Rights Movement. Hours, sometimes even the night before a speaker like Martin Luther King Jr. or Joseph Lowery would climb the rostrum, participants in marches would arrive to sing and chant in order to buoy up their bodies and spirits before facing the water cannons, dogs, tear gas, and batons of the police. Contradicting the violence that would be inflicted on them the next morning, their singing produced a counter-pedagogy, a counterprotest of time-independent reveling in the body, even as it stood at the precipice of violation, an otherwise that did not require a future or the achievement of a solidified liberation. What was being built, instead, was what Abdur-Rahman calls "new relational and representational modes" of joy in the ongoing catastrophe of Black life—an ecstatic relationship to the present, in the song, in the singing.

These defiant possibilities found in singing are notably similar to those associated with lyric poems, which likewise display an ability to contest time and teleology and enact a mode of joy in the midst of on-going catastrophe. As the literary critic Jonathan Culler notes in *Theory of the Lyric*, the lyric poem resists mimesis through its ongoingness, its sense of "now," which does not end. In a poem, an event that took an hour, three days, or a year can be invoked in a single line. Or an instant in time can be expanded or arrested—for instance, through rituality, rhythm, and refrain. As Culler notes in an interview in the *Los Angeles Review of Books*, "While many lyrics do have minimal narratives or events in some sort of causal sequence, the stanzas of a lyric are often not arranged in a narrative temporality; they may be different takes on a situation, or utterances that are not temporally situated in relation to one another. (Think of the case of the refrain as the most obvious.)" Or as Culler puts it in *Theory of the Lyric*, "Nothing need happen in the poem because the poem is to be itself the happening." More interested in evocation, in making something happen in the moment of reading rather than merely representing a memory or history, the prototypical lyric brings us back to Eliot's entreaty on the uses of memory:

> History may be servitude,
> History may be freedom. See, now they vanish,
> The faces and places, with the self which, as it could be,
>   loved them,
> To become renewed, transfigured, in another pattern.

Like Eliot's memory, the lyric poem vanishes the faces and places of history "to become renewed, transfigured, in another pattern"—not through mere erasure but through the ecstatic, which is reified in the imperative, Eliot's "See, now." Eliot liberates memory from the old factions and patterns for the possibility of a renewed, transfigured pattern through the imperative and declaring them vanished in the same sentence, in the present tense. This compression of the past, present, and future reminds me of the "relational joy" of the Black ecstatic in the space of ongoing catastrophe that Abdur-Rahman articulates. For Eliot, the ongoing catastrophe would be attachment, and as he makes clear, the break is not clean. The renewed, transfigured pattern, though liberatory, will bear residue of the past—memory. The instantiation of memory toward a transfigured pattern is not a state of purity but one that plays in and with both "freedom" and "servitude." Like the Black ecstatic, Eliot's notion plays in abjection but is not constrained by that abjection.

Eliot's use of the imperative "See, now"—an implicit apostrophe or address to an unseen presence—makes us, the readers, complicit in the ecstasy, in the vanishing of history as servitude, history as freedom. Without us, the readers, "another pattern" is not made. The act of making the new pattern and vanishing the old patterns, making a larger, maximal freedom, occurs through the operation of reading, which is itself a new pattern. "They vanish" because we, the readers, inhabit the moment of the sentence, enacting the action of the sentence. Through reading, we've helped to open up another possibility, a beyond. It's the glossolaliac wail and chanting of Pharoah Sanders's call for love being everywhere. The invisible made visible.

This is the lyric par excellence. The lyric acts as a way of knowing, as a vocalizing of a way of being that is without order but wholly present. "Me and you, your momma and your cousin, too," say Outkast. The lyric, if played on Abdur-Rahman's piano, resists "the logics of teleological progression by opening an immediate space of relational joy." Yet it is often the space of relational joy that is relinquished in the march, the sit-in, the die-in, the occupation, because in those moments what is prioritized is the teleological, a future-looking, the other side of struggle when the action or result is achieved. Joy must wait for the resolution of struggle.

But why? Why must our joy be delayed to some unguaranteed future? Why not enact it, live it in the moment of the protest *as* protest. After all, our joy is the reason we are there. Here I am thinking of the dancing protests by queer folk when the homophobic then vice presidential candidate Mike Pence visited Philadelphia and Columbus. Much like enslaved Black folks who furtively "slip[ped] off the yoke" of slavery during dances under the master's eye, the dancer-protestors create a space of relational joy in front of Pence's windows, Pence himself a representative of State power and its long history of disenfranchising queer folks in America. Enacting an ecstatic subjectivity, these queer bodies also performed a critique of Pence's homophobia by making themselves radically present. In dancing before Pence, the overseer of power, but not for his pleasure (much to his displeasure, in fact), these queer protestors manifested a beyond in the space of abjection, offering themselves a nonsovereign sovereignty or agency that was not beholden to any normalizing or mastering discourse, not beholden to the State and its governance for recognition. The aesthetic act of dancing does not follow the logic of protest or that of the infantilized citizen who must beseech a congress of politicians or a court of judges for rights and redress. Nor does dancing follow Western notions of sovereignty. Instead, the dancing creates a din, a discourse that is both legible and illegible: a beyond without the necessity of a future.

This dancing in the midst of struggle continues today, despite the ongoing catastrophe of State violence committed against marginalized bodies. During the protests against anti-Blackness in Los Angeles, Atlanta, Newark, Durham, and Washington, DC, following the killing of George Floyd in Minneapolis on May 25, 2020, demonstrator-dancers juked, krumped, and Cupid shuffled in the middle of intersections while holding signs that read: "HANDS UP / DON'T SHOOT" and "LET JUSTICE FLOW LIKE A RIVER." Electric sliding while chanting "No justice no peace / fuck these racist-ass police," the protestors commit themselves to two simultaneous actions: civil disobedience and joy. Their bodies in motion make the case that these two phenomena should never have been separated. Although White supremacy and police violence would literally like to take the breath from Black people (think of Derek Chauvin, the police officer who killed George Floyd, kneeling on Floyd's neck for nearly nine minutes), these protestors, in the luxuriant reveling in their bodies, produce a counterlyric—one that wallows in embodiment, in breath, in the flexed arm, in the arched back, in the hop and turn. Black people dancing while protesting, as protest, in the streets, boulevards, and avenues of America subverts our disposability and ironizes the notion that we must be surveilled to death. This dancing is a refusal to be yoked. Black life will not be curtailed. In taking place in the face of the State, in the helmeted faces of the National Guardsmen and police, this dancing fugitively calls back to the coffle, the internal Middle Passage to auction blocks and slave markets during slavery, reconvening that history while subversively repeating it. Whereas before we danced unwillingly and with fear of the lash, now we dance willingly despite the lash.

> History may be servitude,
> History may be freedom. See, now they vanish,
> The faces and places, with the self which, as it could,
>   loved them,
> To become renewed, transfigured, in another pattern.

I hear something else in Eliot's last three lines: a push toward understanding memory as a way of knowing, an epistemology, possibly even a theory and poetics. That the goal of memory is to find something beyond recollection, something that is both an arrival and a disappearance, a beginning and an end, something "renewed, transfigured, in another pattern." Liberation, a maximal freedom.

Might this push to participate in a beyond that is devoid of attachment, this seeking another pattern, be helpful in writing in persona, writing in and about a body, language, culture, social position, and class that is not the poet's? I am referring to the appropriation and misappropriation of Black, brown, and disabled bodies, their conflicts, and aesthetics, in text and other media. Over the past several years, social media has erupted into heated debates over the question of who has the right to write and make art about Black and brown bodies—from Kenneth Goldsmith's found-poetry-performance-piece appropriating the autopsy of Michael Brown to the dustup over Anders Carlson-Wee's persona poem spoken in the voice of a homeless person and published in *The Nation* to Dana Schutz's painting of a mutilated Emmett Till in the 2017 Whitney Biennial. Often there are two sides: the free-speechers and the authentics or strict constructionists. The free-speechers believe we should allow artists to say and make whatever they want and any attempt to curb this right is to censor. The authentics or strict constructionists believe that to deploy the materials of another culture, whether it be its linguistic or vernacular patterns, history, or struggles, is a type of colonization, further proliferating Westerners' extraction of the labor and materials of Black, brown, and Indigenous people. Yet, there are also folks in the middle of this continuum, and it is from this position I want to think. How might we think about deploying discourses, aesthetics, and bodies in our poems and art without reinscribing patterns of colonialism and cultural imperialism? This, we might say, is another use of memory, another pursuit of the ecstatic.

Could this be precisely the problem—the inability to imagine the other in ecstasy? In the examples I've given above, all three artists sought to encounter Black subjectivity or the racial, economically disenfranchised other solely through woundedness, annihilation, and the elegiac—through eradication, as if pain was and is the only way the other can be legible. What if the pursuit of writing about the other means understanding the other as a body in possession or position of ecstasy, rather than sorrow or only sorrow? I am not arguing that the racialized others' sorrows or struggles should be off-limits to a writer or artist from a different subject position; rather, what I am petitioning for is a rendering of the other that allows ecstasy, pleasure, and joy to be comprehensible *within* moments of struggle and sorrow. In other words, to think of the Black, brown, or disabled body not simply as a body *only* in pain but also as one complicating and contesting pain and subjection. Think again of the testimony of Toby Jones, the enslaved man from Hartman's *Scenes of Subjection*, who describes the brief moments of pleasure and agency stolen while under the surveillance of the slave master at Saturday dances. Even there, in the most brutal of situations, we find a complicating of the bifurcation between pain and pleasure.

In pursuing this line of thinking, I would like to put Eliot's passage about the uses of memory from "Little Gidding" in conversation with Christopher Gilbert's "Listening to Monk's *Mysterioso* I Remember Braiding My Sisters' Hair." Gilbert is a poet who died of polycystic kidney disease in 2007, and whose work is woefully understudied and underdiscussed. Born in 1949 in Birmingham, Alabama, he grew up in Lansing, Michigan. A psychologist by trade, in 1977, he participated in the Free People's Poetry Workshop, which was established by Etheridge Knight. In 1983, he won the Walt Whitman Award for his first book of poems, *Across the Mutual Landscape*, which was selected by Michael S. Harper. I knew nothing of Gilbert's work until Terrance Hayes emailed me several poems from *Across the Mutual Landscape* in

2010 and asked if I had heard of him. I hadn't. As soon as I could, however, I found a used copy of his book and immediately was entranced by the thinking, the music, the ability to move in and out of several linguistic registers.

Gilbert's work is suffused by his sense of wonder—wonder at how to be part of something that is not one's own, how that wonder can pull someone into a place of joy. It is that wonder we find in a poem like "Listening to Monk's *Mysterioso* I Remember Braiding My Sisters' Hair." The poem offers us a lesson on how to get to "it"—the lyrical space of the beyond, the not-yet seen but opaquely known. Gilbert's and Thelonius Monk's "it" is also the "it" of the other, the other's pleasure, the other's ecstasy.

The poem begins with, and in, the illegible, the unknowable:

> What's it all about is being
> just beyond a man's grasp,
> which is a kind of consciousness
> you can own, to get to
> be at a moment's center
> and let it keep on happening
> knowing you don't own it—
>
> which is moving yourself close to, being
> particular to that place. Like my two sisters
> taking turns braiding each others' hair—
> hair growing against their weaving, . . .

The enjambment of the first two lines emphasizes the first half of the declarative statement—"being" as opposed to anything else. There is no desire to traverse—to subject—this unknowable territory. What "it" is all about is being, not knowing. This "being" that Gilbert is describing reminds me of Eliot's nonattachment to memory and history, in that Gilbert does not call for an "owning" of the unknown, the ungraspable, but rather allows for its mystery, its unfamiliarity. It is this which then allows one to become "particular to that place," which I read as akin to Eliot's renewed or transfigured pattern because it creates a relationship that did not exist before. The term *particular to* is important here because it nods to a type of nonhierarchical simultaneity that Gilbert will later call a "mutuality" existing between the foreign and the native, between two disparate entities, in his poem "Kodac and Chris Walking the Mutual Landscape." This mutuality transfigures and critiques the American notion of tolerance, that "I tolerate you and your ways, and you tolerate me and mine," which always seems to carry with it the connotation of disgust and disapproval, our tolerance erecting a fence between us. In contrast, Gilbert's way of "being / particular to that place" as a form of not-knowing implies a broader openness. One does not have to be *of* that place, one does not have to be native to be particular to it; one can be "of" it via invitation and one's consciousness. One might think of this being particular to a place, this type of consciousness that Gilbert offers, as a type of immigration rather than a colonization even if the consciousness is in doubt. Doubt becomes a way of being at home.

I read this moment as an intensification and augmentation of Keats's "negative capability," the ability to sit in doubt and allow doubt to be part of the creative process. The augmentation is in the moving of negative capability from the realm of the poetic to that of the social and political. In this way, Gilbert's meditation on doubt, what I would call a heavy, intense, or maximal negative capability, becomes a type of political theory, a theory of sociality, and an ethical statement on the production of knowledge.

Pause. I know this moment in this essay might sound jargony. Some might even call my attempt to close-read Gilbert in this fashion "academic" and excessive as a means of disparaging this sort of interpretation and critical engagement, but I assure you it is not. I'm trying to address the complexity of Gilbert's opening in the poem, meet him and his poem where it is he asks me to meet him. And if it is academic, so the fuck what? I don't think Phillis Wheatley or Frederick Douglass or any enslaved Black folks who fought for the right to read would mind my parsing Gilbert's poem with such a precise and critical eye. As poet Nikky Finney notes in her 2011 National Book Award acceptance speech, the slave codes in South Carolina in 1739 levied a one hundred dollar fine and a penalty of six months in prison "for anyone found teaching a slave to read, or write, and death is the penalty for circulating any incendiary literature." Yes, let's begin with history and the fact that enslaved writer Jupiter Hammon, the enslaved poets George Moses Horton and Lucy Terry Prince would encourage me to read and read and read since it was once considered subversive, illegal, and radical for Black folks even to fantasize about let alone cultivate an intellectual life. They understood reading was an act of self-making. Autonomy. A risking of freedom. An embracing of a masterless future. Maximal liberation. Maximal freedom. Ecstasy. And, it would not be denied them. They would read and read and read however they saw fit, in whatever fashion or form it required. Ecstasy now. Ecstasy whenever. So back to reading, back to circulating "incendiary literature," back to Christopher Gilbert and his calling to us to embrace doubt as a way of being home, as a type of ecstasy. Unpause.

Gilbert would have us think of doubt and confusion not only as a way of knowing (epistemological) but as a way of being (ontological). A way of knowing and being that allows the unknown its opacity and illegibility without recasting that illegibility as dangerous and reprobate. Gilbert starts his poem in statement, a statement that contests the notion that knowing something requires being able to hold it, possess it completely. As such, he addresses the by-product of knowledge production and accumulation. Often, in the pursuit of knowing, we fix or arrest the event's—"its"—motion. This pursuit foregrounds the desire of the pursuer and reifies what is being pursued. Often, this reification of the thing pursued takes the form of objectification. The objectifying then leads to a type of fungibility that moves knowing into the territory of commodity and control, thus bringing us back to the subject of subjection.

Gilbert finds a way around this ethically fraught territory of possession and knowledge. Rather than focusing on the confounding, "ungraspable" event, he would have us think about our consciousness, about the inability to grasp as a type of consciousness, a type of place to be, something to own, as in claim, rather than possess or administer. The move toward claiming a confused consciousness rather than the event is a shift of burden and an offering of grace. Often, the confounding event is blamed for its perplexity, its opacity. Gilbert wants us to understand that such a transference is misplaced, not because the event (in this case the braiding of hair) is inherently ungraspable but because the "you" (the narrating poet) lacks sufficient skill and experience in braiding hair. The hair slipping the grasp is not a failure of the moment but the moment as it should be.

It might seem as if I'm arguing that the Gilbert poem is offering two competing models of ecstasy, one that involves sitting in the position of the outsider and allowing the ungraspable aspects of the moment to be the way into ecstasy, into knowing and being, and the other model that suggests that ecstasy resides in not corralling or arresting the unknown but allowing its illegibility. What I am pushing us toward is embracing both. Ecstasy in the ungraspable, in rendering the unknown, is recognizing one's outsiderism while simultaneously understanding or embracing the ineffability of the act itself—the hair resisting the braid, for example—which skilled practitioners of the act would know. It is thus that Gilbert offers that confusion, that inability to grasp, as a place to dwell. In the unreachable, the unattainable: grace rather than anxiety.

What Gilbert also acknowledges in that long first sentence is that being a stranger does not necessarily mean being estranged or alienated, conditions often accompanied by discourses and technologies of violence and containment. In letting the event "keep on happening," allowing ourselves to be nonnative to the event and yet at its center, Gilbert offers a distinct kind of arrival. This is an arrival that critiques the expansion of Europe into the erroneously named New World, critiques Europe's colonial and imperialist move into Africa and Asia. Gilbert's arrival is an arrival that does not require mastery, mastering, or extraction. His sense of arriving at the center of a moment has to do with a mutuality of differences, but the differences do not require a reconciliation. They happen alongside each other without contestation. They co-perform. They exist without seeing the other as impinging or threatening. In arriving without the need to subject or control, we arrive at the center of the event because the event is large enough to invite in the uninitiated. There is no outside or outsider.

But where are we? What is the impetus for this claim about consciousness and knowledge at the outset of Gilbert's poem? Gilbert grounds his philosophical assertion in a narrative scene:

> Like my two sisters
> taking turns braiding each others' hair—
> hair growing against their weaving, they formed
> a flow their hurt and grace could mean
> as each took turns pulling the comb through
> the other's knots and their little Vaseline.

Whereas the poem begins in the public realm of the rhetorical and philosophical, the simile moves the reader into the visual and the domestic. This switch vernacularizes the opening sentence and stanza, locating the philosophical and the conceptual in the realm of the banal. And as such, it indicates the intellectual rigor and possibility in an act such as braiding hair, an act many might mischaracterize as without intellectual substance or difficulty.

The "two sisters / taking turns braiding each others' hair" teach us to sit in the unknowable and be. In the sisters' braiding, in their patterning, they materialize the ineffable of "hurt and grace." For a moment, they make a motion, "a flow," that allows the "hurt and grace" to be known, to "mean." It is an improvisational moment, a moment of pinched ecstasy. In grasping each other's hair, they create a new consciousness, a transfigured pattern, to call back to Eliot, even as their hair resists the legibility of the braid. In their braiding, they create an epistemology, "a knowing which makes the world / a continuity."

Just like the speaker of the poem, we are constantly embarking upon a process that is amorphous, vanishing, renewing, and transfiguring itself into another pattern. Gilbert's wave metaphor at the bottom of the third stanza addresses this process of constant change:

> As in your core
> something calls to you
> at a distance which does not matter.
> As in the world you will see yourself
> listening to follow like water
> following its wave to shore.

The water following the wave back to shore must take on the shape of its varying formations, rushing toward what calls it even as it is moving toward its dissolution. In the fourth stanza, Gilbert declares that this following of one's calling is a type of "letting," which we are to understand as a type of being. In following this process of being, we move into "something else," into becoming an "other." I would argue that this is the position and disposition of the writer. This becoming other is neither smooth nor easy. In fact, Gilbert describes it as a type of drowning: "it flows into always something deeper and / over your head." Though he lightens the moment a bit—likening the one in this state of "letting" to "a kid with 'why' questions"—Gilbert swiftly submerges us again, transforming the "'why' questions" into something that can drown us. Yet the drowning is the only way to come into life:

Your answer is a moment struggling to be
more than itself, your straining for air
to have the chance to breathe it free.
It's alive you've come to,

this coming into newness.

In what might seem like a contradictory moment—coming into life
while drowning—we encounter another echo of Eliot's notion of the
transfigured pattern that results through nonattachment. We also witness a moment of ecstasy. This ecstasy is one of relational joy, in which
struggle is not banished or eschewed, an ecstasy that accepts contradiction, the oxymoronic. For Gilbert, this oxymoronic moment—the
struggling for air, the struggle for answer—is the quintessential moment of being alive. Whereas earlier in the poem Gilbert suggests that
this process is illustrative of the continuity of the world, he now presents it as simultaneously discontinuous: a way one comes into newness,
into a mind that can perceive an otherness. One becomes fractured,
transfigured—though into what?

Here again, at the poem's moment of greatest abstraction and uncertainty, Gilbert moves us back into the world of the real, of his sisters' offering: "'You want to learn to braid my hair.'" The request moves
him into the center of the event, and recognizes his desire to be part of
it, a mutuality signaled by Gilbert's use of a period rather than a question mark. The sisters' offering is both a request and an acknowledgment, a moment of ecstasy. It is at this point that Gilbert presents, for
my money, the poem's humblest and most sublime insight:

there are circumstances
and you are asked to be
their member. Not owning but owning in—
a participation.

Here again, I hear an echo of Eliot's notion of nonattachment, trans-
formed into a way of being part of an event without colonizing it.
Liberation. Ecstasy as "not owning but owning in," a getting to "it."
Learning "to / be at a moment's center / and let it keep on happening."

For those interested in writing about people and lives other than
our own, this moment is instructive because we must be asked or

called to the task the way Gilbert's sisters requested and acknowledged him, his call: "'You want to learn to braid my hair.'" The writing of the other, then, is the learning of what is beyond desire: "not less of love but expanding / Of love," learning to braid, walk, talk, love, cry, run, and hurt like the other without usurping the moment. So liberation. So ecstasy. Ecstasy becomes not a possession of the other but a mutuality, a recognition of a simultaneity such that "The moment of the rose and the moment of the yew-tree / are of equal duration," as Eliot writes. Another pattern, another love. Ecstasy. "If you can," writes Gilbert, "get to it."

Letters to Michael Brown

August 11, 2015

Dear Michael Brown,

We do this now: write letters to the assassinated, to the dead—the dead who do not want to be forgotten, the dead who are still with us, the dead in us. Yes, I said in us. How else are we to remember you, know you, converse with you, touch you, if not by touching ourselves? Actually, we've always done this—fumbled and groped with sound, written to the dead in us because in the writing we put our hands and mouths to something that only exists in the ephemerality of language, the ability to bring the unseen close. This, this is why I come to you this way—with language, with sound, with touch so that I can get to you who was killed one year ago at the hands of the police. You whose death has moved so many to take to the streets and boulevards of this country and risk death to protest your killing. You whose death witnessed by your people sent them pleading for us—*FOR US!*—to do something about it. I worry, though, that in the doing, in the doing something about it we are making you labor in death. You who were made to labor and labor for breath at the end of a police officer's bullet. You who should not have been made to labor this way at all.

Too often, flesh and blood and death are turned into spectacle, into material, into memorial, an artifact laid at the altar of history, and the body of the dead—your body—becomes a vessel for the anxiety, fears, and hopes of the living. I do not wish to do this to you, to empty out your body, which was more than flesh, and turn you into a device, something for me to latch my own imagination and intellect to as pack mule and chattel in service of political exigency, in the service of transforming your death into something redemptive; though a laudable act, redemption is sometimes also a very destructive one in that it requires and demands a double absence of the victim of State violence. The very act of redemption enacts and necessitates a double disappearance because what is redeemed—the nation, the laudable ideal—is prioritized and takes precedence over the dead in order for redemption to be achieved, in order for us to shut away that gruesome moment of the political death for the bright dawn of the future, which we would like to believe bears no remnants—no blood or murdered body—of the past.

Your death is your death. Though it was provided by the hands of the State, it does not belong to this country. Your death does not belong to everyone though we claim it and smear it across shirts and banners and computer screens and stages and essays and chant it. Your death belongs to you, your kin, and your community, first. This is why I ask your permission because I am not of your community though I am Black, living in Chicago, and experience an America and Midwest that is similar to yours. I was not raised in Ferguson, Missouri, among the flat plains and tumultuous sky of Middle America. Until recently, I had experienced neither a tornado warning nor a tornado. I have never hidden in a basement or school classroom in fear that something would snatch the walls from the very foundation in a whirlwind of rain and noise. I am from a small town on the East Coast, born in a hospital surrounded by fields of cattle and apple orchards.

My first experiences with the police may have been similar to yours; however, when I ran from them and hid in the darkness of a shed in the backyard of my grandmother's house, they did not find me there, sweating and being stung by all sorts of insects. Maybe you, too, had friends who had been stopped by the police, beaten and left like a sack of unwanted pots on the side of the road. Perhaps you, too, were followed up and down the white-linoleum aisles in grocery stores by security because of what they feared your body capable of. Perhaps you have watched White women clutch their purses and children to them when glimpsing the outline of your body at a mall exit, the sky awash in roiling oranges, reds, the twinkle and pink of twilight. Yes, we share—we shared—a similar America, a similar shackling—forced to grapple with the rancorous and disingenuous projections of others' imaginations onto our bodies.

But you are not here. You could not outrun the police and hide in your grandmother's shed. There might not have been a shed for you to hide in. You belong to a different community, a community that should arbitrate and secure what redemption means for them. And besides, there is no salvation for the dead.

And so I ask for your permission to reflect on your death, where it sends me wondering and wandering. I am not trying to be overly respectable because I do know the dead, especially the dead that come to their deaths via violence, want to be remembered. However, in the remembering, I am trying to honor you even as you are no longer in the corporeal form of the flesh. I am asking for your permission because there were so many privileges taken with your body—which you may remember and which I don't want to recount but am so doing right now in not recounting. You see the double bind, the difficulty of addressing how some of us are left on the side of the road, are taken up as art and spectacle—our work on the road.

Brotherly,
Roger Reeves

July 22, 2022

Dear Michael,

I am in a parking lot and cannot convince myself to start my truck and drive home. The fear of dying, being killed by a police officer, overwhelms me. I lean on my one leg hanging out of the truck, my foot stuck against the pavement. The pavement glitters as if some intergalactic glass or star exploded and emptied its corpse all over the asphalt. When I'm done tracing the slivers of glass with my eyes, I look up. The evening sky casts off its intense blue of the day for softer pinks and oranges. And there I am below it, despite distracting myself with the grace of shapes and colors, thinking of you, Philando Castile, George Floyd, and Sandra Bland—Black men and women whose death waited for them, found them on the road, their assassins taking the shape of the police.

Dusk dips its head and yields to night, and I am still here, remembering your deaths, not wanting to leave because at least here I am alive. And the police nowhere near the warm aroma of cedar and chlorine burnishing the evening. Sometimes, I lift my head and try to drag the smell of cedar into me, but the fumes of the chlorine, which is used to sanitize the water jumping out of spray nozzles in the ground, water pouring down from pink and yellow umbrellas and mushrooms at the little water park across from the parking lot we call a splash pad here in Texas, is too strong. So, tonight being alive but being paralyzed in this living smells like chlorine with a faint hint of cedar beneath it. And, beneath the canopy of the late summer heat, a shirtless man sitting at a green picnic table, his back to the splash pad, a cigarette in one hand, his small dog at his feet pulling at the leash tethered to the metal legs of the table—this, this will be living and serve as distraction from dying. The man's finger whisks along the screen of the phone, and for a moment I forget about dying, meeting my death out on the road, and become absorbed in watching the man scroll through whatever causes the five o'clock shadow around his mouth to lift, lift into a smile. What does he love? What makes him smile so? Clearly, he loves the dog at his bare feet that he shushes after it yips and yips at the children who chase each other beneath the umbrellas of water, leaping through the water shooting up from the ground. And obviously the man loves an evening cigarette in the middle of a drought, the smoke lifting up from his face, curling, and disappearing. For a moment, I want to feel the relief that an evening cigarette brings.

Instead, the white cigarette in his hand throws me down in memory, into thinking about the black-and-white television footage of Palestinian novelist, playwright, journalist, and political leader Ghassan Kanafani discussing his people, Palestinians, "defending themselves from a fascist government" and "Zionist terror." I don't quite know why the cigarette reminds me of Kanafani. In none of the television footage is he smoking though someone next to him at a news conference appears to be holding something like a cigarette though there is no visible smoke wafting from it. Maybe, it's the barefoot man's face, the tilt of his head, the bushiness of his moustache, the way he balances the cigarette between his fingers, the tenderness of it that reminds me of Kanafani. If you listen to Kanafani's interviews, to his firmness, you might question and reject my assertion of tenderness, but even in his unyielding persistence, in the dipping of his head toward the reporters who interview him as if he might suddenly lock shoulders with them and wrestle them to the floor; there, in that motion, in that wrestling, lives a gentleness, a love, something that I might call soft and pliant—something like the way smoke wreathes and bends itself around any hard thing it encounters. Maybe, it's the whiteness of the barefoot man's cigarette that reminds me of Kanafani—the whiteness of the cigarette very much like the whiteness of Kanafani's shirt in an interview with Richard Carleton, an Australian journalist who dismissed the Palestinian struggle for self-determination as a "conflict," as a civil war in 1970 rather than as what it was and is—"a liberation movement fighting for justice." It is in that interview where Kanafani declares that talks or discussions of peace between Palestinian peoples and the Israeli state is a conversation between the sword and the neck, a conversation that ends in liberation or death.

The sword and the neck—this, the conversation between Black people and America, a conversation had and a conversation to be had. However, while sitting in this parking lot, watching the first daubs of night smear across the bottom of the sky and enfold a barefoot man smoking a cigarette into its cloak, it is Kanafani's strange feeling that he wrote about in a letter to a friend that has sent me thinking of you, writing to you, Michael, after all these years.

"My feelings are very strange," writes Kanafani. "They are the feeling of a man who was on his way somewhere in search of suitable work when he died suddenly—on the road." When I read this quote, I thought of you and George Floyd who had died on the road. And, then I thought of Sandra Bland who was on her way somewhere and died on the road. Did you too have a strange feeling? Kanafani's uneasy feeling anticipated his death thirteen years later. Mossad, the Israeli national intelligence agency, planted a bomb beneath his car that detonated, assassinating him and killing his beloved, young niece. Like you, he was a man on the way toward something and suddenly found his death on the road. Neither of you had the privilege of a calm death but rather the death of the sword and the neck, a death that comes about because you live in a time of hostility.

"In war," Kanafani writes, "the winds of peace gather the combatants to repose, truce, tranquility, the holiday of retreat. But this is not so with hostilities which are never more than a gunshot away, where you are always walking miraculously between the shots." This without-the-hint-of-peace, this lack of repose is where I find myself, miraculously somewhere between the bullets, and the winds of peace fettered and jailed somewhere else is what keeps me staring out into the dark shapes turning in the night, watching a man smoke a cigarette in the dark.

Where am I between the bullets? Where are the bullets, and do any of them know my name as they knew yours?

While the nation might pretend to know our names, calling us "urban youth" or "super predator," the bullets of the nation *do* know in that they rush to tear our lives from our flesh, leave us as the refuse of safety, of progress, the bullets plowing the fertile landscape of our bodies. Our deaths, the blood that causes the corn and wheat to rise. I hope none of the bullets are calling out to me.

Sometimes, I am dizzied and overwhelmed by the echo of deaths like yours, deaths that come by the assassin in his blue uniform and contempt for our lives. Your death, the memory of it, comes upon me with the rush of a slamming car door. While driving home one morning after a run along the Colorado River last summer, the summer after George Floyd's murder, the sky's new blue sprawled out and wet before me, the last words of George Floyd flooded me; Floyd, a man choked to death by Minneapolis police officer Derek Chauvin. His assassin knelt upon his pleading: "Mama, I can't breathe." Floyd's mother no longer alive but the only solace he could request or reach for as his life was being throttled from him. Sitting in the cage of the car, the car whisking over the newly laid asphalt on the highway, I could not turn from the phrase, his voice: "Mama, I can't breathe." I drove down the highway with the thunder and gray of that sadness moving inside me, the irony of such a blue sky in front of me, and could do nothing but cry. And drive.

Today the sadness over the seeming disposability of our lives will not let me up, will not let me out of this parking lot. I don't allow myself to cry; because if I do, I might not be able to get up from beneath that darkness and go home. Once, I let myself fall beneath such a sadness, a deep-down sadness that kept me latched to a newly made friend's bedroom floor, crying for a whole day. A sharp pain that ran from my ear down into my neck wouldn't let me rest, kept me up at night clutching my head, unable to cajole or bring down any semblance of peace or relief. It was the first time that I had felt an ailment, a suffering that seemed to have no end. I started to cry because of the pain. Other pains, other emotional aches showed themselves and demanded to be accounted for. I sunk down in them—the pain of feeling abandoned by my mother because I had departed from the path of Christianity she had set me upon, the impoverishment of feeling rootless and without my people. I had just moved to Atlanta after failing at my first attempt of college and had no job, no money, and was depending upon the kindness of strangers to get me through a rainy winter in Georgia. Desolate and without a god or a family—unsure, confused if I wanted or needed a god or a family—I thrashed on the floor of that strange house and wept from one moon until the next. Michael, have you ever cried like this? Has something every hurt so badly that you had to stay on the floor weeping? Who did you call? Who did you ask to accompany you in the suffering?

I call my partner. Normally, I sit wherever I find myself with these memories and disturbing thoughts until they dull or I become distracted or can force myself to jab the key into the ignition and allow my feet and hands to guide me home, my brain turned off, languishing in the malaise of weathering this visitation of those spirits. But today I couldn't get past the memory of the dead and my potential dying.

"You think these thoughts because you're alone," my partner said.

Alone, as in you're nót with your people. Community keeps the graveyard and the potential bullets that seek to push you beneath its lawn at bay; muzzles and measures grief; allows us to touch the lives we've been denied. Like Baby Suggs in Toni Morrison's *Beloved*. In the novel, Suggs takes everyone in the community, a community of runaways and survivors of slavery, out to a grove in the woods near their homes to cry and laugh so that they can get closer to themselves, closer to what was denied them and what they denied themselves during slavery—their lives and love unfettered, messy. We share our sadness, our griefs, our hurts, our lives, our love with our community, so in order to reckon with them, which is to say feel them, we have to do it with others. We have to laugh a hysterical laughter while crying hysterically in the next moment. And, we must do it together—in a grove sometimes and in the streets and boulevards of America at other times—in a sort of study group.

In the parking lot, I am by myself, without directive, without a grove of my people, so my grief is just running wild all through me without anyone to adjust or help me understand its darkness. I am neither sitting on a porch nor in the bottom of a church with an elder who has been down to the river and down at the cross to retrieve what was left after America was through with it, which makes me think of James Baldwin and the stories you hear of him sitting in dorm rooms with college students after giving a lecture or reading, all of them grappling with the consternation, difficulty, and grief of trying to live, love, and thrive in a country that seems to want its opposite.

I can see it: James Baldwin sitting on a couch in some dormitory apartment building in Washington, DC, or Atlanta, his legs crossed, a burning down cigarette in one hand, the smoke wafting above his head forming a large, lazy halo. A gaggle of students leaning toward him, peppering him with questions. One student asks: "Why must Black people die in order for the nation to live?"

I imagine Baldwin leaning toward them saying, "Because that, Baby, is what it means to be a nation." And, he'd take a drag of his cigarette, blow it out across the living room and the students, and let the words and smoke settle over their shoulders and eyes before continuing. "And America, while it's sure it wants to be a nation, deludes itself daily about the costs of that ambition. The costs being you and me—and itself. America will kill itself in order to become itself. But what will it have, what will it have?"

Is this the work that you—we—have found on the road—the cost, the price of the nation? Must our lives always be remanded to symbol, to spectacle, to commodity, to exchange, to historic marker or announcement for some cultural or political shift needed? When can we find ourselves on the road, without the strange feeling of our deaths at the back of our necks?

"Come home," says my partner.

I couldn't—not yet. I'm still thinking of Baldwin, the road, my death possibly on it, and wanting to be like the man who sits shirtless in the evening smoking a cigarette in a park.

I hear the question again: when can I find myself on a road and only that?

"You can't," says a voice in my head. As long as it is an American road, you will find yourself running between burst of gunfire.

"Keep [that boy] running," writes Dr. Bledsoe in a letter handed to the unnamed, naive Black protagonist in Ralph Ellison's *Invisible Man*. And from there on, the protagonist finds himself on the road—running for his life through New York City until that running finally sends him beneath the road, sends him underground.

Is that where we are being pushed—beneath the road? I can't help but think of George Floyd—the police officer pressing his knee into his neck as if trying to plant him in his grave. And, he successfully does—plants Floyd in his grave.

Beneath the road, the nation gathers itself. But why must the grave be the birthing ground of the nation? Why must death be the means of exchange?

The cigarette is no longer in the man's right hand. Both hands clutch his cell phone. The screen commands his full attention. And the dog that once darted about his feet yipping at the children has resigned itself to curling into a ball at the man's feet. The spray jets and nozzles are quiet, merely dripping. The children gone. Somehow, I missed their leaving. The only remnants of their play, the smell of chlorine and the large wet spots on the asphalt disappearing. The day is calming, and the heat backing down to something reasonable.

Yet, I'm still here, listening to the cicadas that seem to be churring more intensely now that everyone else is going inside and bedding down for the evening. I'm still here, one leg in the parking lot, one leg in the car thinking about the nation and its cost, its fetishization of origins and how the fetishization of origins is also a fetishization of death and annihilation. Our deaths.

Origins allow us to propagate the fiction of sovereignty, of independence, which in turn allows us to create disingenuous narratives of land undiscovered and unused therefore appropriable, the land enclosed and owned by the nation then the sovereign citizen. Ownership traffics in the ideology of "mine," and anything that might come up against this *mine*, this nation, is an other and a threat. Through the excoriation and denouncement of an other we create a national identity and a murderous righteousness and ethos to uphold and proliferate this identity. In the nation becoming itself, it decides who is citizen and who is barbarian, who and what must be subdued and who must do the subduing, what constitutes *in* and *outside of*, what is normal and what is aberrant, who is central to the project of making nation and who is marginal, what is healthy and what is unclean and who bears these various marks. The nation decides who is worthy of life and who must constantly be put to death in order for the nation to thrive; thus, the nation is in charge of annihilation. The sturdiness of a nation requires the nation to mete out these titles and destruction. And this nation has decided that we—Black folks, Native folks, nature, Latin America, the Middle East, Asia—have all become those that must bear this annihilation, must find our work beneath the knee of the nation. The conversation between subdued and the subduer is the conversation between the sword and the neck.

Ironically, this potential for annihilation is why Black folks have taken to the road despite possibly meeting our deaths there. It's why we run and have run. The road permits us to be unlocatable for a moment, potential, neither here nor there, outside the cage of the nation while being inside. The road is motion, is where the nation is most vulnerable and least gathered. In fact, when I think of Black folks' freedom whether expressed in literature or song, it is always achieved on the road, in some form of itineracy or nomadism, grappling with exile, toggling between being made to run and running out of a desire for liberation. From Harriet Jacobs's slave narrative to Ralph Ellison's *Invisible Man*, our freedom is improvisational, fugitive, errant—against Western notions of origins. It is the ability to be *in* a place but not *of* a place and yet *be*. In the Pentecostal church I was raised in, parishioners often testified that the measure of one's holiness, one's soul, was the ability to be in the world but not of it.

But we are, we are in this world and partially of the nation even while being designated as those that must be subdued and exterminated by the nation. If I were W. E. B. Du Bois and interested in pronouncements, I might say: The problem of the twenty-first century is the problem of the nation and the fiction of sovereignty. It is how we get us, Michael, and you dead on the road. And me slipping between the bullets, running between hostilities. It is the nation that makes my daughter ask each time she hears a siren if they are coming to kill her.

My partner's voice echoes in my head: "come home."

Home—is that where you were running when you ran from the police? When I've run from the police, I've always run in that direction—toward home, which was my grandmother's house, the rusted shed in the corner of the backyard. The crabapple tree in the center of the yard. It was an evening like this one when I ran from the police. Luckily, I had hopped the curb and disappeared on a bike before they could clear it in their vehicle. They did not shoot at my fleeing back.

"Come home."

Home—exactly where I want to go, but I don't want to travel on Parmer Lane or Lamplight or Highway 45 or Lamar or Guadalupe or Cesar Chavez. I want to be already in my house, watching the evening sky in the limbs of the live oaks in the backyard, my daughter cartwheeling about the living and dining room pretending she's a gymnast, her long brown legs thrown into the air. It is the thought of my daughter—the brown curve of her face—that gets me to pull my leg into the truck and start it.

I want to put her to bed, which is to say I want to live (though I keep mistyping *live* as *love*). I want the simple task of watching my daughter brush her teeth, pull a book from a shelf, wrestle her twists beneath a pink polka dot bonnet. I want to lie down in her bed, feel some of the twist that escaped the bonnet rub along my cheek. I want to read whatever book she's shoved into my hand, whether it's a book about the Pleistocene period or a dinosaur who eats her classmates or a dystopic planet that uses hip-hop and turntables to settle its political disputes.

While this list of simple tasks might seem to verge upon the sentimental, I assure you it is not. There is nothing spurious or excessive about the task of wanting to be alive and in the presence of my daughter. Nothing easy about trying to gird oneself for a drive home. Nothing easy about staying alive on the road. Driving home requires a calculus that turns every endeavor into a series of complicated measurements. If I take Parmer Lane to Brushy Creek Park, for instance, it requires me driving by or circling around a local police station on Lamplight, which means putting myself in the direct line of sight of the police; but if I take Mopac or 45, I put myself on the highway, which is the domain of the state police who like to camp out on the corridor of the highway near my house. These are the calculations Black folks have had to make throughout our history in America. When traveling through East Texas to Louisiana—Vidor, Jasper—I've ridden in cars where the driver says, "we're not stopping until we get to Lake Charles." That means eyes trained on the road and no bathroom breaks or fuel breaks until we get across state lines and out of these towns where Black folks have been known to disappear or dragged behind trucks and cars to their death. These are the calculations—this is the calculus of merely driving in America.

Who is watching? Who is preparing to kill me in the name and under the auspices of the nation? I simply want to get home and be with my daughter—without incident.

But being with my daughter will always require me to risk encountering my death because being with her is not merely making it home without being stopped by the police or encountering one of my White countrymen who believe they are standing their ground when they shoot at me because I spoke to loudly or knocked on the wrong door or asked them for an apology or found myself jogging though their neighborhood. Being with my daughter requires me to always confront America—either in my art and writing or in the streets buying groceries, getting the mail, or protesting this country's inequities. Being with my daughter requires being on the road. And being with you, Michael, and the memory of your death.

Yours in Brotherhood,
Roger

August 1, 2022

Dear Michael,

Why have we not talked about your love in reflecting upon your death at the hands of the police? In our remembrances, in our various autopsies, in our sifting through the bones, trying to divine the significance of your dying, rarely did we turn to what sustained you, what was your beauty, what did you make of the earth?

What we forget here in America is that we learn as much from the dead as from the living because what the dead have loved cannot be loved in the same way any longer—death removes the dead's love from the world. Or, at the very least makes that loved thing opaque. That love, that attention paid to someone or something acts as a type of statement, acts as both art and artifact of that love. That residue, the artifact of that devotion should be studied because it will show us, the living, how to bring what does not yet exist into existence, which is to say again, love; the dead teach us how to love. Maybe this artifact of love and the studying of it is the gift of death, of the dead. These artifacts of love are why we memorialize people like Martin Luther King, Fannie Lou Hamer, Malcolm X, Ella Baker, and James Baldwin. They teach us something about love— they teach us how to exist—in their devotion to us, to art, in their grappling with the trap of the nation. They offer us the possibility of ourselves and more abundantly so because they will not allow us to turn from ourselves at our most beautiful or most ugly. They ask us to be naked, which is to say lovers, without the scales about our eyes, bound, ironically, to seeing—truly seeing—someone else's beauty as well as our own. These great leaders, thinkers, and artists are afforded this attention, our attention, but not you, Michael. We don't interrogate or study the love of the regular dead—the dead who happened to die unfortunately on the road between here and there. The dead to whom we pay attention only momentarily because of the salaciousness of their death—not for their living, their love, for what they brought about into existence.

Men and women like you, who have been killed by the State, lose this love in their death. They lose their bodies and what their bodies made in the world. Or more so, this love is removed from them, from you, in becoming symbol, in becoming redemption, narrative, memorial.

Earlier in the week, Natalie Diaz read a poem where she asked: "Let me be lonely but not invisible." As in let me exist but don't annihilate me. Let me have absence, even emotional deprivation. Let me have rejection, unhappiness, sadness, and even isolation. But don't remove me completely from your field of vision. Don't remove my echo, the trail of my spirit from the landscape, from the water. Let me have these flawed moments of living on the earth, but let me have that living. Alive. Diaz is a Native poet, and annihilation has befallen her people, and it has befallen ours as well.

Befallen—a strange word. I must be careful with this English and its grammar, the ways in which it and I can hide culpability in a verb, in its predication. Befallen, for instance, creates a sense of innocence, naturalness. Almost as if an event that befalls someone or a people is without cause, without origin, merely progress. The word as innocuous as *rope* or *age* or *weather*. Something like the stars moving down the sky or a pine tree suddenly collapsing in a stand of pines. When in actuality the tree does not suddenly fall; the tree is cut down by a saw and a man at the end of it.

It's not mere progress or fate that brought about your death, Michael, but the nation's pursuit of itself, its frightened and deadly sense of order and safety. I wanted to wander, wonder in what you loved, what your hands touched, what was comfort and what was loneliness for you. Perhaps a cousin that sat on a couch with you and perhaps in the sitting with you, you felt something—that almost indescribable sense of warmth that comes with belonging to something, to someone without the necessity to name or call it or to know it as anything other than what it was right then—you being near them.

Or, what about your loneliness? How did you negotiate it? Was it ever in sitting next to a cousin on a couch, having something you wanted to say, wanting to reach out to touch their wrist, get their attention, but rather than reach or touch or fumble your way through explaining a sadness that was almost inexplicable, you sat there and allowed the distance between you and your cousin to be that—distance. Or, did you turn to your mother, sit with her in a kitchen, and talk and talk and talk of isolation? I have. It was my grandmother, not my mother. On a pay phone in the rain. She, in New Jersey. I, in college in Atlanta, Georgia. *Without* is the only word that comes back to me to describe the desperation and deprivation of the night, the gray pall of it, my heaving into the receiver of the phone. I felt so *without* and walked and walked and walked up and down the red-bricked promenade in front of Steagall's, the little market I often bought chicken wings from, past the library, proceeded down the promenade to the crosswalk that separated one section of the Atlanta University Center from another. Nothing was in the streets except for the swaying traffic lights hanging over them, which were red. I crossed anyway, continued my walking. The walking brought no comfort, brought nothing near, so I stopped at a pay phone and dialed my grandmother, who lived a twelve-hour drive away in New Jersey. I don't remember what I said, but nothing my grandmother said soothed me (in fact, I remember becoming more inconsolable the longer I talked with her on the phone). But she stayed, she stayed on the phone *with* me. Michael, have you found yourself in such a wet and gray place? Did you know this sort of loneliness, and what did you do with it? Who stayed with you?

My God, the loneliness of dying on the road. Death already seems as if it is lonely enough but to have to face it against the asphalt and without any warning or company other than your own fear in your ears, in your chest. "My God, my God, my God" is all that I can mutter to myself.

I am trying not to put my imagining of your dying in place of your actual death, but the mind is a promiscuous animal, one that turns the body in all sorts of directions, provides all sorts of transgressive feelings and visions. I'm worried—in the writing to you, in the thinking about your death, about your love and your possible loneliness—that I've overstepped. I've come to know who you were through a headline, your mother's weary face emblazoned in my mind, your neighbors and friends recounting your death, the cell phone footage of it, and the blood, your blood on the pavement. I'm holding my eye as closely to that blood as possible, to its running. My God, it ran. My God, I want you here. Alive.

Missing you,
Roger

August 4, 2022

Dear Michael,

Two years after the killing of George Floyd and the uprisings that surged and grieved his death in the avenues of America and the tear gas that shrouded and followed the grieving masses and the car aflame beneath the highway and the rubber bullets shot by the police putting out the eye of a boy protesting their brutality here in Austin, my seven-year-old daughter turned to me in her bed and confessed that she still fears being shot when she hears sirens.

"Why?" I asked.

"Because I'm Black," she answered.

Two years before, she confessed this same fear when walking to the mailbox and hearing sirens in the neighborhood, but it made a sort of sense then. It was the summer of the uprisings, and every city in the United States that had any population that had to deal with an unjust police force streamed into the streets and boulevards, grieving the death of Floyd, which was really about grieving their inability to breathe in their own homes and communities. My daughter's mother and I took her into the streets to protest, to march behind cardboard signs we made at the dining room table, to listen to the speeches from mothers who had lost children to police brutality, to watch the policemen's horses paw at the pavement and the men on top of them behind their plexiglass shields and masks refuse to return my daughter's gaze or her raised hand when she said "hello" to them.

We took her to play in the blocked-off streets where folks had painted in yellow lettering "BLACK LIVES MATTER." There she ran and hopped from letter to letter. We spoke all summer about the police, the brutality they sometimes brought to people who looked like us, brutality she might someday face, brutality her father *has* faced. And when the sirens struck up throughout the city and she heard them, she asked: was everybody safe, who were the sirens coming to kill, were they coming to kill her. I answered each question honestly: I wasn't sure everybody was safe . . . I hope the sirens will kill no one . . . No, the sirens were not coming to kill her.

These questions continued at every wail and turn of a siren but as the autumn came and the leaflets passed out at the protests wilted, becoming as brown as the leaves falling from the trees, my daughter's questioning diminished. Because she was no longer vocalizing her worry, I thought my daughter had long left that fear of being shot, left it with the toy microphone she no longer uses to pretend she's conducting a rally against police brutality.

For weeks after going to protest with us, my daughter conducted many rallies in our living and dining room. She'd call us to attention, and we had to gather at either the dining room table or on the couch. Sometimes, she held a blue clipboard with white paper on it and announced that this particular rally was "to keep Black people safe." Other times, the rallies were to bring people together "against the killing of Black people." The rallies always began with a poem, one that she often made up on the spot. Sometimes, she'd ask me to read a poem, and I would. Then, she would call a speaker up to give a speech. Again, she was that speaker, and she improvised the speech. Her mother and I often sat and watched, tickled but also wary.

What had we done? I also wondered if she might be showing some sort of gift, some early talent. I, too, had orated and preached as a child about her age. To encourage me, my mother built a pulpit out of discarded wood and old vacuum hoses and tubing. From my little pulpit, I would proclaim "I AM A PREACHER . . . OF THE BAPTIIIISTTT," which meant I came to bring the gospel like John the Baptist, though I was unaware at the time that John the Baptist lost his head for declaiming his gospel.

There, in the hallway of my grandmother's house, which is where we lived after my mother left my father, I banged my fist and orated and shook—shook down whatever "word" I could get from heaven. And, now look at me: once a teenage minister, now a poet—with a lot less fist shaking and pulpit thumping but nevertheless declaiming and speaking of visions. I wondered if my daughter mimicking the speakers who climbed the dais in front of the capitol was a sign of what was to come. Maybe an activist, maybe a poet, maybe one of the leaders we're always looking for. One day, she might be climbing somebody's rickety stage in front of a gold-domed capitol trying to urge people "to keep Black people safe," a phrase she often uttered at these rallies she conducted in our house. But slowly, she left that play and pretending behind as the winter came with its ice storms, and the Rosa Parks doll her *tío* bought her to encourage her nascent activism remained buried beneath her other dolls in the darkness of her doll box. The poems she "wrote with her mouth" no longer about Black life but about the trees and the shifting darkness of winter.

So, it was a surprise the other night, while putting her to bed and preparing to turn the light out, when she admitted that she was still scared of being shot for being Black. It was almost a whisper. Her announcement had come after a long conversation that began with her asking me why we don't stand for the national anthem when it's played at the soccer stadium before Austin FC games. I would have said, "Because of this, your fear." But she had admitted this fear only after I explained to her that "The Star-Spangled Banner" as written by Francis Scott Key, himself a slaveowner, has a verse that we do not sing but is nevertheless in the song, and that verse celebrates the terror of slavery. And we will stand for nothing that celebrates the terror of slavery, which sent us tumbling down and reckoning with the long history of slavery and Black folks counted as three-fifths of a person and what all that might mean for her almost three hundred years since our founding aristocrats and slave traders penned that now sacrosanct document called the Constitution.

Through a summer camp on acting and musical theater, my daughter has become acquainted with the Constitution because of the musical theater work of Lin-Manuel Miranda and his career-defining Broadway production *Hamilton*, which tells the story of founding father Alexander Hamilton through singing and rapping. Every morning and evening, between brushing teeth and swimming and traveling to and from camp, Naima sang the catalogue of Miranda's work—from *In the Heights* to *Encanto* to *Hamilton*. We did not talk about Bruno as one of Miranda's most beloved songs announces, but we sure did sing about Bruno. In the car. In the bed. In the bathtub. At the pool. While eating carrots. But it was not Miranda's "We Don't Talk about Bruno" that echoed throughout the house the most. It was Miranda's "You'll Be Back," from his musical *Hamilton*, that bewitched my daughter the most. "You'll Be Back," sung by Jonathon Groff who plays Mad King George, skewers the Mad King and his tyrannical taxes levied against the American colonists. My daughter sang the tune wistfully, sardonically, loudly, brazenly, enjoying what the song allowed her to feel in her body. I watched her swing and swagger about in the song, sometimes practicing the choreography she was learning at the camp that accompanied the song. After the recital, which was a sort of pageant of Lin-Manuel Miranda's most admired songs, my daughter asked if we could watch the musical. Because none of the household had seen it, her mother and I agreed that we should all watch it together, though I was already skeptical of the musical because I knew of Ishmael Reed's and Toni Morrison's critiques of the play. Morrison provided financial backing for Reed's play *The Haunting of Lin-Manuel Miranda*, a satire that has Miranda visited by historical figures of the past that Miranda has left out of his play, à la Charles Dickens's *A Christmas Carol*. In two previous critical essays, Reed had described the musical's cross-racial casting as "whitewashing" and fraudulent.

After watching the musical, I agreed with Reed. We cannot body swap our way into freedom. Replacing the founding fathers with Black and brown actors does not graft us onto the American vine, slip us into the American dream. We are still laborers—no, slaves and former slaves—in the vineyard, not yet invited to drink the wine from the casks we built, from the harvest we gathered, from the grapes we've pressed. Laying our swagger and style and music over the founders' genocidal politics will make neither the wolf any less wolf nor the dead lamb in its mouth any less dead. And the heartbreak of it all, hearing the character of Thomas Jefferson who's played by a Black man flippantly order Sally Hemings (the enslaved Black woman, Sally Hemings!) to read a letter from George Washington. Pause. Sally Hemings . . . Sally Hemings! The Sally Hemings that Jefferson owned—the bondswoman Sally Hemings—the bondswoman Jefferson took as a lover? You want to have her read this letter? The character casually tosses this line out as if it were the most natural thing. And the musical written by a Puerto Rican man, whose people are still colonized by the United States.

I sat stunned in my living room, my daughter beside me, the bulb of her eye glistening with the images of this American travesty, this American mess flickering across it, her singing along to "You'll Be Back," my daughter, unaware that her fear of being shot for being Black begins in this historical moment. Yesterday's musket and ball and flintlock and the grand speeches of liberty and death and the peculiar institution and three-fifths human becomes today's police car and siren and the bullets entering us and our hands up and our necks knelt upon and her diving beneath her bed in the evening when she hears a police car bouncing over the hilly streets of Austin, Texas, just outside her window.

The musical obscures the nightmare and annihilation and savagery that would transpire in the wake, in the triumph of the American Revolution. One man's revolution is another's prison. We sometimes forget that revolutions are not revolutions for everyone. Some of us are put into the dungeon, kept in the basements, chained to walls, hidden in the homes of the revolutionaries to do the work of cleaning the bed linens, wringing the chicken's neck, nursing the revolutionaries' children at our Black and bonded breast.

Michael, I thought of you when my daughter confessed her fear of being shot. Did you have that fear? Had you sensed your death as a boy, worried that you wouldn't make it past twenty. As a boy, I had no expectation of living past twenty. While playing tee-ball and singing in the church choir and going to school, the thought of my death sloshed about my head. I don't know when this expectation concretized in my mind, becoming a type of semiregular thought, but I had fully expected to die, most likely violently and before I could climb out of my teenage years. Shot by the police. As a teen, the thought arose much more frequently, but I was never scared of it. My death at twenty felt as imminent and banal as a dandelion or the skunk that sprayed its odor into the night outside our house. Every night the odor and the casualness of getting used to the stench. And when my twentieth birthday came and I was not dead, I was shocked. I had not planned to live, and now I was faced with what to do. What do I now do with my life?

Who and what am I now that I lived past my death or what I thought was to be my death? I remember it felt as if a door had suddenly been thrown open. No, not a door. I felt as if I were standing by a set of long windows, windows that I hadn't realized were there. And now I could look out of them, and there was some light and the sky coming in. I have lived my life since then as if standing next to these windows, the sky filling in the room with possibility (of something else, something outside). Michael, what do I do with my daughter's impossibility, with the deadline of her death wailing and running toward her? How do I help her hold the strange feeling of one's death being there on the road, awaiting her and the feeling of an open window, that she, too, is standing next to a wall of windows? Which is to say: at the end of suffering, there is a door.

Thinking of you—in love,
Roger

Singing into the Silence of the State

1

What is the song that can be sung to soothe a fretting child in a bomb shelter? What is the song sung to disrupt a State-imposed curfew? What is the necessity of singing during catastrophe, whether State-created or virus-induced? Bleary-eyed, my head pandemic-heavy, I watch protests erupt all over Austin, Texas, after the murder of George Floyd, a Black man, by Derek Chauvin, a White Minneapolis police officer. My daughter sits beside me, and I'm fumbling to find a poem to read to her, as I do every morning, a poem that will allow us both to enter the day. But, the day appears much like the day before in this early part of the pandemic: she is huddled over a tablet, watching an Australian cartoon about a family of red and blue heelers, and I am furiously trying to write on a small pad of paper. However, I'm distracted by the growing number of deaths in my neighbors' houses and in hospitals. How did we get here? And, how long will we be here—the purple-blooming crepe myrtle tree tossed by the wind, its branches touching its trunk as if making sure it is still whole, still there in the ground, and in the city, the people burning and the city burning too?

What is the poem, the singing that can console and be with us while a city burns, and the people die in the burning, die on gurneys in the hallways of the hospital, die and disappear because our politicians are too in love with their mouths, which they mistake for beauty? But, their mouths are not beautiful things. They are the mouths of dogs in love, addicted to trash, pulling down the cans in the alley at night, running into the shadows after they've dined and swelled their bellies, leaving garbage strewn everywhere. They leave, they hide. And, we must be with this absence, be with this silence.

How might we sing into this silence?

In late October of 2019, I woke up early in a hotel room in Minneapolis after a long day of traveling from eighty-degree weather in Austin to a milk-white midwestern sky and its welcoming cold. I was there for a conference on human rights, which I always look at askance—these gatherings that remind me of church meetings where we must whip ourselves into a fervor before we enter the fray of the real world, only to find out the real world is gently and not so gently ignoring us. I am not the best hotel sleeper, so by 5:00 a.m. I could no longer delude myself that a restful night's sleep would usher me into a long day of forum-going. I stumbled toward a long desk that sat opposite the bed, opened my laptop, drowsily browsing Facebook. I came upon a video posted by a former student. Atop the video, she wrote: "The beauty of Resistance," which was followed by a rose emoji and a Chilean flag. Beneath her post was a caption and link from YouTube. It read: "This is the chilling moment soprano Ayleen Jovita Romero defies the silence curfew, imposed under martial law by the government of Sebastián Piñera in Chile and sings the song 'El derecho de vivir en paz' (The right to live in peace) by Victor Jara."

I clicked the link, but neither the caption nor my former student's declaration of beauty nor the rose emoji prepared me for what I was to encounter: a cell phone's camera pointed at a window; beyond this, night and, across the street, more windows in a high-rise apartment building full of light; finally, a soprano's arching, effortless voice suffusing the air. It was as if her voice created a tent of sound that floated up over the buildings and yet somehow found its way into the camera, into this rented room, into my body. I thought to myself, *This is power.*

No, I was thinking nothing. I was too full of sound and trembling. Her voice was somewhere in the left side of my body, moving up from my stomach into my chest. The ambient noise of the street—dogs barking, car horns bleating, even the shushing of those who try to speak during the impromptu recital—did not interrupt her singing. In fact, it was another iteration of the silence that she was and is singing into, singing with. Romero sang, sings on into contemporary silence. Though we have only the perspective of a single cell phone pointed at a window and cannot see the rest of the city in curfew—in kitchens, noiselessly sitting in their living rooms and bedrooms, we can tell the whole city is listening not only to Romero but also to Jara.

Jara's "El derecho vivir en paz" was written in 1971 to commemorate Ho Chi Minh, the leader of Vietnam, but the song eventually became an anthem of protest against the repressive Pinochet junta. Pinochet's death squads eventually detained, tortured, and murdered Jara for the song at the infamous Chile National Soccer Stadium, cutting off his hands and displaying them for all those that entered. Romero covering Jara is a double-singing, a double-haunting. Through Romero and those musicians gathered in squares all over Chile, Jara sings into the silence of the State, sings not only into the curfewed silences of Piñera's government but also into the silences of Pinochet's dictatorship, into the silence the dictatorship tried to make of Jara's life.

Romero's version, then, is a co-performance of resistance against the curfew of silence imposed by Piñera's government. By listening, Santiago's citizens have reclaimed their silence, have repurposed it, leveraging and legislating it toward a subversion of a State-imposed passivity. Their silence resists in the form of paying attention to pleasure, to life, to the anarchy and ecstasy of a voice singing into the mandated silences of the Chilean State, a singing that thrusts the city and country into the future.

It is also an ironic resistance, the people's silence surrounding Romero singing because the people's resistance subversively deploys what the Chilean State wants—quiet, silence—but does so in the opposite fashion. The people's silence does not confirm the government's power but actually circumscribes it. It is like the moment in Cornelius Eady's poem "Gratitude" where Eady's speaker surrounds and overwhelms the bullies, the elitists of poetry. Eady writes:

> And to the bullies who need
> The musty air of
> the clubhouse
>
> All to themselves:
> I am a brick in a house
> that is being built
> around your house.

Signifying on Audre Lorde's famous admonition—"the master's tools will never dismantle the master's house"—as well as signifying on the long history of the objectification and commodifying of Black flesh in this country, Eady's "Gratitude" deploys the master's materials—the brick—but against the master's wishes. The line breaks in the second stanza of the above quoted material clue the reader in to the subversive but playful and deadly serious resistance. The line "I am a brick in a house" literally encloses or bricks in the two lines that come after— "that is being built / around your house." Eady visually builds a house within the stanza. Through syntax and enjambment, Eady's house surrounds, overwhelms, and interrupts the other house, the clubhouse that wouldn't let him in. If we examine the adjectival clause that follows the house, the house that Eady built, then we understand that the bullies' clubhouse has been subordinated to his grammatically. It's a hostile takeover but done with the master's tools. Because truth be told, the master has never understood the full range of his tools nor their volition. The history of Blackness teaches us about the unpredictability of tools, their will, their range, their desires that often run counter to their deployment. We have always (and by we I mean Black folks), we have always been the tools tearing down the master's house even as we built it. Though Eady seems to be loud-talking the American literary tradition, canon formation, and canonicity, the use of the brick metaphor opens up the philosophical and ontological field to understand his declaration as political manifesto and theory, as a speculative, vernacular enchanting of the future. A making a way out of no way. Or, making visible a liberation, a possibility that exists but lives shrouded and chained by the circumstances of racism.

Eady's "Gratitude" echoes and anticipates the subversive silence in the YouTube video of Romero singing into the Chilean night. Similar to Eady embracing his brickness, embracing the abject history of being an object, a tool, with subjectivity and subversively deploying that abject subjectivity, the citizens of Santiago embrace and signify on the State-imposed silence through resistance, circumspection, and subversion. They build an outside-of, a house, a nation that envelops and swallows the government and its curfew, the State's house. Santiago's citizens surround and neutralize the State's control through no longer attending to the State's imposed silence. They leave the imposed silence of the State as an artifact, an emptied and empty memorial, thus removing its power, its efficacy, its control, and run off with the resources. If it were money or a train, one might say, the citizens of Santiago remove it from circulation even as it appears to be in circulation. It is a takeover but without hostility or force, without prior agreement, arrangement, contract, or law. It is power. The power of the people to decide. The co-performance of silence and the soprano's arching singing dismantles the State's sovereignty, its belief in its sublimity and omnipresence. The curfew, pierced by one solitary, intentioned voice, offers the opportunity for something beyond—a beyond-sovereignty, which the people of Santiago inhabit if only for the video's two minutes and nineteen seconds.

Their subversive silence, even if fleeting, does not require a forever in order to succeed. It is not a failure if in the next night, the military or government's soldiers in their black Kevlar vests and rifles rapaciously patrol the streets, spraying tear gas into the faces of protestors and bringing their batons to their heads. While the soldiers and police officers may be able to disperse or counter the resistance, they cannot counter or disperse what was made visible and inhabited the moment before, the night before, in the singing, in the silence. The subversive silence announces and corroborates the possibility of an impossibility—a captureless and curfewless future. A future that might have seemed diffuse, unsayable, ungraspable but felt in form rather than in fact. A future improvised and yet known.

In Romero's singing and the silence that surrounds it, welcomes it, helps to author it, we glimpse the emergence of what Sun Ra calls *the impossible*. According to critic Brent Hayes Edwards, the impossible for Sun Ra is "the recognition that the radically different, a radical alterity, is inconceivable, and yet paradoxically exactly that which *must* be conceived." The impossible is the unimaginable, mythic in scale, yet simultaneously imagined, worked for, and reified on earth. Sun Ra conceived of the impossible in terms of space travel and the intergalactic; however, the speculative and mythic technology of space travel is akin and cousin to the political, resistant act of imagining and enacting an alternative organizing of community and nation, an out-there, an otherwise; like Romero singing into the Chilean night, an oppositional sound that ushers in a new regime of political reality—the impossible.

When has a city remained quiet enough that one voice can be heard for blocks upon blocks? Is that cessation of noise not an impossible made possible? That impossible made possible reminds me of Sun Ra's poem that commemorates Apollo 11's landing on the moon, first published in the July 1969 issue of *Esquire*:

> Reality has touched myth against myth
> Humanity can move to achieve the impossible

Because when you've achieved one impossible the others
Come together to be with their brother, the first impossible
Borrowed from the rim of the myth
Happy Space Age to You . . .

In Sun Ra's poem, we glimpse not only an encomium for the Space Age but also a political and metaphysical theory as well—how to live and enact the not-seen, the not-achieved. Enacting these impossibilities requires reality to touch myth, putting potential opposites into relation, bringing the unseen (but possible) into the banal, into the everyday. It's a closing of distance between the speculative and the present. It's a proposal of intimacy. In Chile, reality "touched against myth" in the guise of the soprano's clarion call and its authoring silence. It is a friendship, a brotherhood, but of the most political sort—this intimacy of silence and sound, of myth and reality.

This intimacy is the beginning of art, which is the beginning of politics. It is the notion that something must be said, must be marked, and that marking, that said thing, listened to within silence as it aspires to collect and articulate that silence, that desire for an invisible, the unspoken but known. The future. This dual-authored text brings about a contradictory future, one that seems impossible or invisible because of the current reality; and in bringing the other closer, in touching the other, in this intimacy, it produces an impossibility. Us. And the future—now.

You can't see what I'm doing with my hands, but I'll try to describe it. I'm holding my left hand out and away from me, the fingers spread and curved as if preparing to grip the handle of a mug. My thumb points upward. My right hand is held close to my face, chin level. Similar to my left hand, my fingers are spread as if to grip the handle of a mug but my thumb points downward. My hands are mirror opposites of the other, and I'm bringing them toward each other, stopping just before they touch. It's the only way I can bring the notion of intimacy, impossibility close to you, to me. This motion I'm making with my hands is gesture and the motion of looking, of becoming intimate, of becoming friends, of the future, of reality touching myth. It is like the Giovanni Serodine painting of Peter and Paul meeting briefly on their paths to martyrdom. The Italian philosopher Giorgio Agamben offers a beautiful interpretation of the painting:

The two saints, immobile, occupy the center of the canvas, surrounded by the wild gesticulations of the soldiers and executioners who are leading them to their torment. Critics have often remarked on the contrast between the heroic fortitude of the two apostles and the tumult of the crowd. . . . What renders this painting genuinely incomparable is that Serodine has depicted the two apostles so close to each other (their foreheads are almost stuck together) that there is no way that they can see one another. On the road to martyrdom, they look at each other without recognizing one another. This impression of a nearness that is, so to speak, excessive is enhanced by the silent gesture of the barely visible, shaking hands at the bottom of the painting. This painting has always seemed to me to be a perfect allegory of friendship. Indeed, what is friendship other than a proximity that resists both representation and conceptualization? To recognize someone as a friend means not being able to recognize him as a "something." Calling someone "friend" is not the same as calling him "white," "Italian," or "hot," since friendship is neither a property nor a quality of a subject.

Not only is the painting a "perfect allegory of friendship," it is also the perfect allegory of the intimacy of bringing two entities—reality and myth, silence and sound, the future and the past—into proximity, into relation. Like the two saints, Peter and Paul, nearly touching foreheads, thus unable to see each other yet shaking hands, Sun Ra's notion of the impossible produces a similar opacity and ironic intimacy. Reality and myth, which seem to stand on opposing walls, gaze at each other from their respective positions and must traverse the distance of their respective gazing. Though it might seem that I traveled quite far from Romero singing out of her apartment window, I assure you I'm not. The silent gesture of Peter and Paul shaking hands is a metaphor for Romero singing into the streets of Santiago and the silence that surrounds it. Her singing and the authoring silence is reality touching the myth of an autonomous, capture-less, curfew-less future. This co-performance is Sun Ra untethering myth and reality from their restrictive and circumscribed grammars, breaking them from the chains that keep them tethered to opposite walls. A future, a beyond, that "resists both representation and conceptualization." That's how you know you're in it.

The future is like Agamben's notion of a friend—you will recognize it and simultaneously you won't. Graspable and yet resisting or slipping your grasp. Vocalized and yet silent. Speechlessness, the inability to name the place, the feeling, the moment you're in, are hallmarks of residing in that future. And, even as you're in it—reality touching myth—you might be put out of it. Residing in it forever is not guaranteed.

The fiction writer Gabriel García Márquez would say this dispatching of the people from their oppressionless future is the job of the counterrevolution, to dissolve intimacy, the new thing created by the revolution. The counterrevolutionaries, the cockchafers of order, will recognize the dissolution of their reality and will respond violently.

Piñera and his government were no different. The Chilean state sent more tanks, more police, more rubber bullets into the streets to beat back the protests of its citizens decrying the severe economic straits they find themselves in—an unreasonably low minimum wage, the privatizing of pensions, a transit-fare hike that would require low-income workers to spend more than 13 percent of their income that is already allocated to traveling to and from work on public transportation. As poet Daniel Borzutsky notes in his November 2019 *New York Times* op-ed, "Chile has one of the highest costs of living in South America. Today, the country is considered one of the most unequal in the Organization for Economic Cooperation and Development group of nations."

The *New York Times* posted a video and interview with photographer Rodrigo Palavecino Escobar, who was shot by the military during the protests for taking photographs of the uprising and the military's repressive response. Firing rubber bullets, tear gas, and water cannons at protestors, the Chilean military indiscriminately assaults local reporters and even human rights watchers wearing bright yellow vests that identify them as such. Human rights advocates, activists, and writers such as Borzutsky rightly note that the violent repression by Piñera's administration is reminiscent of General Augusto Pinochet's regime, one that disappeared and murdered over three thousand people as well as violently torturing tens of thousands in a seventeen-year military dictatorship from 1973 to 1990.

"El derecho de vivir en paz" acts as an open doorway, a joint that connects two sublime moments of unchecked, repressive governmental power. The song acts epistemologically. The present-day protestors remind Piñera and his government that they are being watched and measured; that their actions are not free of or untethered to history; that they are bedfellows with Pinochet. Again, it's a circumscription, what critic and writer bell hooks calls an *oppositional gazing*. In the singing, in the song, protestors witness against the cruelty of the military's suppression, of economic hardships, offering testimony to and before the future through the past, through history.

Romero and the protestors in Chile sing a long continuous song that deploys Jara's song "El derecho de vivir en paz" as a suture, a bridge that brings two different historical time periods into relation. When Jara's song declares, "where they ruin the flower / with genocide and napalm," we think of the war in Vietnam, the horrific photos and television footage of incineration, children running out in the road away from American soldiers, the twenty long years of death at the gun and missile of the United States. We also think of Jara killed and dismembered by Pinochet's junta. However, when sung during the protests in 2019, we also see and smell the tear gas, the rubber bullets of the military in present-day Chile. The moon exploding in Jara's song is the moon exploding beneath Romero as she sings out of her window. The nouns of history, of violence, of war sung by Romero call back to Jara, Pinochet, and Vietnam and simultaneously resist the current regime, its noise ordinances, curfews, and tear gas.

Maybe this is the purpose of art or, at the very least, how we might identify transcendent art—it promises another possibility, a revolution even if only the size of one blade of grass. In "The Ideal Critic and the Fighting Critic," John Berger, the artist, novelist, and art critic, suggests that it's the artist's way of looking, of seeing, that allows a piece of art to transcend its period, its historical moment and not some universal, fixed, or sublime embodiment of any artistic ideal. "The important point," Berger writes, "is that a valid work of art promises in some way or another the possibility of an increase, an improvement." Later, in the essay, Berger clarifies that "the meaning of the improvement, of the increase promised by a work of art, depends upon who is looking at it when. Or, to put it dialectically, it depends upon what obstacles are impeding human progress at any given time." Increase or improvement depends upon not only who is "looking" but also who is singing or

reciting the work of art and where because context shapes consciousness, shapes the material, sometimes changing a tool—a screwdriver
suddenly becoming a drumstick, the metal fender of a car becoming a
drum when the breakdown on Outkast's "Rosa Parks" comes stomping
out of the garage speakers and you suddenly feel the need, the desire to
tap out "Ah ha, hush dat fuss / Everybody move to the back of the bus."

Or, take the rapper Future's notion of "fucking up some commas,"
for example. Take the hook of the song out of the context of flipping
bricks (cash) and weight (drugs) and, through quotation, place it in a
new context—say a poem about time, perspective, looking, and slavery. Future's fucking up some commas no longer is merely about drug
culture and conspicuous consumption. Instead, the commas meto-
nymically stand in for Black folks coming over in the cargo holds of
ships spoon-fashion. In this new context, Future's notion of "fucking
up some commas" is a critique of racial capitalism, a playing on the
abjection of slavery, a reworking and razing of the grammars of exploitation, a call to reimagine our, Black folks', relations to markets and
self-commodification.

Whether impediments or the desire for improvement, context ar-
ranges consciousness. In Berger's notion that it is the obstacles that
impede the human that makes past art relevant to the present, we see
Jara's "El derecho de vivir en paz" and his life become a vocalization
of the present and future. In the lyrics, in the historical circumstance
surrounding the song, Jara offers protestors in Chile a language, an
affect, a possibility, a poetics.

Jara offers what my four-year-old daughter, Naima, would call "a
louder voice." This morning, while taking a break from writing this
essay, I helped her prepare for school, which entails all of the rudi-
mentary things that you'd imagine—eating breakfast, brushing teeth,
dressing—but in my house, preparing for school also requires the reading of a poem. Since I will not be raising a religious child, I figure I'll
indoctrinate her with a little secular religiosity in the form of the promiscuity of art and language. Profligate, there go I. And my daughter
to the bookshelves. My daughter's recent obsession: Jorge Luis Borges.
So, every morning she ambles over to the shelf and pulls the gray-and-
maroon book with Borges's young face on the spine. It has been this
way for the last two months. Every morning. Borges. In English. And
sometimes in Spanish. The Borgesian obsession, I believe, is due to

the fact that the black-and-white photograph of young Borges with his dark hair and dark, deep-set eyes on the spine of the book looks, according to my daughter, like Mr. Snehal, a family friend. For a while, she referred to Borges as Mr. Snehal and would point to the spine of the book and say, "I want you to read Mr. Snehal."

I also believe my daughter's obsession with Borges's poetry has something to do with the way the words feel in her mouth. Often, at some point, in my reading of one of Borges's poems to her at the kitchen table, she will begin repeating the words after me, sometimes staring out the kitchen window. This morning, when reading Borges's "Odyssey, Book Twenty-three," she began repeating the lines back to me quite early on in the poem, around the second line: "The work of justice, and revenge is done," said Naima. Usually when she repeats the lines back to me and the kitchen windows, I slow down, give her the lines in smaller chunks, often breaking the line in two or three pieces, something that can fit inside a four-year-old's mouth. As a child, I learned this tradition during Sunday morning devotional service, sitting on brown folding chairs that bore the name of our Pentecostal church on their bottoms as Sister Spencer, a Jamaican woman with a muddy voice, stood in the pulpit and lined out a song about Naaman dipping his leprous body into a river and coming up clean. In the African American church community, we call this method of breaking down a song or poem *lining out* or *hymn lining*. Though the practice can be traced back to seventeenth-century Scotland and England, enslaved Africans and formerly enslaved Africans used this method to worship in the ante- and postbellum South because of low literacy rates. The few parishioners who could read a hymnal would do so publicly during church service, doling out the words to the rest of the congregation, and the congregation would sing them back.

I did not set out to teach my daughter this tradition. She began it quite naturally, almost instinctively, when I was reading Walt Whitman's "Leaves of Grass" to her over the summer. She would stare at my mouth and repeat every word. And, she continued this recitation practice with Borges and his "Odyssey, Book Twenty-three": "Where is that man now," she said, "Who in his exile wandered night and day / Over the world like a wild dog, and would say / His name was No One, No One, anyhow?"

After we finish reading the poem, I always ask her if she liked it or what did it make her feel. This morning, when I asked why she enjoyed the poem, she said something peculiar—the poem made her voice louder. She didn't mean "louder" literally because she never raised the pitch of her voice during her recitation. This louder was a figurative loudness, one she signaled only with the raising of her eyebrows and forehead. Despite the fleeting gesture and her running toward the door, ready to get into the car, I was struck by her use of "louder," particularly in conjunction with her recitation practice, her receiving the line, her co-performance with me, the epic poem to which Borges's poem alluded, by extension the book itself. This "louder" conspired with many partners, assumed several valences, enacted multiple histories, aesthetics, literary traditions, polities, and politics. I read the raising of her eyes as not just a signal of magnitude but also an expression of the ineffable and opaque tether between her and the thousands-year-old tradition of poetry; that poetry, in some way, imagined her, imagined us before we arrived here, thus was always enacting and imagining a future, a possibility. I know I'm being a bit promiscuous, but isn't that indiscriminate mingling, union why we come to art—for the untethering, the flight, the fugitivity it allows?

Maybe this fugitivity, this radical reimagining of ourselves is what poems do to us when they are in our mouths, when the lyrics of another are sung operatically into the street against the government's order—Romero singing Jara into the night of Santiago, for example: they offer us a promiscuity. We become—to borrow language from my daughter—loud, louder. Fugitives. Ourselves. Many. In the doubling, tripling, and infinite refraction and augmentation that occur in a recitation, in a performance, the text fills in where our voices might be metaphorically thin or cracked, where they might waver, where we, ourselves, might not fumble to access the register, metaphor, or language for the future we imagine. It is the open history of the past, those unseen holes and interstices in songs, that allow for this possibility. For us.

This potentiality, this future that Jara's song embodies reverberates beyond Chile. The singing into the curfewed silences of the State moves across Latin America, moves north into the Caribbean archipelago. In a gesture of solidarity with the Chilean protestors and uprising, Puerto Rican guerrilla artists projected the title of Jara's song all over the capital of San Juan, Puerto Rico. In Santurce, a district known in San Juan as a hub of culture and activism, DERECHO DE VIVIR EN PAZ strobed in white light on the overpass. In Viejo San Juan, the symbolic center of political power, a projector cast the title onto signs and the sides of buildings. These same Puerto Rican guerrilla artists extended their message of support for Chileans fighting the demagoguery of Piñera's government and the reprobate constitutional inheritance of Pinochet's dictatorship. In white light against a brown stone wall at the Centro de Bellas Artes in San Juan, a message read: BASTA DE TERRORISMO ED ESTADO EN CHILE (STOP CHILEAN STATE TERRORISM). Together, Romero, Chilean protestors, and these unidentified guerrilla artists sing a long song that travels across borders and histories of exploitation. They build an alliance that exhibits the dynamic relationship between two peoples who are fighting two distinct and different fights—Puerto Rico for a decolonized, autonomous future; Chile, a de-neoliberalized existence—yet see their respective struggles entangled and singing, speaking to one another across the chasm of their differences. They are fighting for the lives and the lives of their children, but they understand their fighting is coordinated and not sequestered to one spit of land.

It is not a coincidence that all over Latin America, from Puerto Rico to Peru, protests abound. They are lining out, singing to each other. All over the map, the imposed silences and violence of the State are being sung into, filled. Challenged. Obliterated. Especially when the police and military forces repress the future-authoring protests of the people with clubs and baton and water hose and dog.

Tear-gassing nonviolent protestors, shooting reporters. These tactics are not only being used by the police in Latin America but in the United States as well. During the protests that sprang up all over the US in response to the police assassination of George Floyd in Minneapolis, police shot, harassed, and tear-gassed local reporters in major cities, in towns, in municipalities all over the country. These sorts of fascistic responses are not located in foreign or exotic locales, a corroboration of the so-called primitivity of South American politics, a politics that we, the United States, has often participated in and corrupted through the propping up of dictators for close to two hundred years. No, authoritarian regimes all over the map from Santiago, Chile, to St. Louis, Missouri, utilize and deploy the club and water cannon, these methods of terror and control to beat back the future. We are not exempt from genocide. Nor are we exempt from having to imagine and author a future, a beyond-genocide while inside it.

2

These bomb- and curfew-sized craters of the State are being laughed into as well. In late February of 2020, a video of a Syrian father and his three-year-old daughter went viral. In the short clip, a father laughs with his daughter as bombs fall all around them. You can hear the father ask the child, who stands on the couch next to him, if the sound they hear whistling overhead is a plane or a bomb. The young girl titters with excitement. In her face, you can see that she hopes that it's a bomb. "Yes," she says. "When it comes, we will laugh." After the muffled explosion, the girl jumps up and does just that: laughs, not a *tee-hee* or short, controlled chuckle but an unrestrained laugh, one that runs toward the high end of pleasure, maybe to ecstasy. She grabs at her fingers and leaps up and down on the couch, her mouth thrown open in what can only be described as sublime joy. Her father asks, "Does it make you laugh?" And the girl responds, "Yes, it's funny."

Watching the video for the first time troubled me. How could she and her father laugh as their potential death fell from the sky? Insane, their laughter seemed to me at first. But, then I thought of Frantz Fanon in *The Wretched of the Earth* and *Black Skin, White Masks*, his embracing of the crazy in dealing with the insanity of colonization, oppression, war. That to claim life, the beyond-genocide of it, the magic and enchantment of it, something like laughter will seem crazy particularly when what is being cultivated as normative as your death. That in order to subvert being constantly imprisoned in catastrophe, made to sup with one's death at every turn and meal, one might have to embrace the abjection of craziness, appearing nonnormative—laughing at bombs falling in your neighborhood, potentially crashing through the roof of your house, exploding against your living room floor.

I watched this video over and over because I was and am trying to figure out how to talk to my daughter—my Black, five-year-old daughter—about the most recent killing of a Black man at the hands of the police in Minneapolis and the protesting that sprang up around the country because of it, including here in Austin, Texas. I am asking myself if I should take her to a protest down at the capitol where she will see men in riot gear huddled behind plexiglass shields or on horseback or on the roof of the capitol building with sniper rifles; and those men may decide to shoot tear gas and rubber bullets into the crowd where she will stand because they are the counterrevolution, and the counterrevolution will always bring violence. But it is necessary to meet the dogs and soldiers of the counterrevolution in the streets, even if our backs are against the brick-and-red-granite walls of the statehouse, even if we cry tears brought on by tear gas and anger. It is necessary, absolutely necessary for her to be there, with me, with her mother, with her *tío*, with her friends who will be in strollers and asking if they can take off their child-sized masks. Racism and oppression care little for virus-induced disaster. Or children. The counterrevolution will bring its police officers, its suffocations, its lynchings, its National Guard, its tanks and dogs, and it will continue its assault, its push to annihilate Black life. So we must be crazy, we must go into the streets, with our masks on in the middle of a pandemic and risk our deaths so that we might risk our lives. We must laugh like this father and his daughter at the tear gas and rubber bullets. We must be a disturbance and disturb ourselves as a way of catapulting ourselves into our lives.

While debating whether to take my daughter into a protest, I am also debating if I should send this video of the father and daughter laughing at falling bombs to some of my friends who have Black children, their children who are now fearful anytime they hear a siren. At a car-caravan protest, shortly after the video of George Floyd being choked to death by Minneapolis police officer Derek Chauvin, my friend T's five-year-old son L—, who can rap and sing Lil Nas X's "Old Town Road" with a Texas drawl while slurping down a bowl of macaroni and cheese with real aplomb, feared joining the caravan because he worried the police were going to "shoot-ed" him. His father told me all of this from behind a blue surgical mask, leaning against my car, all of us waiting in a parking lot to caravan up a hill toward the city manager's house, where we would blow our horns in hopes that this organized noise would signal to him and the city council that we did not want our tax money going toward funding the city police. T— assured his son that the police wouldn't kill him. I was not so sure that I could have offered that same consolation to him, or to my daughter if she asked the same question. In fact, I know I couldn't. I wouldn't. When I had the opportunity, I didn't.

There is no safety here in America, and to pretend as such would be akin to offering false hope—a fairy tale when the country in which we reside is something like King Solomon's court and what has been brought before us is a dilemma—one baby and two mothers laying claim to the child. In order to preserve the life of the baby, Solomon must put the baby's life in question. It is the contradiction of wisdom, of offering it, of receiving it, of moving toward something like justice. So Solomon offers justice by calling for his sword and telling the two mothers that he could divide the baby between them. Being the wise king that he was, Solomon understood that the baby's birth mother would not want to see her child killed, would not want that sort of justice (which is not really justice at all). So she spoke up and said, "No, no, give the child to the other mother, the other woman. Don't bring any harm to it." And in the version of the Bible I was raised with, the woman who falsely claimed the baby as her own was not sad to imagine dividing the child between them. Her lack of consternation at the thought of cutting the baby in half corroborated for Solomon who the baby's mother was. In the end, Solomon gave the baby to the woman who cried out to save the child because only a mother would be willing to give up the child in order to save its life.

This crying out to save a baby's life is what it feels like to be a Black parent in America. That I must give away what is of my flesh in order to save it, to save my daughter. But what I'm giving away is not flesh necessarily but the illusion of safety, that a Black childhood can exist outside of the knowledge of its annihilation.

We must sever our children from the dream of safety. We must deliver our babies into the hands of another mother, who will not be as gentle with them, but at least they will still be alive. We've had to cry out, we've had to teach our children the police are not here to protect them. America is not interested in their survival. And when it is interested in their living, it is so that it can wring something from their lives—some labor or entertainment. Some pulse and circus. And, there is no sword of justice, no Solomon with his judicious wisdom to provide an iota of recompense.

No counseling or consoling stories or parables of wisdom. We live in the nightmare of the West, what they might call history, trapped in the hold of some ship, bound slaver to slave. The ghost of something captaining the vessel.

When ship captains, masters, and capitalists stuffed Africans below the decks of schooners and clippers named *Hope, Wanderer, Wildfire, Care*, they had no idea they were also throwing themselves and their children and their children's children down there into the holds with us. Yes, they could walk about in the dark, tiny cavern, but they would never be allowed out of the hold again until they were willing to free who and what they bound and held down there. Themselves. Us. But, rather than reconcile with the dark, they decided to extend and rewrite their tragic myths with our flesh. They tried.

They tried to fashion Black folks into Sisyphus, Tantalus, Pandora. In those holds, they said, "Here, here, I will make your body and the body of your children your burden, your boulder. Now push it up a hill. Search for them when I have sold them from you. Go, go, push your body after what I have taken, turned into coin, and hidden in labor." After Emancipation, "Here," they said. "Here is your fruit, your water to slake your thirst. All you must do is but pluck it from the branches, lean down, and drink from shore." But the tree, heavy with golden pears, continues to elude our grasp, the branches pulled away in the form of redlining, underemployment and unemployment, lower wages, inadequate schools, our communities occupied by the police. I am continually opening a box of destruction that I am told is my salvation, and I am to counsel my children, my daughter toward this myth of opportunity and safety.

Or, am I? Might I be releasing her from the Sisyphean task of trying to make herself—her love, her body, her mind, her intellect, her beauty— legible to an America that will constantly goad her, beseech her to code-switch, explain, and translate herself in order to, in the end, tell her they don't understand, that she's incomprehensible, nothing but din, all rabble and foolish noise, sending her back down the hill with a boulder that was never really of her choosing? Maybe, the golden pears in the tree, despite their sheen and seeming plentifulness, seeming answer to her hunger, our hunger, belie the dust and ash they become in our mouths.

Severing Black children from the American dreaming tradition might be one of the fundamental, foundational jobs of Black parents in America. Not allowing our children a tradition that requires the hard work of the dream to be done by immigrants or Black folks un-seen behind the kitchen walls or just outside of the frame digging the trenches, laying the brickwork for the foundation of what will become a rat's nest of American pleasure. An American pleasure not even worthy of rats. An American pleasure that requires Black folks and Black children to enjoy and look forward to their own exploitation, to labor on behalf of a future and a country that returns what it has always given us—nightmares and death.

In severing our children from the American dreaming tradition and its delusions of safety, we actually teach them to love themselves. Loving themselves requires knowing what is and is not for them, what contradictory principles of justice they must uproot even as they are planted in them by well-meaning preschool teachers who want to believe that the police are interested in protecting Black children long after they are no longer children.

Black parents must teach their children to see, nurture, and love a self that others, particularly the White world, might teach them is funky, reprobate, profligate, ghetto, janky, clumsy, rough, uncultured, and unmannered. A self that might like to lie down in a field in the rain and take a nap. A self that might want to cuss and cut up on a Saturday night and go to church on Sunday morning and be holy all in it. A self touching and seeing a self in a way that a self wants to be seen, touched—without the veil. In lowering the veil for our children and for ourselves, we allow them, we allow ourselves, to see, to know, to diagnose power and its abuse. We give ourselves a world, a sound for the sense and tense of our lives.

"It matters what you call a thing," writes the poet Solmaz Sharif in "Look." A Black parent must teach a child to know how to call the State THE STATE, abuse ABUSE, and power POWER, particularly when at a protest at the state capitol on a Sunday afternoon and men in brown uniforms stand hunched behind plexiglass shields and refuse to return your child's hello. You must teach your child that the thing calling itself power is an abuse of power. Violence. Fear But knowing how to call a thing a thing also requires knowing the ends and beginnings of things—that "they are not always," as my mother would say. Knowing where the beginnings and ends of love are, the beginnings and ends of the State, of capitalism, of belonging, of citizenship. That one is not bound to something merely because of circumstance or condition, but there can be a slipping of a yoke even while under it. Learning how and what to call a thing is not merely one axis of the poetic, but it is also, I'm coming to realize, bringing a child into language. In this way, raising a Black child is rearing a poet, rearing someone who can embrace loneliness. This statement is not a romantic, escapist gesture; this statement is not refusing the abjection of being Black in America—it's a wallowing in it.

"I think it must be lonely to be God. / Nobody loves a master. No," writes Gwendolyn Brooks. This loneliness, which Brooks attributes to being a master, I believe stems from the notion of naming, of having to call a thing a thing. Because in naming, one distances oneself from what one has named, what one has called forth. And what is sometimes called forth is a critique. Looking askance at the nation, at its democracy and myopic fantasy of justice. So in teaching a Black child to name, to identify power and be able to call it such, a Black parent is also rearing a Black child not to fear solitude, alienation, being separate and apart from the nation.

"It matters what you call a thing." When calling a child *child* in a Black household, it means so many things. It is calling them *love, young, be here with me.* It is calling forth a hedge of protection around them not as a way of absconding from danger but because of the awareness of it, because there is no out from danger. In this way, a Black parent is a poet; they call a thing into being. *Child.* But they have also called their child into language. In this way, a parent is always their child's first poet; an announcement of liberation—"not less of love but expanding / Of love," to borrow from T. S. Eliot's "Little Gidding." The parent becomes the child's first instantiation of ecstasy, of knowing how to use language, to author an invisible future into being.

But my daughter is also co-mothering with me. Standing before Solomon's throne, she, too, must give up something in order to save something else. That something else being her life.

She must relinquish a certain idea of childhood innocence, relinquish the notion that the police are vessels of safety as she had been taught beneath the halogen lights and fluttering pieces of blue and gold construction paper in the shape of a carp at her preschool. She must become less American if she is to survive America.

She must understand that the police car parked in the lot of the day care, its black fender kissing the concrete retention wall, does not mean safety for all equally. In fact, the police car inspires a sense of terror and fear in her father because it reminds him of the times the police have threatened to shoot him or have jumped the curb and pinned him against a bus stop shelter, accusing him of robbing a house or stealing a car. That when her father pulls into the lot, he must be careful of what tension his face does or does not hold. That he must not slam his car door too hard. If he glances in the direction of the police car, he must hold nothing that seems like anxiety or worry in his face, to offer nothing more than a nod. And sometimes, not even that. All of this anxiety and stress to be managed while trying to pick up a child who could be in any type of mood, one that ranges from exuberantly-happy-to-see-you to obstinately-resisting-any-attempt-to-take-them-home. And all of this consternation and childrearing witnessed and judged by a state trooper who could decide at any moment that holding your child by one arm as you try to catch their writhing body, preventing it from falling into a large puddle in the parking lot, is abuse. My child does not understand this anxiety, this pressure embedded in a banal activity such as picking her up from school, but she must. I must teach her this finesse, this awareness of the terror in the everyday lives of Black folks in America.

I can hear someone say, "Ignore it, just ignore it. You're giving too much power over to this object, to the police in general. If you've done nothing wrong, what do you have to worry about?" My life has been a forced accounting of what is there but not there for others—what is danger for me but for others is merely the blandness of the day, something as banal as a blade of grass. I reckon with the invisible, with nightmares, particularly the nightmares of others: me, as a loaded gun. For instance, when stopped by the police, I, Nightmare, keep my hands on the steering wheel, and narrate every movement as in "Officer, you asked for my wallet. What I'm going to do is reach down into the cupholder and pull it out . . . ," I must anticipate and account for the nightmare that I've been made in America and what this country has done to protect themselves from the nightmare they've made of me and my people, the loaded gun that is, in fact, not loaded at all. A gun that was never a gun but a life. The nightmare, a vision in the mirror—the American state looking at itself.

The police car in the lot of the day care seeks to soothe the sleeping American dreamer, but violates the dream and anyone who is not privileged to walk through America asleep. Maybe this is why the police car in the lot of the day care cannot be ignored. It is meant to disturb, to say ironically, "Welcome to your Life, Black Man."

In welcoming me to my life, the police car in the lot demands my attention. To believe it can be ignored is absurd. It is there to be noticed, ogled, even marveled at. The car represents the alleged beneficence, largesse, and supervision of the State, and, simultaneously, it functions to intimidate. I am supposed to feel both cared for and threatened. And, I do. I feel supervised toward terror.

When Black folks in America are counseled to ignore the police cars docked in the parking lot of their child's day care, asked to ignore the casual racists at our jobs, the weather of White supremacy that feels so much like the blue-eyed sky that arches over our heads on a cloudless Sunday covering this vast land, White, conservative America is asking us to refuse the veracity of our sight and good sense, our rational minds—to believe in the nightmare that they have made for us, which is really a nightmare they have made of themselves. A nightmare that greets them in every cup of coffee, in every mirror and door handle. And because they feel the creeping fear everywhere, this nightmare of themselves, this violence, they must create an antidote, an amulet to ward it off. The police car is America's amulet and apotheosis created to reckon with this fear. And they leave it everywhere, littering the streets and grocery stores and day cares and universities and parks and ball fields and basketball courts. In its audacity and militancy, the police car keeping vigil in front of every movement of our lives enacts the hyperbole of power, its omnipresence, its seeming benevolent omniscience. This simple operation of leaving this talismanic, symbolic object in public is how the power of the State becomes like spirit, like the weather—everywhere and always. Immortal.

The police car grooms my daughter and me toward this understanding—that the specter of the State haunts every endeavor. And, this haunting done so casually, with sprezzatura. A nonchalance that belies its insidiousness, its sweating to make itself seen but surreptitiously and gracefully so. To get you accustomed to its hiding in plain sight. To appear as inevitable as the weather. In the police car sitting outside of my daughter's preschool, in the policeman parading the police dog in front of her and the other children seated on the playground during Community Helpers' Day, their faces and eyes level with the dog's snout and caged maw, the school and the police are preparing the children to think of this violent display of power, of its presence, as normal, as necessary as farmers and doctors, the other community helpers who visit the school on the same day. The dog tearing at his handler's padded arm as necessary as food.

If my daughter uncritically imbibes this performance of power as safety, then she will only feel any measure of security when power is displayed in this fashion—a German shepherd lunging at the arm of his master. His master, the officer, explaining that the dog attacks at his command. This display is not safety but a perverse orientation toward power, toward safety, especially when she, a Black child, will watch the evening news in the coming years or scroll through timelines and newsfeeds and learn that she and other Black people are what cause this country's feelings of danger. Which is why she, too, must sever herself from the desire for a certain type of American safety. Because safety in America requires the eradication of Black people—and if not the eradication, then the management of them by coercive and mostly violent means.

Power in America works in these clumsy, ostentatious, and, contradictorily, subtle ways, through something as simple as a police car—sometimes with an officer in it, sometimes not—waiting in front of a day care, waiting to greet you: *Welcome to your life, Black people of America.*

This welcoming to my life, to my daughter's life, is why I must counsel her toward the hysterical, the crazy, to laughter in the middle of hostilities, in the middle of a protest where the police horses dash their hooves against the curbs and the glint of the sun caroms off police shields and my daughter waves hello to the police, to the State, but it will not wave back. Because safety in America is absurd, and by that I mean that it doesn't exist for the Black child, which means it doesn't exist for the White child as well. Or the Asian child. Or the Latino child.

To survive requires a lyric, ironic, improvisational sensibility, which my people have always had. Some call it the blues, others jazz. Some call it side-eye or oppositional gazing. It is inhabiting the vulnerability of a mother who must give up her child in order to save its life, in order to rear it. It is knowing that in order to save our lives, we must risk them; that some silences must be sung into or subverted with silence; some bombs laughed at even as they fall around us. In other words, make a joyful noise.

Peace Be Still

Hush. You could be whipped to death for being out here among the trees, on your knees at the edge of a stream, holding the hands of other enslaved folks and praying at the edge of a plantation, praying to a possibly unsanctioned, non-Christian god, worshipping life as you saw fit, without having to suffer through the guile of a sermon sponsored by White masters whose only interest was in your obeying them and having that obedience corroborated by Ephesians as in be obedient to them that are your masters . . . knowing that your Master is also in heaven. These were the circumstances of the hush harbor—sneaking off into the woods, breaking branches and trunks of trees then pointing those broken limbs and bodies in the direction of these clandestine and invisible meetings by bodies of water. The water used to hush the sound of Black folks celebrating their notion of God, imagining and praising a captureless and masterless future. These were the circumstances of life—risking it. This was the cost, the price of freedom—being whipped to death for *imagining* yourself in possession of it.

All over the Caribbean and the southern United States, Black folks waded out and off of plantations, stealing away, in search for some time and space to be themselves, among their own, in community with their bloodlines, Gods, and traditions. This practice of gathering— sometimes called a hush harbor or brush arbor or bush arbor—is the beginning of the improvisational practice of Black folks imagining themselves outside the deracination of slavery. Freedom's first expression is that of a hush, some quiet in the maelstrom of plantation life. Some elsewhere, some otherwise.

I have been searching for where I might go, how I might bring myself some measure of peace, some quiet in the middle of what feels like catastrophe—the coronavirus pandemic, the ratcheting up of racism and anti-Blackness in the United States, the killing of Black folks by the police, state legislatures seeking to pass laws that forbid the teaching of the several genocides that our forefathers and -mothers used to hew this country from the alleged wilderness, from the nothing that was already something. Our deaths seem to be in every siren—whether ambulance or police. In the floodwaters and forest fires. In going down to the rambles of a park to watch birds or merely sitting at the edge of a river and reading a book. Sometimes, our deaths are in walking to the mailbox. Shortly after Derek Chauvin pressed his knee into the neck of George Floyd, my daughter asked me, while walking down the street to collect the mail, if the sirens we heard were coming to kill us as they had killed Floyd. A few days later, more sirens, and my daughter pulling her face away from peering into a bird's nest that had taken residence in our little pines in the front yard, my daughter, again, asking if those sirens, too, were coming to kill her. Since the death of George Floyd, when my daughter hears sirens, this question follows: who have the sirens come to kill? My answer: I don't know. Hopefully, no one. I never promise her that the sirens don't mean death, that someone's death may not be at the end of them. I cannot offer her this easy solace. Nor do I want to. Our deaths from sea to shining sea. All of it gratuitously displayed on screens in bars, at our jobs, in our homes, our deaths, the deaths of our kin traveling in our pockets.

Where is there to go when our deaths feel so imminent, as if waiting for us in front of the case of oranges in the produce aisle at the grocery store, when they're in my daughter's every question, in her face when a siren comes blaring past the car? How did our people build peace during slavery when they were spied on and speculated flesh? How did they dredge it up from swamps, lift it out of rivers in the midst of banal and sometimes rather outlandish and savage forms of subjection? This peace was not a calm, after-the-disaster-is-over peace, one that came after one weathered the storm. The hush harbors built in hollows, dug out from ditches, erected in the middle of forests existed within the confines and borders of the plantation. Sometimes, hush harbors appeared in the middle of a slave cabin. The peace, the hush enslaved folks sought was dirty, impure, catch-as-catch-can, enacted in the middle of disaster. How did enslaved Black folks create peace right there in the din and deracination of slavery?

And might we, we whose community is occupied and patrolled by the police, we who die at higher rates from disease because we cannot access the medicines or infrastructures of health that our White peers can, we who are the center of the carceral state's dreams, might we need to call on this tradition of seeking a hush, some peace in the middle of our dark days? What would the architecture of our peace look like? What is the practice? What would our ecstasy look like? In *Slave Religion: The "Invisible Institution" in the Antebellum South*, Albert J. Raboteau cites archival records that describe the ecstatic nature of these clandestine meetings during slavery: "If anyone became animated and cried out, the others would quickly stop the noise by placing their hands over the offender's mouth." Shouting, courting ecstasy were essential to the hush, to the peace enslaved folks sought while subjugated. It's ironic, for sure, that one must seek quiet, some peace through noise, through ecstatic movement, but this irony is the vernacular physics, the vernacular subversiveness of surviving and imagining life inside a nation that thrives through its genocides, through deciding if and when you will live and if and when you will die.

Might we need to go down into the wilderness again, reconvene what our ancestors knew resided there when we collected ourselves near those bodies of water? I've been thinking quite a bit about what this might look like, what we might need to know and feel with the warming up of the planet, with our children being attacked in schools, my daughter told her skin was "feo" by one of her White classmates? What might we need to bring again to each other that cannot be hewn out of a marching down the brightly lit thoroughfares of our city shouting "NO JUSTICE! NO PEACE!" or petitioning our negligent legislators for rights and redress?

So down into the rambles and hollows of books I went, looking to find what our ancestors left in the archives, in their recorded testimony, in the opacity, pauses, and ambiguity in their description of hush harbors. I went looking to understand how I might cultivate not only a little peace for myself but for friends here in Austin: Starla, Ashante, Tyson; for Naima, my daughter, and her mother, Monica. For us. How might they and their gifts help bring peace close, hold the ever-roaming peace still for a moment? Starla whose singing voice sounds as if scooped up and out from the earth's inside, a knot of flame, brown and rich as muddy diamond. Ashante who practices care as an art, who brings fish and loaves of bread and water to the mouths of the hungry, who gives and gives even when they have little to give. Tyson who hunts and knows the earth, whose large hands are never diminished in caring for the sick in his nursing job. Sometimes, I see in us a hurt, a desire to heal the hurt in others. But when we get together, what rejoicing sometimes spills from us, rings in the house, shakes the very walls of our dungeons. So I searched in Raboteau's *Slave Religion*, Noel Leo Erskine's *Plantation Church*, Paul Harvey's *Through the Storm, Through the Night*. I searched in what archival material and secondary sources I could find. But, I was not prepared for where the archive, where my ancestors would send me.

When my grandmother moved from South Carolina to New Jersey as a teenager in 1954, she went from attending a white, clapboard two-room schoolhouse in a small, one-road town where a King James Version of the Bible was the only school book to Burlington City High, a high school on the Delaware River, Philadelphia's skyline there just behind the chemical plant and factory smog. There at Burlington City High, a school several hundred times larger than what she grew up with in Black Creek, my grandmother fell in love with physics, graduated two years early, and fielded scholarship offers from various colleges in 1956. Her father, however, did not allow her to go to college. He said women who went off to college just got pregnant, brought the baby home, and he would be responsible to raise the child. And, he was too old to be raising one of his daughter's children.

My grandmother often told this story in the evenings, while my mother, who was in college, and I would be eating dinner or doing our own schoolwork at the dinner table beneath all those spider plants that hung from every available shelf and cabinet in her house. Since my grandmother wasn't allowed to go to college, she did what most young women in her position did. She married, started a family with my grandfather, who in his navy uniform would come by the high school and court her, his smile and laughter what drew her to him. Because there were very few job prospects, she sought out any employment she could. Her sisters and cousins who had also come north had become domestics, cleaning house for wealthier White folks in Medford Lakes, Moorestown, and Cherry Hill; they suggested she do the same and brought her along to help them clean the larger homes. Eventually, my grandmother started to build up her own list of clients—the Lazars, the Parones, the Goldsteins, the Rostans— but she also cleaned house for Black women who taught at Temple University and Trenton State College (now the College of New Jersey); these Black women she dusted and mopped for were some of the first

Black women to earn PhDs from universities and colleges like George Washington University.

Whenever my sister or I was sick, or there was an unexpected day off from school, my grandmother would take us to the houses of Dr. Gloria Dickerson and Dr. Bettye Collier-Thomas. With a vacuum cord coiled in her hand, she'd urge me into their libraries, to look at the books on the shelves, not to be afraid of the African masks on the walls, the wooden faces, their open mouths. Papers spilled from the desks, all sorts of scribblings that I didn't understand, but my grandmother would later tell me were the beginnings, middles, and ends of books and essays they were writing. They wrote on Black women and slavery and work and about other books, other writers. Often this work on Black women sent them off to libraries and to archives, a word I wouldn't learn until graduate school. When they weren't away sorting through old books and dusty file folders, these educated Black women worked from home, which I had not seen before. My grandmother and mother—and all the women I knew really—left the house for the majority of the day, worked in somebody's office, bank, restaurant, grocery store, beauty salon, hospital, or house.

After school, I let my sister and me into our house, making sure homework was complete, snacks were eaten, and only then were we allowed to traipse about the neighborhood, jumping fences, playing jailbreak, kill-the-man, and hot peas and butter—all games whose reward was dodging violence: a belt, a slap, a tackle. None of the academic Black women my grandmother tended house for had children. They spent their time researching or hosting parties that my grandmother sometimes worked. Like my grandmother and great-aunts, they spoke loudly when on the phone. While my grandmother cleaned, I sat quite still in their living rooms or studies if they weren't occupied, listening to their voices on the phone, ear-hustling, trying to catch a little gossip, though mostly getting quite bored.

Over cups of tea, my grandmother sat with them, the Doctors, at their kitchen counters or in their living rooms, talking and laughing. They were never without their titles despite the intimacy my grandmother shared with them. In fact, their titles invoked or realized an intimacy for her. It might have been my grandmother bringing something far-off near: her reifying her desire to go to college and get a PhD; her defying her father's proclamation and order that women who went off to college became a burden. Saying their names—Dr. Gloria Dickerson, Dr. Bettye Collier-Thomas—defied the yoke, the burden my great-grandfather had placed upon her, made the impossible not just possible but reality. The invisible visible.

It was Dr. Bettye Collier-Thomas's name that would lead me back to my grandmother in my search for peace, for evidence of the hush harbor. While reading Erskine's *Plantation Church: How African American Religion Was Born in Caribbean Slavery*, I happened upon a quote that looked as if it might lead me to an important primary source. Hush harbors were clandestine meetings organized by folks who were not always literate, and the possibility of a record or some archive existing was unlikely. I was prepared to read absence—not to fill it in but to actually *read* it. To allow absence its opacity and fragmentation, to live with its ruptures and raptures, its discontinuities and disquisitions. To take what little the archive gave me and make it two fish and five loaves of bread, a full-belly feast made of abundant scarcity. I didn't need much, just a little direction. And here was a little direction in the testimony of a formerly enslaved woman named Della Briscoe, who herself attended hush harbors. "Brush arbor meetings were common," says Briscoe. "This arbor was constructed of a brush roof supported by posts and crude joists. The seats were usually made of small saplings nailed to short stumps."

Here it was, the architecture of an arbor. Because I hadn't read much on the design of these makeshift, quickly erected sanctuaries, I did what most researchers would do. I dove into the endnotes looking to see if this quote might take me to a primary source where I might learn more about the arbor, how it worked, who was there, what was said, what people felt, and how that feeling was cultivated. I flipped to the endnote associated with the quote. Note 28 read: "Collier-Thomas, *Jesus, Jobs, and Justice*, 6–7," which meant that Erskine had quoted Collier-Thomas somewhere earlier in the chapter. But was this—no, it couldn't be, I thought. Was this the same Collier-Thomas that my grandmother had cleaned house for all those years ago? I scrambled to find the full citation. And there it was, there she was—Dr. Bettye Collier-Thomas in note 24: "Bettye Collier-Thomas, *Jesus, Jobs, and Justice* (New York: Alfred A. Knopf, 2010), 5."

I couldn't believe it. The archive, my search for what helped my ancestors survive the genocide of slavery was taking me back to my grandmother, which I thought it might, which I didn't want to do. It wasn't that I didn't want to travel back to my grandmother as much as the difficulty of facing what I would encounter when I got there. Though we talked over the phone every few weeks, the conversations were light, tentative. My mother had warned me that since my grandmother's stroke she wasn't the same—her memory, her intellectual acuity. She stumbled where she once was sure-footed and loped through all sorts of thorny discussions about politics, the South, the history of our family. I worried that her memory and lucidity might have been taken from her, erased. I grew up, no, I was fed on my grandmother's wild, sometimes heartbreaking stories—the mudpuppy down at the well who licked children in the face if they got too close, jumping down out of a tree onto the back of a horse named Old Dan, the "as-a-fizzy" carried in a pouch and hung around a baby's neck to keep away evil spirits, the black snake she once rode on as a frail and sickly child, her older brother lifting her from the back of the snake before it disappeared into a brackish swamp. My grandmother taught me about the medicine in water, how to use a spider web to heal a cut. Were these stories, these knowledges still with her, in her? Was she still the same woman who called White folks devilish to their faces, who taught me to ask "what about your beauty?" before I ever read James Baldwin, Toni Morrison, or Aimé Césaire? Since the stroke, I tiptoed in our conversations, not wanting to corroborate any of my fear—that like a hurricane, the stroke had blown everything down in her and dashed it to splinters and fragments.

To delay calling my grandmother, I called my mother. I told her what I had been working on—this essay on hush harbors, underground political action, freedom—and that I had found a woman that Nan may have worked for who has written on hush harbors. I was thinking of calling my grandmother to ask about the scholar, I told her. My mother said that indeed the name sounded like the woman my grandmother may have worked for and that I should call her. "You think it'd be all right?" I said to my mother. And my mother said, "Sure, she's probably at home." What I didn't ask was—is she good? Is Nan up for such a conversation? Would she even remember working for these Black women scholars? If my mother heard any tentativeness in my voice, she didn't let on.

I waited. I sat in my bedroom looking out of the window. It was December, one of those rare overcast, bloodless, chalk-white-sky days in central Texas. The day in its cold, in the rain running down the window reminded me of sitting in my grandmother's Nova, pulling up to one of the houses she cleaned, her flinging the door open, dragging out vacuums, spray bottles and sponges, cleaning cloths and feather dusters, and finally me.

I called her landline, which my grandmother is dedicated to keeping as much as she's dedicated to her ever-growing garden of plastic bags beneath her sink, her jar of rubber bands on the counter, and her drawer full of twist ties. Her collecting is the result of being a child of the Great Depression—nothing wasted because you never know what you'll need.

After a few rings, my grandmother answered. "Hello, Roger." It was the ebullient, fluvial voice that had greeted me since I was a child, one that always pronounced the second syllable of my name as "jah" instead of the hard "jer" that most did. Because of my grandmother's pronunciation of my name, in third grade, I began spelling it differently—Rajah—instead of Roger.

Surprised she answered, I stumbled in saying hello back. Though my mother told me my grandmother would be home, that was not a guarantee. Despite the worldwide pandemic, my grandmother is the type of woman for whom staying in the house is anathema and against her nature. She is constantly moving water. Like most Americans, she did her requisite few months of lockdown, but with a vaccine in sight, lunches at the church, doctor appointments, and soup kitchens to staff, her social calendar could no longer endure the virus or our federal government's inadequate response to it.

"Nan," I said. "I have something to ask you."

Though she said nothing, I could tell she was smiling on the other side of the line.

"I'm working on this essay, a project really, about hush harbors, about enslaved folks sneaking off into the woods to have church service by themselves, on their own terms, and I came upon a name. And it sounded familiar." I was rushing at this point from the excitement of finding Dr. Collier-Thomas's name in the archives, and in fear—several fears really. I feared that my grandmother would find what was exciting to me insignificant, would be just her grandson bellowing on about something; I feared that in trying to get her to remember a decades-ago past I would expose her decline, what of the past was lost to the past, to her aging, her stroke. "Did you used to work for a woman named Dr. Bettye Collier-Thomas?" I asked.

She said, "Yes."

"Well, her name and her book are in this other book I'm reading on Black churches called *Plantation Church*."

"That's her," she said. "I just spoke with her two weeks ago."

"Yes, yes, yes," I thought to myself. My body tingled. The writing, the thinking about Black folks, freedom, our invisible institutions, and our peace had taken me back to my grandmother, to the Doctors.

"You should call her," she said. "Let me get her phone number."

"She wouldn't mind?"

"No," my grandmother said. The "no" held much longer than the normal beat of one syllable. It was a "no" that said "you're a fool for asking."

Before I could get a pen, my grandmother was rattling off Dr. Collier-Thomas's phone number.

After receiving the number and promising that I would call, I said, "Nan, have you ever heard of a hush harbor? Have you ever heard of any of the old folks, your mother and grandfather talking about it?"

She said she hadn't, but when I described it—Black folks meeting in the woods, in swamps, in ravines, near bodies of water, streams and rivers, arranging thickets and canopies made of branches over their heads to have church by themselves away from the supervision of White folks—she said she had heard of it, just didn't know the name of it. My mention of water, in particular, jogged her memory.

My grandmother started to tell me about going fishing at night with the old folks when she was a girl, and how'd they sit on the water and tell stories in the boat—stories about the past as well as secret things, things that could only be told at night, while on water.

Did she remember any of these secret things—any of the past, I asked her.

"Code names," she said. "They used code names."

In the background I could hear my great-aunt Jewel, who lives with my grandmother, repeating my grandmother's name, "Elloree," and urging her to tell me something. What it was I wasn't sure.

After a moment, my grandmother said, "Roger, they went into the woods and used code names. 'Wade in the Water.' When White folks were coming, they would sing 'Wade in the Water,' and all the Black folks would get in the water to throw off the scent of the dogs. The water would protect them."

In the background, I could hear Aunt Jewel saying, "That's right, that's right" and goading my grandmother to say more. My grandmother said that's all she could remember, and besides, she had to take Aunt Jewel to an eye doctor appointment so she would have to call me later when she could remember more.

"But call Dr. Collier-Thomas. She'll talk to you. You might have to call her a few times. I just call her and call her until she answers," she said.

And with that, she hung up. My first call wasn't to Dr. Collier-Thomas but to my mother to relay what happened on the call, the feeling of awe still overwhelming. I had been coming to this essay, to this thinking for more thirty years and had not known it until December of 2020. My grandmother had been leading me here my whole life. My mother and I marveled at the revelation, at the sublimity of it, which we expressed back and forth to each other as "wow." Nothing else could be said.

After getting off the phone with my mother, I called Dr. Collier-Thomas. Like my grandmother instructed, I let the phone ring and ring. And ring. And ring. Dr. Collier-Thomas never answered. I called and called and called, but I never spoke with her. I emailed her as well—no response.

I called my grandmother a few days later. She had just slipped on her boots, coat, and gloves. A winter storm dumped several inches of snow on her driveway, and Mr. Ted, her neighbor across the street, had come over to help clear the snow. My grandmother had been shoveling her driveway since 1958, as long as she had been in the house, and no stroke or age would keep her from it. Though she said she'd take a moment to talk to me, I could hear the impatience in her voice. She wanted to get out into the cold and shovel. She feels most alive when she's in her body, sweating, even if it's struggling with several inches of snow. Though I couldn't be certain, I'm almost sure that she sat down on the step of the small landing in front of the back door, her white cordless phone in her hand.

Because I couldn't get Dr. Collier-Thomas on the phone, I realized—more so decided—that my grandmother would be my guide in thinking about hush harbors, in the research, in the quest for how to design some measure of peace for me and mine—for *us*. Besides, she told me to call her back, and it felt like—I felt like this project had to go through her. It was the course of things, fashioned outside of the rational. It was in the blood. Something had to be taught, carried through, and whatever it was had to be brought from her body to mine, her mouth to my ear. So I gave in, gave myself over to her, to whatever it was she was going to bring me in pieces or whole, well or sparsely remembered.

Again, I asked her if she remembered anything about hush harbors since our last conversation, what she might have learned about enslaved Black folks and their religion as a child. She started to answer my question but opaquely so beginning with her grandfather Walter Crawford, whom I also met before he died. It is one of my oldest memories, meeting an old tan-colored man with big hands lying on his deathbed. Later, I would learn from grandmother that he had been enslaved into the 1890s, that he was the son of his master. This memory of the room, his bed in it, there in the corner, comes back to me, and sometimes I wonder if it is actually my memory or a memory that I have been told about so much that I have made it a memory. Regardless, my grandmother starts from where I know—Walter Crawford, his slave-master father wanting him to bear his name, wanting the world to know that he was indeed his son. I found this desire of my slave-master great-great-great-grandfather peculiar, but I said nothing, kept listening as my grandmother continued.

My grandmother speaks in monologues. She is not a conversationalist. You don't interrupt. You listen. And, when you can, you pierce the conversation with a "is that right?"

When I could cajole her to tell me more about the family's history with slavery and the church, she said she didn't know much because her mother didn't really talk about it. "My mother didn't complain," she said, which I interpreted as her mother didn't want to talk about the hardships of slavery, Reconstruction, sharecropping, and her life intertwined within this brutal history. But what my grandmother said next brought me back to hush harbors and the need for subversive worship in the middle of the ongoing catastrophe of abject poverty and racism, although I didn't see it at first. "My mom instilled prayer in us, to pray with your family." To pray as a way of confronting the brutalities of anti-Blackness and terror.

At first, I thought my grandmother's monologue about the importance of prayer was a veiled attempt at proselytizing me, nudging me to get back to the church—me, her sin-sick grandson who wore locs, that "girl's hairstyle," for all those years. She wasn't moving away from my question about slavery, religion, hush harbors, and finding peace. She was moving toward it. In emphasizing her mother's belief in prayer, my grandmother was describing the logic, history, and efficacy of the hush harbor but not explicitly so; its traditions, sensibilities, holdovers, and retentions adapted and transformed by my family. The harbor, its subversiveness, its quiet was all there in my grandmother's monologue. The hush harbor was speaking, and my grandmother was speaking as hush harbor. She was answering my questions, my wonderings, but in the way that archives and elders answer questions, which is to offer the gift of the answer, then to offer the gift of the question that you didn't ask but was underneath or to the side of the originally asked question. Which is why elders often take this monologic opaque form to answer questions. They are answering the question you mean to ask, in all its fullness, in all its opacity.

Outside of my grandmother, I've witnessed this form of question answering before, this hush harbor sensibility. Ericka Huggins, a founding member of the Black Panther Party and former political prisoner, sat at a dais at the University of New Mexico in 2006 practicing this sort of discernment. The Black Panthers' archives were being rehoused at the university, and there was a weekend-long celebration in honor of the fortieth year of the Panthers' founding and their archives' finding a permanent home. Huggins, along with several other former Panthers, including Elaine Brown and David Hilliard, fielded questions from the audience. The questions were sometimes maligned with fear and anxiety. One woman in a long, brown winter coat stood up, walked to the microphone in the center of the ballroom, and recalled being a young girl, watching the Panthers drill and practice formations on an asphalt basketball court, their guns and berets overwhelming her. Too much, too much for her. Rather than meet the woman's fear and disgust, Huggins stealthily turned from it, from the accusation in the woman's question toward what was below it. If I remember correctly, Huggins said, "What you mean to ask . . . why were those young men drilling on the court only understood as fear?" In the redirection of the woman's question, she highlights the irony of Black people defending themselves from the brutalizing occupation of their communities by the police as dangerous to other Black people. Then, Huggins proceeded to answer the question, to delve into the fear of seeing Black folks armed, the misinformation campaigns that the FBI and local law enforcement deployed in Black communities to squelch the effectiveness of the Panthers' civic outreach, the food and education programs, the radical reimagining of Black communities as autonomous and in control of their lives.

I sat and watched in awe. Question after question, Huggins peered into the confused, trepidatious darkness of the conference attendees' questions, into the misinformation and smear campaigns, and found the kernel of what was being asked, what the longing was. I was twenty-six at the time, and although I couldn't name it then, I gropingly understood that her ability to see into people's questions, to find the question below the question was not only a gift of discernment but necessary in the struggle for Black folks' freedom in the United States—seeing what was obscuring freedom and its articulation and getting underneath it, unshackling freedom from fear.

Harriet Tubman understood this practice, this necessity to love opaquely, difficultly; that in order for Black people to be free, you must see below their doubt, their fear—what might make them turn back toward their captors and masters—and place a pistol to their fear, to their back, and tell them to keep walking toward freedom, toward themselves. "Live free or die," she was known to say to enslaved folks who tried to turn back or would not go on in their journey, frozen in place in some hollow or dugout.

Journeying toward freedom and peace requires an ironic relationship to disaster, to death. By that I mean you must walk toward disaster, what will seem like certain death. I've come to realize that the walking, the stealing away from slavery is a type of prayer. Each step both a question and an answer. Tubman's pistol, a type of prayer and an answer to prayer; it, too, was a kind of hush and harbor—as in "hush up and keep moving," harbor as in "shelter is at the end of this. I am pointing toward the peace you seek."

Listening to my grandmother talk of prayer is pointing me toward my peace and back to the hush harbor. The harbor, like prayer, was a place of practicing the invisible, allowing the imagination all its theology, orthodoxy, and profligacy—to wander, wonder, and be. For the enslaved, prayer became a preparation, a tilling of the ground for the future in the present, an articulation of the sequestered or unsaid, what had to be hushed or hummed about while working in rice fields and in rows of tobacco and cotton underneath the watchful eye of the master, overseer, and even other enslaved folks. Prayer, like a spell, reifies a potential through the apparatus of the voice, through sound gathered and bent toward presencing what is absent. What does not exist in form, something like freedom, can exist in practice, in the trying out of one's voice, in throwing one's voice toward what one desires. It's bringing down the walls of Jericho, or in this case bringing about freedom, peace, a sense of wholeness before one can achieve it in the physical realm. The hush harbor offered a place, a physical location to speak of the invisible and imagine a bondage-free future.

In *Slave Religion: "The Invisible Institution" in the Antebellum South*, the late scholar Albert Raboteau writes of the subversive nature of prayer and the subsequent penalty for being caught praying, citing Gus Clark, a formerly enslaved man. "My Boss didn' 'low us to go to church, er to pray er sing," says Clark. "Iffen he ketched us prayin' er singin' he whupped us."

The penalty for getting caught praying or singing in a hush harbor was particularly severe. Henry Bibb, a formerly enslaved man, reported that he "was threatened with five hundred lashes on the naked back for attending a prayer meeting conducted by slaves on a neighboring plantation, because he had no permission to do so." Ironically, his master, who threatened him, was a Baptist deacon. If there was anybody who believed in prayer, it would have been his master it seemed. "Charlotte Martin asserted that 'her oldest brother was whipped to death for taking part in one of the religious ceremonies.'" According to Raboteau and the oral records of the formerly enslaved, White folks worried that enslaved people might be praying to God to lift them out of bondage.

Of course, enslaved folks were praying for such escape. In testimony after testimony, enslaved Black folks reported retreating to a "private praying ground, 'a ole twisted thick-rooted muscadine bush'" or "huddl[ing] behind quilts and rags," which had been "thoroughly wetted to 'keep the sound of their voices from penetrating the air.'" The blankets would then be hung "'in the form of a little room, or tabernacle."

The forms of subterfuge and masking of sound in these vernacular zones of study were vast. "On one Louisiana plantation, when 'the slaves would steal away into the woods at night and hold services,' they 'would form a circle on their knees around the speaker who would also be on his knees. He would bend forward and speak into or over a vessel of water to drown the sound."

Iron pots turned upside down, teakettles placed at the thresholds of cabins, teakettles placed at the threshold of the harbor in the woods, washtubs and pots hung bottom upward from the eaves overhead in the "little brush church house"—any- and everything was used to court privacy and silence. In fact, privacy and silence were presiding principles over the hush harbor and Black spiritual life. One formerly enslaved person remembers his parents telling him not to reveal to the master what went on in the slave quarters at night when they prayed for deliverance. "'My master used to ask us children . . . 'Do your folks pray at night?' We said, 'No' cause our folks had told us what to say. But the Lord have mercy, there was plenty of that going on. They'd pray, 'Lord, deliver us from under bondage.'"

When I asked my grandmother if she had ever heard of folks courting privacy in hush harbors, she said she had, although she herself never experienced a hush harbor. Her father and grandfather both spoke of these clandestine meetings in the woods, and they sometimes spoke of them together. "If we ever go back south," she said, "I'll show you some places they used to go." She meant, I'll show you the old dugouts and hollows; I'll take you behind the old Baptist church near the creek where folks would gather secretly before a white clapboard church sat on the grounds; I'll show you where in the woods near the old school-house folks used to go to holler and praise and pray.

Something in my grandmother's promise felt weak, as if we might never again go back south together, as if she were throwing a line toward me that might disappear on the water, in the air between us, a line that I would never be able to pick up, but nevertheless the line must be thrown. I grasp at it and try to hold it, imagine us back south together—even if just in the space of this call. I desperately want to go back south with her, to go back to Black Creek and sit again in the schoolhouse and eat shrimp and grits with her, and now that I'm old enough, sit with the elders and older folks behind the Baptist church and fry fish and listen to the stories, the history, the myth and folklore of the mudpuppy, of old Dan. This is not nostalgia or sentimentalism. My grandmother is disappearing behind the ravages of a stroke. The plague of time. And though I know that her eventual passing from this world to the next does not end her ability to pass knowledge to me, I do want to sit with her one more time on a morning where the sun comes through the windows in that old schoolhouse and the wooden floorboards are catching against my socks, and maybe we'd say nothing at all. Just be together—back south.

As it happened, during another phone call with my grandmother in which I asked her about family history and hush harbors, I was in the South, in Savannah, Georgia, sitting on the edge of Forsyth Park where a spiked, wrought-iron gate protects a tall, stone Confederate monument memorializing Lafayette McLaws, a general in the Confederate Army, his iron head sitting on a pedestal in front of the obelisk stone structure. There, beneath the oaks and magnolias hawked in moss, I read my grandmother the portion of the essay I had written about the courting of secrecy in hush harbors: "The forms of subterfuge and masking of sound . . . were vast. . . . Iron pots turned upside down, teakettles placed at the thresholds of cabins . . . any- and everything was used to court privacy and silence." What she said next, I had not and could not have expected.

"God taught Reverend Crawford and my mom to read the Bible."

I asked what that meant; could she explain a little more. She told me that no one had taught them how to read. That they both had sat before the Bible, and through divine inspiration, divine communion, God revealed how to read not only the words but the message in and below the words.

At first, I didn't quite understand why my grandmother was revealing this piece of family history to me and how it might relate to hush harbors and the courting of secrecy, but then I began to think of the hush harbor as a space of revelation, a space of study. My grandmother's revelation of her mother's and great-grandfather's learning how to read was another enactment of the hush harbor, was her studying with me. Her taking me down to the waters, to the hollows and dugouts, to knowledge produced in those spaces. She was unveiling the history of the sorts of visions produced in those spaces as well as escorting me into the wilderness for me to find my own vision. Her revelation answered how one resurrects peace out of what feels like scarcity or lack. That there is an abundance, a surplus even in depravation, in the illegible. A knowing, ways of coming to an understanding that are improvised into being. The hush harbor courts and resides *with* and *in* the invisible. Within this invisibility, nowhere, and no place, whole worlds reside. Finding one's peace requires a communing in this sort of opacity, study, solitude, communing with what might look like a jumble of letters scrawled on an onionskin page.

My grandmother's mother and great-grandfather wanted to know something—how to read, how to feel connected to the Christian God—

and did not believe that it couldn't be revealed to them even if it sat obscured in something called a text. No knowledge could be kept from them. All one must do, had to do is to sit with one's desire, one's longing, and the answer would come, the desire reached, the longing fulfilled. Again, solitude. Again, another way or method of reading. Being. Help me, Holy Ghost! In fact, that's what the knowledge turned upon. The knowing came from spirit, from the metaphysical, from something for which language had to be improvised through feeling—out and from nowhere.

The hush harbor turns upon this nowhereness, this making of language, a way of knowing and transmitting knowledge through improvisation and opacity. Peter Randolph, a formerly enslaved man who escaped from a plantation in Prince George County, Virginia, describes the use of signs, improvisation, and subterfuge not only to communicate to other enslaved folks about harbor meetings but also to keep the hush harbor outside of legibility, to keep it safe from surveillance and infiltration:

> Not being allowed to hold meetings on the plantation, the slaves assemble in the swamp, out of reach of the patrols. They have an understanding among themselves as to the time and place of getting together. This is often done by the first one arriving breaking boughs from the trees, and bending them in the direction of the selected spot. Arrangements are then made for conducting the exercises.

Pause. Something tells me to stop, to end this revelation, this quoting of Randolph. It has nothing to do with style or making the text more readerly, friendly. It has everything to do with the ethics of revealing a secret, one that for hundreds of years allowed Black folks zones of privacy and productive illegibility.

I take my cue on resisting legibility from Randolph himself. Look again at what I have decided to quote. Randolph says, "They have an understanding among themselves as to the time and place of getting together." Randolph does not tell us how they come to this agreement, this "understanding" about time and place. He gives none of that process, discloses nothing about the rationale of enslaved folks. Who are the organizers? Who is invited? How are folks invited to the harbor? What was the regularity or irregularity of the meetings? All of this information is left out of his description. In this way, Randolph's deft disclosure of the organizing of the hush harbor reminds me of the purposeful gaps and lacunae in the slave narratives of Frederick Douglass and Harriet Jacobs. Randolph gives us an approximation of the organization but divulges nothing of use, nothing that would compromise the harbor's most efficacious and subversive practice— secrecy, withholding, and knowledge production. Randolph published his account of hush harbors in his slave narrative, *Sketches of Slave Life: or, Illustrations of the "Peculiar Institution,"* in 1855, six years before the Civil War began and ten years before slavery was abolished in the United States. Unlike Henry "Box" Brown, who mailed himself to freedom and then gave interview after interview about it, Randolph understood that the harbor must be preserved despite his being freed in 1847. In disclosing too much one might foreclose the strategy for others—get in the way of someone else's freedom . . . which sends me thinking about our hostility to silence as a useful form of protesting the slings, arrows, and police bullets of anti-Blackness and racism in America today.

We live in a loquacious age, one in which silence gets mischaracterized as passive, as noninvolvement, as capitulating to subjection. Everyone's in their feelings and talking about it. On Facebook, Instagram, Twitter, LinkedIn. In fact, talking—talking shit, talking slick, talking about politics, talking about how to make more money, talking about how to get more likes, garner more retweets, more followers, more more more (whatever that more is)—might be one of the defining characteristics of the twenty-first century. Talking as an infinite credit, as a speculation and rebundling of debt. It is as if, in the talking, in loquaciousness, everyone is putting their pain to work, to labor in the marketplace of ideas. If you're not speaking up and out about your pain, your marginalization, putting your grievances into the social and political marketplace, compelling them to labor and work for you, you're viewed as somehow deficient, reprobate, socially negligent, and politically irresponsible. Loquaciousness is valued as a sign of political zeal and commitment and "being on the right side of history." Apocryphally and incorrectly attributed to Zora Neale Hurston, folks love to recite and offer up this clickworthy, everywhere-on-the-internet quote as evidence of the need to speak up and about one's oppression: "If you're silent about your pain, they'll kill you and say you enjoyed it." Hurston never made this statement. It is actually a reworking of a sentence from Alice Walker's novel *Possessing the Secret of Joy*. Regardless, the sentiment rather than its source is the zeitgeisty admonition of our era, but I wonder if this constant announcement of pain, putting one's subjection to work isn't a sort of gimmick, a trafficking in a type of disaster capitalism.

I wonder if our loquaciousness isn't sinking us further into exploitation, a further fashioning of our bodies and pain as commodity, as that which should be laboring rather than freeing us from market and work. In *The Undercommons: Fugitive Planning & Black Study*, Stefano Harney and Fred Moten characterize this phenomenon of loquaciousness as gregariousness, as a type of labor and exploitation rather than as an access to citizenship and democracy because one must labor in the telling, in the trying to get people to understand your pain. It's an extending of the workplace, of exploitation rather than a reprieve from it. And that telling can become an immaterial labor that is transformed into a commodity, a product not within one's control, that eventually can be deployed by a corporation—the National Football League or Pepsi, for instance—to make actual capital, to extend their brand. As a result, nothing happens for you or alleviates or redresses your pain or your subjection.

The violence experienced by you and your people in the streets, violence legislated on senate floors continues, and all you got was a commercial and some promises. Senators taking a knee in a capitol rotunda with kente cloth draped over their shoulders while outside the rotunda the police continue to gun down and kill your people. Police officers on the steps of the mayor's office kneeling in a show of solidarity against police violence and a few hours later tasing and tear-gassing the protestors they just kneeled with. Irony of ironies. Ice storms and the electrical grid of Texas goes down because it can no longer respond to all the requests for power during the storm. Where are your senators when folks are huddled around propane fires in their living rooms, ripping holes in their walls and trying to warm pipes that will burst anyway, flooding their dining rooms and kitchens? Where are your senators? Answer: Heading to the "indigenous spa rituals" and amenity-laden hotels in Cancún, Mexico.

Disaster comes and comes and comes. Everyone acts surprised, acts as if it were the first time, acts as if you and I were somehow deficient in expressing our discontent, our sufficient and understandable rage. If we could have only spoken up more and better and louder or more forcefully or more eloquently or . . . or . . . or . . . This is the seduction of talking and our affliction, our subjection. We think if we talk enough we will be released from it. But we have been talking. Have we yet to be released?

What is the place of silence, subterfuge, illegibility in our struggle for freedom? What if it's in the hush? Recently, I read an interview where someone said, "No change has ever come about by people being silent." And I thought to myself, "That simply is not true." What about the hush harbor? Though Black folks shouted, prayed, laughed, ministered, and studied together while in the harbor, they also courted and deployed silence as a fundamental part of the ritual, as a hedge and gate that protected them, allowed them to carry on behind it, and envision an autonomous future.

I think of Sixo, a minor character from Toni Morrison's *Beloved*, as the orisha or archangel of the hush harbor not only because he steals away at night from Sweet Home, the plantation where he's captured, and goes into the woods to "keep his bloodlines open," but also because Sixo stops speaking English because he sees no future in it. Sixo's refusal to speak, his withholding becomes the avenue to his peace, to his freedom. His illegibility authors or creates the possibility of him being able to know himself. "In America, the color of my skin had stood between myself and me," writes James Baldwin in *Nobody Knows My Name*. Could this also be said of talking, speaking? The talking, the always explaining of one's self to others—one's pains and aggrievements—are a type of barrier, the thing keeping us from ourselves? Talking, then, functions as a capitulation to racism rather than a resistance to it. As Toni Morrison noted, the goal of racism is "distraction," a manipulation that ultimately recenters the oppressor rather than the oppressed. "Somebody says you have no language and so you spend 20 years proving that you do," says Morrison in a keynote address at Portland State in 1975. "Somebody says your head isn't shaped properly so you have scientists working on the fact that it is. Somebody says that you have no art so you dredge that up. . . . *None of that is necessary.* There will always be *one more thing.*" In other words, keep that Black boy, that Black girl running. Keep them trying to prove themselves to be human. What if we jettison or opt out of the human project as defined by racism, White supremacy, and the nation? What if we forgo trying to speak, make ourselves known or legible in the language, in the poetry, in the laws, in the science of our captors? What if when our captors said or say, "you're not human," we said, we say, "fine," and turn from them. Let them have the human. Better yet, what if we said nothing at all—like Sixo? Withholding, then, acts as a critique of the coercive transparency that comes about because of racism and the multiple modes of surveillance deployed to deracinate Black life in America.

I worked in a barbershop as a boy—sweeping hair, shining shoes, running to the pharmacy on the corner to buy cigarettes or to the bank to get one hundred dollars in ones. Mr. George and Mr. Tom, two of the older barbers, used to say, "Roger, never let your right hand know what your left hand is doing." Sometimes, they'd laugh or wink after. Other times, they'd look down at me, a left eye cast toward me and large, as if they wanted me to understand something below the words, something that had to be gestured at with the body and not just with language. I hadn't thought much of those moments in the barbershop, but they were trying to communicate the necessity of subterfuge, of withholding. They weren't just trying to talk slick or teach me how to hustle, but in between shape-ups, box fades, and the clouds of talcum powder that rose when they popped the barber gown or knocked the wooden handle of the neck duster against the top of the chair, they were transmitting to me the centuries-old tradition of the hush harbor—withholding, moving discreetly.

Moving elsewhere. The writer James Baldwin himself improvised a hush harbor. Europe and Asia acted as his dugouts and hollows, his sojourns into elsewheres. Leaving America because he felt he couldn't and wouldn't survive the racist brutality of the country, Baldwin took up residence in London, Paris, Istanbul, in places as far-flung as Spain, Corsica, and Scandinavia, which allowed him an opportunity to tear down the barrier between him and himself that America had erected. Baldwin likened it to being released from an affliction, but, as he notes in the introduction to *Nobody Knows My Name*, "Nothing is more desirable than to be released from an affliction, but nothing is more frightening than to be divested of a crutch." Who was he now that he no longer had this barrier between him and himself?

Who are we?

Who are we when we are beyond talk, when we have thrown off the lights, the definitions and we are in the dark? Isn't this the question we've been meaning to come to? Isn't this the question we want to answer, and, if we cannot answer, sit with? Here, here is our silence—our peace and our beauty. What will we make with it?

Might this be what Black folks saw, knew, experienced in the hush harbor? Might this be the ecstasy that greeted them down at the water, on their knees, in ravines, beneath tubs and over the open bodies of teakettles. Might this be the way toward freedom and peace? Might we need to be still? Might we steal and still our peace?

Might we need to court and abide with stillness—not forever but for a moment? As Baldwin notes in *Nobody Knows My Name*, havens are temporary and fleeting, but they do allow you to figure out who you are and how you might want to be in the world. The silence in havens and harbors allows you to ask about your beauty, to travel deeper into it, to give yourself what the world would deprive you of—you, you, and us.

Coda

It is February in Austin, Texas, and rage is everywhere in the country. Ice shags the pines, the crepe myrtles, the neighbors' trash cans, the streetlights, the thin and shedding bark of the junipers. I am walking with my daughter down, out of the neighborhood into the woods because I'm in need of a hush, some quiet that is not constructed of noise-canceling headphones or the hum of a hot water heater, something to get in the way of the chaos of the country: impeachment trials and the recent unsuccessful coup on the federal government in Washington, DC.

Here, in Austin, rumors abounded that there was a similar plot afoot—a plan to attack the gold-domed capitol building that sits at the top of the hill on Congress Avenue. Helicopter blades bludgeoned and ripped the sky above me on January 6. I was beneath it all, unaware, running through the streets of the city on a jog on the day of the coup. Then chaos, sirens, black cars streaking through traffic lights—the sudden anarchy of uncertainty. I felt as if my life was once again being prepared for the gallows. That feeling stayed with me for several days after the coup, so it was time to go down into the woods, to go seek some quiet.

The neoprene of my daughter's pink boots brushing against each other and her chatter are the only sounds around us besides the branches overhead clattering against each other and the earthbound, wind-swept, ice-shrouded bushes ticking against each other when the wind brought its occasional small gusts. My daughter stops, takes off her glove, and rubs the icicles stretching down from one of the bushes. The bush looks as if it's been caught midblow and frozen there in the drama of having been blown. She performs this ritual with each bush she meets hanging over the path: stopping, pulling her glove off, rubbing the ice encasing one of its leaves, putting her glove back on, and moving to the next one. Sometimes, she scurries and squats under their cascading limbs, amazed that she can now hunker down beneath what only days before stood upright, sentinel, and unbothered on the side of the path.

"The enslaved would have used these bushes as signs," I almost say to her. "They would have come down here to get away from their masters." Instead, I say nothing. I allow her to skip down the path, touching the ice with her bare hand, talking loudly, exclaiming into the quiet woods, marveling at how different the branches look with all the ice over them. Everything alabaster.

"Daddy, look, Daddy, look."

Though I seek some quiet, I give in to her excitement, say nothing. Allow her to praise the natural world, allow her this wonder, allow her to be whatever noise she wants to be and make. I give myself a hush. In fact, I give her one, too, and allow my eyes to follow her from wonder to wonder—all of it covered in ice and her voice.

Down the path we go until we come to the entrance of a narrower path, one that leads to a small waterfall. We slip into the darkness, beneath the overhanging limbs, the brush and loose rock. This path is the path I've been meaning to come to because at the bottom of it is where I imagine a hush harbor taking place when Texas was an infant of a state, before it became a state of sprawling cities, oil and gas conglomerates, petrochemical complexes heaped up high on the shorelines with thousands of miles of pipeline running beneath its swamps and estuaries into Louisiana. I also imagine, there, beneath the waterfall and limestone, convening a contemporary hush harbor, an alcove where I might invite those who need some peace in the middle of this most recent catastrophe of America—the coronavirus pandemic, the coup, the Texas legislature's attacks on voting rights, women's bodily autonomy, and teaching American history. Here, we might gather and bring down the wall that keeps us from ourselves. Here, we might rest and study and plan. And love, love, too.

I say nothing about this desire for peace to my daughter, who's running about in this new world the ice has made of the old world. She is five, delirious with what the wooded world looks like encased in ice. She has not yet been fatigued by the violence of the noisy world and cannot yet understand that noise can be a type of violence. Her noise is the joyful noise, the noise of discovery—not the coup, the mob, the war, the bomb. Racism, sexism, malignant forms of nationalism and patriotism. All noise. Distraction. Death. There, in the wilderness, I allow my daughter this moment of childhood, though, there in the wilderness, I wrestle with myself about the ethics of that allowance, that sort of privilege in a world where some children are not allowed and cannot afford this sort of easeful tumbling through it. The truth of the matter is that she, a Black child, can only bear this caul of innocence for so long before the world snatches it from her and reminds her that she, too, must survive America; she, too, must develop a beauty, must bear one name in the streets and another at home. And this bearing and moving will be what it is to be Black in America. America has yet to try to kill her and call that killing love.

For a moment, I wonder: could I tell her of hush harbors, discuss their history with her? Would she understand this place we have come to before, mostly in the summer, to float homemade boats and sit and look at the water as anything other than that—a makeshift playground during the pandemic? Would she understand why I have come here with her today, the quiet thrall of the place, its hollows, outcroppings, hideaway places, perfect for housing a hushed sound, for gathering and being undetected in the gathering?

My daughter calls for me to come and run with her through the frozen underbrush. I tell her go ahead, that I want to stay up on the rock and look out for a bit; but, she's free to run. She does. She hops and runs and yells, plunging down the short hill on the north side of the falls where the water gathers in a small, dark pool. "See," she says. "It's not scary."

"I just want to be up here," I tell her standing on the outcropping of rocks.

She can have the snarl of bushes, rock, and refuse down there. I want the water, the trees encased in ice, up here. I'm imagining an invisible tabernacle of enslaved Black folks praying, praising, and getting happy. I don't say the last part out loud to my daughter, though I am thinking about how Black folks might have come over the rocks, down to this outcropping. I can see someone standing there—as I am—keeping watch over the folks huddled beneath the falls or crouched in the hollows.

One danger gets me to thinking about another. My mind drifts to an email about a bobcat spotted in a park attached to the woods. Where was it now? Could it be close? The enslaved folks who hunkered down in hush harbors must have encountered all sorts of wild animals: bobcats, javelinas, skunks, possums, snakes, the occasional bear. Those Black folks would have to go down in prayer with bobcats if they were going to come up with their "bloodlines open"—by that I mean greater than their enslavement, with a semblance of their beauty intact. Wrestling bobcats and bears was the cost of imagining freedom.

My daughter comes back up the hill, and I tell her it's time to go back. The thought of the bobcat in the woods begins to overwhelm me. I point to the stream between us, tell her to help me find our way back home, which is our custom. I lead on the way to wherever we're going during these hikes and sojourns in the woods; she takes us back. However, as we both step into the stream, I stop her, make her stand quietly in the almost still water. She must have anticipated what I was about to ask her because before I could ask her to tell me what she hears, she asks me. "What do you hear?"

The ice in the trees, some of it shattering, the water moving over slate rock beneath us. A few crows cawing in the gunmetal gray sky. In my mind, I can hear Black folks praying, singing, caught up in the rapture of their voices. My grandmother, I can hear my grandmother praying.

What I didn't understand then but I understand now is that we had convened a hush harbor. My daughter asking me to pay attention to my body, to the natural world around us, to be so thoroughly there in the water with her.

I was mistaken in the belief that I needed to give her context, a history of the harbor in order to convene one with her. My daughter needed none of that. The making of the harbor was in the coming down into the trees, standing in the water, and listening for what your body knows, listening for what it wants to remember.

Reading Fire, Reading the Stars

I was born to a saint, someone who heard the light, who heard in the light the voice of God so put down her love of the world, put down her love of worldly music, put down her love of Michael Jackson and his records and the dancing she did to them and listened only for the light, for God, who spoke to her, told her to turn from every wickedness and follow him into small churches heated by kerosene furnaces and to pray for the end of the world. Thus, I was born in fire.

Unlike Frederick Douglass, who said that enslaved people knew very little if anything about the circumstances of their birth, likening their births to those of horses, I would come to know more than just the season for which I clattered down from my mother into the bright hospital lights there in Willingboro, New Jersey, the hospital surrounded by apple orchards and cornfields, squat, one-story brick apartment buildings, and strip malls. It was January 23, 1980, in the middle of a northeastern winter that everyone called "bad," which means I had to come to this earth bearing my own fire if I were going survive the America I entered. An America just five years out of the haze and muck and blood of the Vietnam War, an America still adjusting to the purported end of Jim Crow, an America for which all the great leaders were dead or on their way; Huey P. Newton, the former leader of the Black Panther Party, strung out on drugs and just nine years from dying ignominiously in the streets of Oakland, reportedly looking for a fix. The bullet, cocaine, COINTELPRO, the FBI's infiltration program designed to destroy organizations like the Panthers and leaders like Newton, had done—and were doing—their jobs. Reagonomics and neoconservative politics stood at the door and were about to be welcomed into the house of America, and, with their good manners and patriotism, began to tear the family curtains down from the walls, burn the drapes, comforters, carpets, banisters, mattresses, and the children's toys; strap the dog to the roof of the station wagon, ride out of town, and sell what remained of the land to whoever wanted to buy it.

The burning house of America greeted me every Sunday at the Sanctified Church in the form of a sermon delivered by Reverend Flagg, who brought *the word*, a mixture of exegetical and reader-response criticism that drew as much from Leviticus, Psalms, the Gospels of Matthew and Luke, and Revelation as from the nightly news, gossip, family history and lore, weather reports, folktales, and his life as truck driver and in his younger days, a lothario and scamp.

The *word* brought by Reverend Flagg often found its way into contemporary and world politics, social critique, the problem with Black folks, the problem with White folks, the HIV crisis, which had taken some relatives of family members in the church in the mid- to late 1980s. During testimony service or after church, parishioners stood in the light of those deaths and reported back the horrors, cousins, aunties stripped down to nothing and bone by the disease and no one willing to touch them in their hospital beds in fear of contracting it. Very few of us knew what HIV was at the time, how it was contracted, so ignorance roved over America and every conversation about it. Especially conversations in the church houses of America, the disease becoming a manifestation of God's punishment of the wicked and another sign of the coming apocalypse, the mountains crying out and falling, the blood of the last battle rising to touch the mane and bridle of the white horse of the Lord.

Like James Baldwin, I, too, grew up among the promises of brimstone and fire and wailing and talk of the last days in a storefront Pentecostal church, a church that sometimes had to relocate to school gymnasiums or parishioners' living rooms depending upon landlords and rising rents and, sometimes, malfunctioning furnaces. The son of a Sunday school teacher and Holly Roller, I grew up a dark-skin boy, dark for the Northeast, that is, which made me aware of what America did not want to see (but could not hide) and thus saw everywhere. I was both a veil that one had to pass through to get to the past, and I was the past that some wanted to avoid. I was history and outside history. I reminded America and even my grandmother of its ignominious yesterday—slavery, Reconstruction, Jim Crow, lynchings, sharecropping, and poverty—and the day before that, the past-past—Africa, what G. W. F. Hegel imagined sat outside of history, and what Americans imagined in its wilderness, in the native, in the non-Christian. The past and the past-past, history and outside of history provides contradictory and cataclysmic conflagrations in a Pentecostal church, where the Blackest among us want to be washed whiter than snow in order to be worthy of the star-filled and golden crown awaiting in the afterlife. This was the sort of Pentecostal church where folks from the pastor on down to the parishioners spoke of any number of spirits that could possess a sinner—avarice, lust, gluttony, addiction—though, in fact, according to the Bible there was only one spirit, so a Pentecostal church that had a revisionist bent on biblical literalism and Christianity, a Pentecostal church where the pastor's sermon became more and more politically radical as it wore on and the kerosene-operated water heater lulled everyone sitting in those brown, metal folding chairs into a sleepy-headed "yes." It was there, under those circumstances, that I learned to read. These living rooms and storefront churches in strip malls behind Red Lobsters and Jamesways and Kmarts, holding a Bible or a Sunday school pamphlet on my lap, broken tambourine zills on the floor, were where I learned to be a critic. Because everyone in Full Gospel Church of God was a critic. It was a requirement.

Unlike most churches, Sunday school at Full Gospel Church of God was not separated by age groups. Children at four and five sat in the same room—living room or gymnasium auditorium—with teenagers, young adults, the middle-aged, and the old alike and puzzled over the same biblical texts and lessons. As I child, I was allowed to raise a young hand and contribute with a comment or question if so moved. And sometimes, children did contribute. The adults leaned their head toward the young voice, very seriously listening because the thought was one never knows how God might move or communicate. The Christian God was known to bring messages and revelations through all manner of animal—mule, horse, even a child—so no one dismissed the words of the young because even there, in the soft voice and the unstudied and unsteady grammar, a potential fire or lamp unto the feet of the righteous. So children were often thought of as potential oracles, their words in the space of the church studied, their faces and bodies watched for potential signs of God announcing some need or message, some sign of his coming or disaster. Which also meant that adults misread the actions and words of the children of the church, ascribing to us genius or intelligence that was dubious at best—maybe there, maybe not there—especially around reading.

Sunday school always began with a collective reading. Men, in double-breasted suits and wing tips and Stacy Adams brogues of every hue from watermelon to snakeskin green; women, in feathers and hats of all sorts of styles and shapes, stood up from their folding chairs and read the seven to ten verses that were on a pamphlet distributed down the small aisles of the church. The pamphlet contained the Sunday school lesson for the week. Often, there weren't enough for the children, so we wound up looking over the shoulder or outstretched arm of an adult nearby. My sister and I raised ourselves on tiptoe to read over the arm of our mother and grandmother. We were fascinated by the green and black text in boxes or a map on the back of the pamphlet where words like Cappadocia and Aegean Sea arched over landmasses and bodies of water that did not resemble the continents and oceans and seas we were used to seeing on the small globes at our elementary school.

My sister and I would mouth the words we heard coming out of the mouths of the adults, trying to anticipate them before they could move on to the next. We became so good at pretending to read that Sister Spencer, a Jamaican woman who often led Sunday school, stopped the choral reading and asked if my three-year-old sister and I, myself just five-years-old, were actually reading. The church was quiet in anticipation of the answer. In the space of Full Gospel Church of God, a church that believed in signs and wonders and miracles, this could be possible. Also, my sister and I had gotten quite good at anticipating the words coming out of the mouths of the adults so it must have appeared that we were, in fact, reading. Sister Spencer stared down at my sister as if a mule had suddenly received the gift of speech, and I remember chuckling inside though I tried to look as stone-faced as possible at the moment. My mother was also amused and answered immediately, "No, they were just mimicking folks." Anticipating the sound. But it was shortly after that we were, in fact, reading and often demanding our own pamphlet to follow along. We were never given our own because there was always a shortage of them because we were not a wealthy church. Many of the saints lived in Section 8 housing or received financial assistance from the government so the coffers for things like tambourines and Sunday school materials were often collectively raised and short. So old pamphlets were given to the children to pacify us so that we, too, could pretend to as if we were participating in the experience of group study.

The old pamphlets kept me entertained for only as long as I couldn't read. I wanted to contribute and study with the older saints, which I now realize was a sign that I would probably take up the mantle of criticism and end up in graduate school though then I knew nothing of PhD programs and poetry and halogen lights and the vow of poverty one takes in pursuing writing about others writing. In the early '80s, I just wanted to know what was being said by this mysterious God who somehow made folks tremble, shake, weep, speak in unknown tongues, and fall out on the floor of a living room. I was drawn to mystery, to the power of a word like "yes" said over and over again until it seemed the church and everyone in it lifted up into something beyond the limitations of their sicknesses and bounced checks and empty kitchen cabinets. That "yes," the power of it, began in those Sunday school lessons, in the words in the boxes, and I wanted access to it if for no other reason than to figure out how to deploy them to bring a few more groceries in the house, bring my father out of the mental bondage that kept him from us, bring my mother off her knees at night, the blanket beneath her face wet each time she rose. So, I demanded a pamphlet of that week's lesson.

My mother responded by staring at me through the gauzy white veil of her hat. Her stare and the angle of her brim said "not today, don't test me," and I needed nothing more than that. Not a word, not a "no," not a nothing. I let go of her arm and dropped my supplication because otherwise I would be taken to the back of the church, the bathroom if I were lucky and mother's patience could bear it, and made to feel—to catch—her version of the Holy Ghost and his fire. My mother had the quickest hands you've ever seen on a woman just barely five feet. My Lord, the thunder she could bring! So, I chose relaxing. Or more so, listening.

I'd listen to Sister Spencer, also known as Mother Spencer, sing an invitational song about Naaman, the leper white as snow who went to the Jordan River to dip his sick body in it, and after seven water baptisms, came up from the water, clean, his leprosy healed. After singing, Mother Spencer would lean over the wood-paneled pulpit and start to ask questions about the Sunday school lesson, the themes of the week, which were always sprawling. Sometimes, themes were as philosophical as "justification by faith" or as annual as "arise and walk," which normally dealt with the crucifixion.

"Dearie, . . ." the questions began, particularly if no one quickly answered, because every full-grown adult was expected to participate, even the ones who were not the best readers or stuttered during the choral reading or were inclined to silence or didn't have more than an eighth-grade education. No one could opt out. Everyone had to have something to say, had to engage with the text interpretatively. And that interpretation could take a wide variety of manifestations—reader-response, close reading, a song, a dream, a memory, sometimes an anecdote from one's life that mirrored the scripture discussed that week. For example, Queen Esther confronting Haman and foiling his plot to kill her Jewish countrymen might be likened to a trial and tribulation faced on the job with a boss who was working against you, trying to get you fired. Often, Esther, Job, Ruth, David, Isaac, Joseph were the allegorical companion stories to the saints' and parishioners' trials and hardships for the week. Much like spirituals, which sought to syncretically map enslaved Africans' sorrows and desires onto Christian orthodoxy and worship, many of the saints in the church continued the practice of allegorizing and narrating their lives through the gospels and prophets, through melding the world of the Bible with their working class lives in southern New Jersey at the end of the twentieth century. Many of the saints had people from back south or were from the South and had migrated to the New Jersey and Philadelphia area in the 1950s and '60s, so they were steeped in this sort of amalgamative ritual.

In fact, one of the strongest and most troubling memories of my childhood in Full Gospel Church of God was the pastor, Reverend Flagg's dream of driving a horse-drawn wagon across a desert, the wagon filled with dry bones. Reverend Flagg was from the South, born in Fort Pierce, Florida, in 1929, and was raised Pentecostal as well though he strayed from the faith in his early twenties, only coming back to the church in his thirties when he heard the call of the Lord to preach. His suits were immaculate, often three-piece, tailored and a pair of shoes to match the color of the suit. His hair always finely coiffed and cut, he wore a part in his head that was always crisp. And for special occasions—church anniversary or pastor's aid—he sometimes wore a black robe with two long, blood-red crosses that dripped down the right and left panels of the robe. When I say *mean*, I mean the man was cold in that robe, colder than ice on the outside of an igloo.

His presence was intimidating, and as a child, it was hard for me to read his countenance as he sat in the pulpit, thumbing through his Bible, waiting on a word from the Lord. Because I couldn't read him,

I always felt as if I couldn't predict the emotional direction of the sermons. Sometimes, the sermons were as innocuous as a glass of milk, but they could also veer into humorous takes on politics and everyday life. Or his sermon might careen into a critique of White folks. And Black folks too. Other times they were brooding and shifted from what felt like a fireside chat to fire and brimstone, thunder shaking the heavens loose, in the span of a cough into his hand and looking up to see a parishioner nodding off. His sermons shook the saints of the church into fits, sometimes fits of joy, folks leaping from folding chairs and shouting; other times, fits of wailing, parishioners whispering to themselves between tears for help as in "help us, Lord, help us."

As a child, and I don't know if this is true or not, I felt as if one of his greatest gifts was that he seemed to make everyone in the church want to please him. As an emissary of the great big God in heaven, this makes sense. If one believes that the man standing up before you smelling of cologne and exegetically reading this text for filth in front of you is in conversation and divinely communing with God, then yes, please away. However, it bothered me at times, watching what felt like groveling to me, but again I was a boy. And, I, too, was transfixed, in awe and terror at what he could make people feel through his visions *and* his ability to read and interpret the Bible, which takes us back to his dream of the valley of dry bones—his deceased first wife sitting next to him as he drove this wagon filled with bones through a canyon. As I remember it, he had the dream several times over several months and didn't know the meaning of it. But then he turned to Ezekiel in the King James Version of the Bible, chapter thirty-seven, which like his dream begins with a valley of dry bones. Except in Ezekiel the bones are the house of Israel coming back together, foreshadowing and announcing the coming of the nation. Reverend Flagg's interpretation of his dream was less triumphant. Like Israel, the bones belonged to his community, the church. However, the bones were dead, dry, and there was no life that was coming back to them. He saw this as a warning. If folks didn't get right with God and do it now, they would soon perish, and he would soon be caring for a wagon of dry bones, a wagon full of spiritually dead people.

The church burst into a box of wailing, folks beseeching God, tearing at their throats in supplication. Folks who hadn't yet received the Holy Ghost tarried, dropping to their knees. The children were swept away by an usher to the back of the church, which was the kitchen of someone's home, and there we listened to what seemed like agony. Folks crying for their souls. Many of us cried as well, listening to our parents sound so helpless because of the dream of one man, a man of God.

When the tarrying was over, the folding chairs that had been scattered about the room were put back into some sort of order that resembled a church. Sometimes, the sermon would end there, Reverend Flagg sitting back down, the congregation teetering on the edge of their terror of going to hell, the children, too, awash and trembling in their seats. The offering would be collected and prayed over, the closing benediction given, and our terror carried out of the door of the church house into our cars and back to our homes for Sunday dinner.

Other times, the sermon would continue. The small break, and the storm it released, sewed back up. The saints stroked the pages of the Bibles sitting in their laps anticipating *the word* that was soon to come. Reverend Flagg would get back up into the pulpit, lodge himself behind the rostrum, and turn his Bible to whatever passage the crying and tarrying interrupted—begin again. And there, he'd read and exposit and surmise and wonder along with the scripture.

It was captivating to watch him transform what seemed like an ancient text into a modern living body, to take the dry bones of those pages and through his insight and speculation add sinew and flesh and say, "Rise, rise up and walk." And the text would rise; it would walk. Job's travails suddenly our travails. King David's disobedience, our disobedience. Ruth's faith, our faith. A faith we needed to confront unexplained joint aches, diabetes, high blood pressure, wayward children in various stages of upheaval, drug addiction, and the slings and arrows of being working poor in the 1980s. What was far became near and closer. The faith hewn from these various Biblical narratives enabled so many of us to go into the week, go into our jobs cleaning houses or banks, driving trucks, working factory floors on the midnight shift and to do it all without collapsing in the middle of the street with our bag of cleaning supplies or lunchbox in our laps, refusing to get up because, Lord, sometimes this life was just too much to bear. What was brittle and dusty became wet, renewed, imperishable. I didn't know it then, but this sort of reading, thinking, speaking—sermonizing, really— became both the path and the lamp unto my feet, was the gate thrown open to poetry.

"At the end of my suffering / there was a door," writes Louise Glück in "The Wild Iris," which I take as an announcement about how one moves not only into language and the poem but into a deeper knowledge of the self. I now realize that implicit or opaquely rendered in that statement is a declaration about the necessity of reading, of study. To see the door at the end of suffering is the ability to not merely be assaulted or assailed by the suffering, to be passive in it, but to be able to *read* it, to see it as something beyond mere pain, to see the suffering as a text, as a possibility. At the end of my terror, there was a door; or in the middle of my Black life in America, I learned to read. There was a word. And, the word was not only with God, but it could be with us. With me.

At Full Gospel Church of God, we were very much in the Protestant tradition of study. God revealed himself and his scripture to everyone, not just the elect or the theologian or the pastor. With the help of the Holy Ghost, any- and everyone who believed and put their shoulder to the gospel plow could receive a *word*, some insight that could alleviate current suffering or provide an answer to an ongoing struggle. In fact, evidence of the spirit of God and the Holy Ghost working in your life was best shown through careful study, through the ability to interpret scripture. Though it couldn't be denied that some folks had the gift, or what was called "the anointing" amongst the saints, everyone was expected to show a modicum of ability. Spirit, the Holy Ghost, would make an intercession for those who might lack the critical gifts of others. Despite one's gifts or lack of skills, everyone was a critic. Or at least expected to be one.

My mother became a Sunday school teacher after showing herself to have the gift of interpretation Sunday after Sunday. Throughout the week leading up to Sunday service, my mother sat down at my grandmother's kitchen table or on her bed after coming home from work and read the week's lesson, underlining passages in her Bible and then cross-referencing them in a heavy, green concordance—a word I learned only after asking her what that heavy book was that she wanted me to carry from room to room for her. In my grandmother's attic, which is where my mother, my sister, and I lived, my mother made notes to herself in a notebook. This note-taking and study went on throughout the week, and on Saturday, she'd fall asleep with her notes and books around her. On Sunday morning, I'd wake to the smell of bacon and my mother feverishly rereading her notes and preparing questions, her Bible, dictionaries, and concordances strewn about her in the bed. After a quick prayer, she hustled my sister and me downstairs to the bacon my grandmother prepared, then into Sunday suits, dresses, shoes, and out the door. Since Sunday school was the first thing on the church program, we couldn't be late though we often were.

She'd drop to her knees in the front row of the church, offer a quick prayer, open up this brown briefcase with a beautiful gold lock, gather her notes and all her materials, slide the briefcase beneath her chair, and make her way to the pulpit. My mother was the first scholar I had known though I wouldn't have called her that then. My mother, who had an associate's degree from a local community college, who would, throughout my life, take university classes at Rutgers, Drexel, and various other colleges in the New Jersey–Philadelphia area for thirty years before earning her bachelor's degree. I attended some of these classes with her as a child, sitting in those big wooden desks, my feet dangling above the beige linoleum floor as a psychology professor lectured about God knows what. It didn't matter. I wanted to be there, be in that space of learning with my mother. I wanted to see what took her tired body from the house in the evenings, kept her up late at night, and on the weekends, when she wasn't studying the Sunday school lesson for the week, writing papers, first by hand, then on a personal computer that sat jammed in the corner of my grandmother's attic. I was sure there was a secret there, some sort of knowledge being kept from me in those university classrooms, something only adults could access, and I wanted in.

And my mother encouraged this desire in me: bringing me to her classes when she could, sometimes signing up my sister and me for our own computer classes at the local community college, and, oddly enough, playing records at home on my grandmother's large, wooden console that sat against the wall across from the bay window in her house. Every January and February, my mother sat my sister and me down on the floor of my grandmother's living room, slipped two records from their sleeves—the speeches of Martin Luther King Jr. and Malcolm X—put them on the console, and told us to listen. Not allowed to sit on my grandmother's good furniture at our age, we leaned on our elbows and listened to cheers and hollers from the crowds on those records, listened to King wearily describe his journey there into the church that night, the journey of Black folks for justice, the moral arc of history.

My mother and grandmother sitting on the couches above us would sometimes cry or sigh or begin to reminisce about the 1960s. I listened to them, to the stories of what drove my grandmother north and what kept her there. These records served as my first lessons of history—both personal and collective—as that without-which-I-would-be-lost.

It was my mother who, when James Baldwin died, sat me down and told me, though she didn't agree with his lifestyle, one of our great writers had died, and I should know who he was. It was a Saturday. It must have been 1987. Winter. The weak sun came through the attic and my mother sat at a desk crammed into the corner of the hallway of the attic. Was she writing a paper or was she typing out our family tree, the branches reaching back to the 1700s and the first enslaved African? I don't quite remember. I could even be off about the year of this memory, but it is true—her stopping her typing or writing, her pulling some green, hardback anthology off the shelf and calling me over so that she could read Baldwin to me. I don't remember if it were an essay or a short story. For some reason, I think it might have been "Sonny's Blues," though this might be less history and more the fiction of memory. But what I do know to be true is that the book was small and green and hardback, and I listened.

I sat on the blue carpet beneath her, looking up at her face as she turned the pages of the book and read, that late-afternoon, winter sun coming through the windows. I do remember thinking: this must be important. I must pay attention because my mother only required this sort of attentive listening while she read a chapter of the Bible to us when we woke in the morning and before we went to bed at night. Our eyes were to open and close upon the word of God, and now I was to listen to the words of Baldwin as if it were the word of God. I'm sure my mother hadn't intended to impart this sort of lesson, only wanting to educate me in our people's literature and history, which she was a student and lover of. But there in the middle of the day when I was normally tearing about the house, terrorizing my grandmother's hanging plants and her old black poodle, Dezi, leaving the screen door open or letting it slam shut, allowing my grandmother's good, paid-for PSE&G heat out of the house, there, I was to sit, be quiet, listen to my mother bring a recently dead man's words across her lips. And his words were to be held, were to be known, to be given to others. Maybe this is why I have become a critic, to bring the words of others, the words of the dead to the ears of the living. To read and read and read before you so that you and I might live.

Our lives are, sometimes, records of cruelty. Records of forced and unfair labor. Records of a nation's cruel calculus, the nation deciding who must become the subdued so the subduer can erect his strongholds and myths and legends on our backs and bones. Our lives become records not of our capacity for living but of the capacity for being a threshing floor. Our bodies to labor, to uphold a nation's optimism and cruel dream. But these cruelties can be resisted.

The history of *lectores*, readers, in tobacco shops and cigar factories at the turn of the twentieth century in Latin America, is a history of the revolutionary and radical capacity of reading to subvert the routinized violence of factory labor and the tyranny of colonialism. Hired by factory owners to read everything from newspapers to short stories to novels, *lectores* stood on elevated platforms or sat on elevated chairs and read above workers who rolled cigars and cigarettes on wooden tables spread out over factory floors. To democratize the process of reading, *lectores* often asked the workers to choose what texts they wanted to hear read to them, thus giving them choice in a place they often had very little choice. Despite being hired to perform the innocuous job of reading, they sometimes fomented uprisings and protests against working conditions, as was the case of Bolívar Ochart, who was sent to Juncos, Puerto Rico, by the Free Federation of Workers and the Socialist Party to be a lector in a tobacco shop. Ochart performed his duties of reading newspapers and novels as a *lector* in the factory and he organized the workers, eventually giving speeches to thousands of local workers who often waited for him outside jails after he was arrested for these speeches. The speeches delivered on jailhouse steps infuriated local politicians, which led to an ambush and a shootout with local police. I don't think it's coincidental that the *lector*, the reader, also inspires and foments resistance to economic and social tyranny. Reading gave a *lector* like Ochart access to the workers' imaginations. In the reading he's nurturing and inspiring their capacity to imagine, to envision other possibilities and delivering to them news of resistance from other subdued people from around the world and the island. Ochart's voice quickens something in the workers, triggers contemplation, the what-if of fiction, the capacity to dream, and the record of others dreaming, imagining a world different from their own.

As Frederick Douglass noted in *Narrative of the Life of Frederick Douglass*, reading promotes an imagining, a worldmaking that can directly and emphatically contradict one's present circumstance, contradict the language weaponized against oneself—slave, three-fifths, chattel, property. When reading, one does not passively receive the words of others; one makes—makes a sentence, makes a paragraph, makes a book, makes a world, makes an argument. One authors. And sometimes in the reading, in the authoring, one creates a counternarrative and counterargument particularly when reading something like Thomas Jefferson's assessment of the poetry of Phillis Wheatley or reading the pathologizing of Black families in the Moynihan Report. In other words, one makes a possibility, a possibility that hitherto did not exist. In reading (which is also an act of interpretation), one finds language for what is possible, what is untenable about the present, what must persist beyond the present. Reading, therefore, is always an act of making a future, an act of speculation. Even if one is only speculating about what one wants at the grocery store later. I should explain. In graduate school, I took a course on performative rhetorics with a brilliant rhetorician and philosopher named Diane Davis. In the class, we were discussing the prognosticative nature of language, how we never write for who we are but for who we will be; that language is always imagining us in the future. And she gave the great example of the grocery list. We sit down and write a grocery list in order to remind our future self of what the past self wanted. The list anticipates our forgetfulness, our future self being somewhere else, in some other headspace, after waiting for the bus, for example, or working all day. In this way, writing anticipates need, what the future self needs even if, for a moment, unaware.

This is why reading is dangerous—because it points. Reading points to the necessity of pleasure, of longing, of desire—even if in the words of others, even if desire is nowhere in the text that one is reading. Reading itself is desire, desirous, a playing in and with the illicit because reading allows one to occupy a dream, the not-yet inhabited. Reading points to the invisible, to what must be created that doesn't exist. Reading can also point to what exists but is not always acknowledged—one's freedom, for example. Again, think of Frederick Douglass—his coming into literacy as an enslaved boy. In the act of resisting his master's desire for him not to learn to read, in disobeying the slave codes that made it illegal for enslaved people to learn how to read, Douglass began to cultivate not just literacy but the stuff of his abolition, his self-making. Reading became the introduction and practice for his personal revolution. Reading helped to prepare Douglass and his imagination for the question, What might my freedom look like? And, the practice of reading helped him answer it. Reading points to that which is against genocide. Or at least the reading I'm interested in doing, the reading that begins on the edges of plantations, in small groups of study, away from the eyes, appetites, laws, and codes of the masters and their policing paterollers; reading that announces the future, reading that disobeys, critiques the present through pointing, pointing away to the swamps and marshes where we might convene something like freedom.

Often, this pointing, the pointing of the critic, is disparaged. A very smart, thoughtful, and loving friend once described the difference between art and criticism about art as this: art is the moon, and the critic is the person who points to the moon. The person pointing at the moon should not be mistaken for the moon or the person who created it. As an artist, something about the allegory felt satisfying, even affirming, especially in a world that relegates the arts to the curtains on the house, the wainscoting and trim—merely decorative and of little consequence to the architecture and well-being of social and political life. As a critic who grew up in a community of critics, I see critics, criticism, and the expertise that allows these critics their perspicacious criticism everywhere: the barbers in the barbershop arguing over grades of hair and the elasticity of a boy's scalp and whether he'll go bald when he gets older; the Black Vietnam and Korean War veterans sitting about that same barbershop arguing over the best bait to use when fishing in the Delaware Bay; all these men, barbers and patrons alike, vehemently disagreeing about who's the better singer, Anita Baker or Aretha Franklin. Or, I think of my mother—dictionaries, concordances, reference books, and Bibles spread out in front of her on the bed; or Reverend Flagg in the pulpit, leafing through the Bible during devotional service, preparing his sermon. This dichotomy, this analogy of pointing at the moon versus creating the moon troubled me because sometimes it is absolutely critical that someone knows how to read the moon. In fact, being able to read the moon and the stars might be exactly what saves one's life.

In the family Bible that my mother was transcribing onto a hard drive of a personal computer crammed into the corner in my grandmother's attic in the early 1990s, there was testimony from ancestors about how to read the sky, how to read the moss on the trunks of trees when one was stealing away from the plantation, the songs that carried this incendiary information. I think of my great-aunt Anne standing up at family reunions in Black Creek, South Carolina, or in Burlington, New Jersey, sweat running down the side of her face in those swampy Augusts, reading out our lineage, then stopping the list of who begat whom to read some commentary left alongside an ancestor's name. Those memories and the commentary ranged from farming to the natural history of the area of South Carolina our folks hailed from to how to read the night sky for travel. Despite many of us no longer living in the same conditions—farming or sharecropping, raising hogs and peanuts, or trying to survive the tyranny of slavery and segregation—it was absolutely necessary for us, even the youngest of us who lived in suburbs and cities, to know, to learn how to read the world in this way because the lessons reached beyond their time, reached beyond the northwest corner of South Carolina.

As we were being taught to read the archive of the past, we were learning how to read the future as well. We learned that our survival, our thriving requires knowing how to read many things at once, knowing what the land will yield and how it will yield it, knowing what the moon and the sky say about tomorrow, knowing that in a book about your bloodlines, you can find what might ferry you out of captivity.

Later, I would learn that it was not just my family that had knowledge of the sky, the land, how best to use a spider web to heal a cut. Black folks up and down the Eastern Seaboard built these critical bodies of knowledge and used them to usher folks out of slavery into the North. Reading the sky, reading the land, reading an essay of Richard Sheridan that denounced the institution of slavery, as Frederick Douglass did as a boy in the *Columbian Orator*, was and is a radical and necessary act, a radical and necessary announcement of the future, of freedom. Our future required our being critics, scholars, those who studied. Our present and the past required creating ways of seeing, ways of reading. Pointing at the moon, reading the stars saved our lives. Criticism is not merely the domain or luxury of the elite. Building critical bodies of knowledge is the work of the revolution, of the revolutionary, which is to say love.

"Poetry Isn't Revolution but a Way of Knowing Why It Must Come"

> The twentieth century is not characterized by the search for new-ness, but by the proliferation of nostalgias. . . . Nostalgic nationalists and nostalgic cosmopolitans, nostalgic environmentalists and nostalgic metrophiliacs (city lovers) exchange pixel fire in the blogosphere.
>
> —Svetlana Boym

When did we, our nation, slip into a post-fact epoch? Did it begin with the torture memos and the diplomatic and political sophistry of the Bush administration's seductive and scandalous indeterminate statements about the felicity of engaging Iraq in war in 2003? Remember Donald Rumsfeld's Department of Defense news briefing in February 2002 concerning the lack of evidence that linked Iraq to weapons of mass destruction, yet Rumsfeld affirmed that "yes, yes, we would declare war against Iraq anyway." In the briefing Rumsfeld famously offered this sound bite that reverberated around the world:

> Reports that say something hasn't happened are always interesting to me, because as we know, there are known knowns; there are things we know we know. We also know there are known unknowns; that is to say we know there some things we do not know. But there are also unknown unknowns—the ones we don't know we don't know.

In this contortionist web of statements and follow-up statements that seek to nuance and elucidate the prior statements' lack of clarity but that somehow sink us further into the darkness of knowing-we-don't-know, we might have seen a glimpse of what we now live in: a world in which frank, determined, or impassioned speech, its click-worthiness, matters more than its veracity, a world in which a president (Donald Trump) can constantly make false statements. And, when the falsity of that statement is proven or displayed (the felonious notion of election fraud in the 2020 presidential election, for example), what is held in contempt by zealots and apostles is not the lack of truth but the challenging of that untruth. We live in a world where signs no longer signify or point but are merely broken props that uphold clownish and bombastic pathos.

Maybe the post-fact era in the United States began earlier: in Jim Crow segregation—in the false assertion of "separate but equal." Maybe the post-fact epoch began in the consistently broken treaties between Native folks and the US government. Maybe the United States has always been post-fact: beginning with the constitutional fraudulence of slavery, the *Dred Scott* decision, and the mythos of this being a country where every man and woman had the right to "life, liberty, and the pursuit of happiness." Maybe our post-fact era began with the elided clause that haunts the most famous of guarantees of the Declaration of Independence—that life, liberty, and happiness can be yours *only* if you're White, male, and a property owner, the other sort of aristocracy our founding fathers refused to unseat or dismantle when they chased redcoated British out of the American colonies. Maybe, like Ralph Ellison's famous unnamed narrator, we're "getting too far ahead of the story, almost to the end, although the end is in the beginning and lies far ahead." Maybe I am at the end and simultaneously at the beginning. Maybe we begin here—at the end, at what feels like the end of a certain type of America, the end of a certain type of democracy, a certain type of truth or at least an allegiance to it. Maybe this troubling of truth has been the question of art, art in America, all along—how do we begin democracy, how do we extend democracy to all the animals?

And if you can bear one more subjunctive statement, maybe a poem will show us how to begin or extend democracy to all the animals. But how? Isn't the poem interested in lying, in artifice, in asking more questions than it is interested in answering? How does one enact, perform, *poem* truth in a post-fact era, in an era where democracy seems to glide away from us even as we reach toward it, a Priamesque shade avoiding our grasp in the afterlife? Has democracy always avoided our American reach? Have we finally entered the afterlife of our nation, paid the boatman, and he ferries us off to wherever it is we are now—an America that finds truth secondary to clownish, infelicitous speech, bombastic parrhesia? Is that what the insurrectionists who climbed the white-stone walls of the Capitol building and violently interrupted Congress on January 6 in protest of a legal election hailed—an America so nostalgic for a mythic past that the untruthful declarations of a defeated president could drive them to destroy the vessel they claimed to love?

What is the artifice, metaphor, line length, linguistic register, syntactical deployment, and rhetoric that could subvert the kinds of untruths peddled by a president and his oligarchic regime? Is that sort of subversion possible for a poem? But there again, in the words *poem, metaphor, artifice*, the haint of fiction haunts us. Poem, metaphor, artifice might seem anathema to the reestablishment of truth or fact. These terms conspire to trouble the establishment of fact, objectivity, Cartesian notions of truth. It might seem like a dubious thought that a poem could be an antidote to the post-factual. But poetry, in its swank, flamboyant, and egregious allegiance to artifice, is exactly the type of frankness we need—a frankness delivered through imagining the invisible, through residing in the interrogative territory of speculation, of the fugitive, of the all-too-quickly-given-over-to-science-fiction-and-fantasy "what if."

This type of imaginative frankness is in the ontology, nature, and guts of the poetic line. The poetic line defamiliarizes grammar and denotative meaning. A line break or ending can contradict the sentence that it carries. For instance, a sentence could read: "He knew nothing but what he knew." If we break this sentence over two lines—"He knew nothing / but what he knew"—we now must consider for a moment that the "he" in the sentence actually knows nothing. And when we continue to read on, encountering in the next line that the subject "knew what he knew," we must now think about these two statements separately and collectively. Why might the poet have wanted those two distinct moments? Why might the poet physicalize the irony of the sentence on the page with the line break? Is the poet trying to reify the process of coming into knowledge, the line break enacting the delay of knowing, the uncertainty that the subject felt? Does the line break provide a type of rhythm that bears upon how we come into experiencing the subject and what he knew? The line break in the above example also manifests what I think poems are acutely and fundamentally about—simultaneity—that two things, even two seemingly contradictory things, can exist together, in one body, in one poem. There is a moment in time in which the subject of the statement knows nothing. And there is a moment in which he knows something. Yes, we experience these moments in a type of teleological progression, but we also separate them and demarcate when one tips over into the other. When does the subject know, and when doesn't he know? Does it begin after the "but" or before? Does he know something on the first line when he knows nothing?

What I am pointing to is the way in which the poetic line resists the smoothness of narrative and causality, a smoothness often seen in political rhetoric and nationalist notions of sovereignty. The poetic line asks the reader to hold multiple truths, multiple iterations of a thing, simultaneously. The line also asks us to see below grammar and syntax. In other words, to reimagine the conveyance of knowledge and, more profoundly, power.

The poetic line holds the "word" in question and thus becomes a tool to announce, interrogate, and resist political tyranny and imagine a future that critiques an oppressive and disingenuous past. I am arguing for a poetic parrhesia, something akin to an assertion that Adrienne Rich offers in the poem "Dreamwood": "poetry / isn't revolution but a way of knowing / why it must come." The poem as siren, the poem as embodiment of an epistemological and ontological break, the poem as an enchantment and enactment of the invisible, the poem as Leaders of the New School, the poem as the future, as beyond the future, the poem as inhabiting the unknown and doing so frankly—this "a way of knowing."

The poem must be an attempt to tip us into a truth or knowledge that we cannot turn away from, a terrain that, once stepped into, we cannot feign ignorance of or turn back from. The poem confirms for us "why the revolution must come," why it is already arriving and only awaiting our acknowledgment. The poem in its unabashed and frank imagining and inhabitation defies manners, institutions, institutional rationality, and reformist notions of change, performing a type of parrhesia by subverting the fragility of the powerful and imagining a beyond, an otherwise.

But before we begin running off into the abstraction of an otherwise, a future, what do I mean when I say parrhesia. *Parrhesia*, a concept and term, appears throughout Euripedes's plays and in Greek texts in the fourth and fifth centuries BCE. However, it was not until more recently with the lectures of Michel Foucault at the University of California, Berkeley, in 1983 that the rhetorical figure and its philosophical import garnered more attention and discussion. Put simply, parrhesia means frank speech. But it is not a frank speech winnowed and deduced from a set of procedures, experiments, or proofs, a thought or opinion that one was not in possession of prior to a testing for it. Rather, the parrhesia of Euripedes and subsequently Foucault is a frank speech derived from the body, substance, and life of the speaker. Foucault writes: "In *parrhesia* the speaker emphasizes the fact that he is both the subject of the enunciation and the subject of the enunciandum—that he himself [or she herself or they themselves] is the subject of the opinion to which he refers." Thus, the "speech activity" gains its efficacy through the conflation and flattening of speaker and thing spoken.

But there in the conflation of speaker and thing spoken is danger and peril for the parrhesiastes, or the speaker of parrhesia, because the one who speaks parrhesiastically is often in a socially marginal position to whom he or she addresses. Think: a messenger bringing bad news to a king, or a philosopher addressing a sovereign or a citizen speaking in front of the demos, the people. Think: a slave writing about their experience at the hands, whip, and desire of their master while still fugitive and being hunted. Think: confronting a congressperson in a town hall about an immigration ban while being undocumented. In Foucault's words, "Someone is said to use *parrhesia* and merits consideration as a *parrhesiastes* only if there is a risk or danger for him [or her or them] in telling the truth." In exposing one's life in a "parrhesiastic game," according to Foucault, "you risk death to tell the truth instead of reposing in the security of a life where the truth goes unspoken." Death, reenslavement, loss of citizenship, and exile are risks of frank speech. However, the speaker of parrhesia "prefers himself [herself or themselves] as a truth-teller rather than as a living being who is false to himself." The possibility of a liberating and liberated future that frank speech offers is prefered to the embodied and corporeal safety of the present.

Again, we can hear the haunting of Rich's statement: "poetry / isn't revolution but a way of knowing / why it must come." The parrhesiastic poem is one that risks imagining itself as sanctuary and ideological break, risks censure and censoring, risks the future. The parrhesiastic poet risks their life.

While parrhesia might seem to be a personal politics made public, living one's truth (to borrow from the slogans of today), parrhesia, when done felicitously, expands beyond the personal and gestures toward the demos, the people, the country, the political. The parrhesiastic act is an extending of democracy through welding or coalescing the political body with the personal body of the private citizen. Often, that personal body is a politically marginal body. This coalescing disturbs the policed borders of the State and who the State deems as politically healthy, diseased, or viable. The marginal body speaking and imagining frankly challenges the sovereign and sovereignty's smooth and placid narrative of its supremacy and political sublimity. The parrhesisastes enters where they were not imagined, reifies the limits of governance, circumscribes the power of the State, steps out of order, protests the purity of political positioning and imagining, speaks as the sovereign or with an authority akin to the sovereign.

In other words, the parrhesiastes commits a violence. A violent reimagining of the world. Like Electra's killing Clytemnestra after Clytemnestra killed Electra's father, Agamemnon. (We're about to get into the weeds of Greek tragedy, but stay with me here because this story is great example of parrhesia and the sorts of political risks and world reimagining that parrhesia opens us toward.)

Clytemnestra has just killed Agamemnon. Electra and Orestes are there to confront her, but they have to be careful because the queen, Clytemnestra, is now their superior. Electra asks several times if she can speak frankly, parrhesiastically. The queen, Clytemnestra, assures her that she can though Electra doesn't believe her. When Electra is assured that her mother won't kill her, she speaks. What makes this situation parrhesiastic is that Electra is no longer under the protection of her father, King Agamemnon. She is in the position of a servant or slave and speaks as such. But what makes this situation particularly instructive for us modern readers, poets, and citizens is what Electra does after she speaks frankly, confronting her mother about her involvement in her father's death—she kills her. The inferior, Electra, reverses her position through the radical act of imagining an alternative possibility and enacting it through violence. "The parrhesiastic contract becomes a subversive trap," concludes Foucault. Subversion as trap. Subversion as radical imagining. Participate in the civility and customs of discourse—then undercut them.

Maybe this gesture of undercutting, this act of subversion, is the aesthetic, the vocation, utterance, and imagination that we've been looking for, the pedagogical lesson on how to respond to a post-fact regime. But what would this look like in a contemporary context? I believe we have seen some versions of this sort of subversion of the parrhesiastic game in the women's marches that sprang up all over the world in response to Donald Trump's election, participants in a town hall meeting in Utah chanting to their Republican representative Jason Chaffetz "Do your job" and "Last term." These moments of parrhesia, frank speech, are similar to Electra's moment of embodying parrhesia then subverting it in that they speak and perform. They demonstrate and through demonstration they begin to imagine and enact a future that no longer has unresponsive, lily-livered congressmen at the helm. Their chanting "isn't the revolution but a way of knowing why it must come."

But what might this chanting look like in poetry, this frank speech that we are hearing and witnessing at town halls and protests echoing in the cavernous avenues and boulevards throughout our American cities and towns? I believe we are beginning to see this transformative, poetic parrhesia in the work of Iranian American poet Solmaz Sharif. In fact, Sharif's poetry answers the question I posed earlier: how do we begin democracy? In Sharif's first collection, *LOOK*, she continuously inhabits and interrogates the language of war, particularly the war on terror, through the seeming civility of the lyric poem. Throughout her collection, she signifies upon the US Department of Defense's *Dictionary of Military and Associated Terms*, hollowing out, subverting, reifying, redefining, personalizing, troubling, and politicizing terms like DRONE, DESTRUCTION RADIUS, PINPOINT TARGET, EXECUTION PLANNING via the lyric, the terms rendered in her text in capital letters. The politicizing of these terms is quite an important project because they can function with an air of apoliticality because they appear in something allegedly innocuous and reliable like a dictionary. However, this *Dictionary of Military and Associated Terms* is deployed diplomatically, politically, violently, and even torturously to do the bidding of both American government and business interests in Iraq, Afghanistan, and all over the world. Moreover, when is language not political, always-already carrying with it a nation's mythos, identity, ideas of (in)humanity, civility, and justice?

Through the interrogation of what might seem like idle, perfunctory, or procedural terms, Sharif implicates us, the American citizen, in her grappling with the terror of language put to these uses. These terms, which people the space of the dictionary, are metonyms, substitutions

159

for us. Like these terms, we sit idly in the security of our homes, gathered in the safe dictionary of America, in the belief that we are not the ones droning, bombing, organizing, EXECUTION PLANNING, or measuring the DESTRUCTION RADIUS of recent military operations in Iraq and Afghanistan. But, like these terms, we are not idle placeholders that merely describe an action; we are not mere apolitical metonym. We are the action itself. Our American citizenship is a DRONE, is a DESTRUCTION RADIUS, is a PINPOINT TARGET.

Because we drone and bomb and destroy, we must find a way of imagining and subverting ourselves, subverting our nostalgia for war and the language of war, the language our bodies have become accustomed to. Sharif employs and achieves this subversion through gathering a bevy of voices, what I might call extending democracy to all the animals. In gathering a menagerie of voices that experience war—soldiers' accounts, the accounts and voices of victims of drone attacks and intersplicing it with her own biography—Sharif allows each its solo within the whole of the poem and does so without aggrandizing one voice over another. Rather, they appear behind a colon, adorned only in their frankness, their accounts coming across as the language of testimony rather than what we might consider poetic speech. Sharif performs what the poet and philosopher Éduoard Glissant might call a poetics of relation. Without explicit markers that designate race, age, nationality, or rank, the voices accumulate into a drone or chorus. They blend to sound or sing a jagged song about war and the bodies upon bodies that lie at the bottom of it. Through the accumulation, through the droning, what Sharif calls "singing," we gain both the particularity of the individual while having to wrestle with the collective. The parrhesiastic force lies in the sublimity of this cohesion, in, as aforementioned, the collapsing or welding of the marginal body and its alienness to that of the civil body, that of the demos. For instance, "Drone" opens with a persona that speaks in the first person, one that we might assume to be the poet's though that might not be necessarily the case:

> : somewhere I did not learn *mow down* or *mop up*
> : somewhere I wouldn't hear *your father must come with
> me* or *I must fingerprint your grandmother can you
> translate please*
> : the FBI has my cousins' computers

: my father says *say whatever you want over the phone*
: my father says *don't let them scare you that's what they want*

Then the persona, the first-person voice, shifts to what feels like witnesses of a drone attack recounting the aftermath, their experiences:

: it was my job to put a cross on each home with dead for
  clearing
: it was my job to dig graves into the soccer field . . .
: from my son's wedding mattress I know this mound's
  his room

Then the poem shifts again to the voices of soldiers, particularly American soldiers:

: I dropped a knee and engaged the enemy
: I emptied my clip then finished the job
: I took two steps in and threw a grenade
: I took no more than two steps into a room before firing
: in Haditha we cleared homes Fallujah-style

Then another devastating shift:

: my father was reading the Koran when they shot him
  through the chest
: they fired into the closet
: the kitchen
: the ninety year old
: the stove
: just where was I

Just when you think that you have located voice, located a narrative, the poem shifts; the poem subverts your familiarity, your desire to get comfortable in voice, in the lyric. The resistance to this comfort is also a resistance to nostalgia and sentimentality, which we might say are the presiding affective conditions of our current age. Sharif's use of the plainspoken helps to destabilize and raze a facile emotional connection to the subject matter, to trauma, to the fungibility of the pained bodies in the text.

Too often in political writing or writing that seeks to grapple with our American complicity in empire and empire building or writing that would think about political and social horror, trauma, and the aestheticizing of it, the pained body in the text becomes a vessel for the reader and writer to fill with their own affect and affective relationship to the described or rendered pain. Think: the many postings and repostings of Black people dying at the hands of the police recycled on Facebook statuses and pages, foregrounded by a comment that expresses the user's dismay, chagrin, heartbreak over the top of the scene of death. Think: a letter from an abolitionist to his brother, a slave owner, trying to dissuade him from continuing his practice of slavery through the exchanging of his body for that of a enslaved person, as in "imagine it was me or my children that you're whipping." In both examples, what is foregrounded is the body and affective experience of the spectator or the reader rather than the actual body in pain. It is as if the body in pain is so opaquely human, so nonhuman, that the only way to understand their pain is to disappear their body, to annihilate it through analogy—in other words—"normalize" it, demarginalize it, de-other it, Whiten it, renationalize the pain through a body swapping. Sharif resists this appeal to insincere affect through the gathering of many voices and the refusal to sentimentalize them; she refuses to capitulate to a narrative and, instead, embraces many through an ethnographic rendering of them.

Sharif's gathering of voices and presenting of victims alongside the victimizers produce a panoply effect that is reminiscent of Kerry James Marshall's three-part photographic series, *Heirlooms and Accessories*. Through erasure Marshall revises a famous lynching photograph in which the lynched bodies hang from a tree while a crowd casually mills about, some pointing to the bodies, others smiling and laughing as if they were at a carnival or circus. As Marshall notes in a video produced by the Smart Museum in conversation with his artwork, too often what is focused upon is the men hanging from the tree, but for Marshall, what is most brutal is the casualness of the spectators witnessing the lynching. Marshall continues: they, the crowd, are all "accessories to these murders," hence the use of accessories in his titling. Because this brutality, the brutality of casualness, can be missed because we are used to focusing on the apparent, pornographic violence of the lynched bodies, Marshall decided to obscure the lynched men in the background and frame the women's faces that peered into the camera at the precise moment the photographer takes the picture. Marshall frames their faces with broaches or pendants, mementos that are normally passed down from one generation to the next, much like racial violence, hence the use of *Heirlooms* in the titling of the piece. Also, as Marshall notes, his use of broaches as a framing mechanism is a critique and subversion of the heirloom tradition of lynching—the photographs of dead bodies turned into postcards, the cut-off fingers, toes, and hair of lynching victims brought back home as memorabilia. Marshall interrupts and intercedes in this long citational chain of transmitting the dead, Black body as the only manifestation, the only heirloom of lynching. This recasting offers another signature to the event, destroys the familiar aestheticizing and politicizing of lynching.

Like Marshall, Sharif performs a sort of obscuring and intercession in "Drone" in that she does not allow the reader to rest in the pornography of American militarized violence or in the victims' testimony concerning that violence. We are made to move and move and move such that the poem at one point asks, "Just where was I?" This inability to locate oneself in the poem is not only the success of the poem but the state of complicity many of us, Americans, find ourselves in as citizens of an empire. Where are we? Sometimes, we are victims, particularly Black folks in this country in relationship to our militarized communities by way of the police. And, at other times, we are the victimizer. Victim and victimizer is not a stable relationship as historican and political theorist Achille Mbembe notes in *Critique of Black Reason*. Mbembe describes these competing subjectivities astride one another in plantation life:

> The Blacks on the plantation were, furthermore, diverse. They were hunters of maroons and fugitives, executioners and executioners' assistants, skilled slaves, informants, domestics, cooks, emancipated slaves who were still subjugated, concubines, field-workers assigned to cutting cane, workers in factories, machine operators, masters' companions, and occasionally soldiers. Their positions were far from stable. Circumstances could change, and one position could become another. Today's victim could tomorrow become an executioner in the service of the master. It was not uncommon for a slave, once freed, to become a slave owner and hunter of fugitive slaves.

Though Mbembe is describing the unstable position of the slave in the sociological atmosphere of the plantation, the logics of this indeterminacy persist today, persist in the relationship of the marginal and nonmarginal subject to the empire, to the State, to authority. Sharif occupies this zone of indeterminacy, this liminal space as a poet and, concomitantly, persuades us to enter it as well as readers. Through the removal of punctuation in the poem, Sharif demonstrates for us that the grammars of victim and victimizer that we have normalized and made normative are now blurred, queered, obscured, and rendered opaque. One voice, one sentence, will bleed into the next. Like Marshall, Sharif seeks to raze the stable and brutal ground of the casual gaze, the casual look at violence. The spectator, the reader in the case of Sharif's "Drone," must become unlocatable, nomadic, must become relocated through complicity, through the act of reading. Sharif stuns us, the reader, away and out of sentimentality and nostalgia. She will not allow us anything emotionally, rhetorically, or aesthetically easy. We must grapple with the shifting of our rhizomatic and opaque relationship to language, aesthetics, witness, and empire.

Sharif teaches and demonstrates for us the poetics of parrhesia: how to speak back to the empire, to a post-fact regime and nation. It is not in a singular voice but in a gathering of voices. This gathering is not without tension and conflict; it is not the uncontested territory or epistemology of tolerance and saccharine notions of democracy. Rather, in the gathering, in the proximity of one voice next to another, the reader resides in the muck of war and frank testimony concerning its horrors. Terms like *NSA* and *FBI*, apparatuses and agencies of the nation, sit next to more traditionally understood poetic language like *bone*, *singing*, and *wedding*. This coalition of traditional or received poetic language and the banality of US acronyms for federal agencies performs a double renouncement and simultaneously an embracing. First, it renounces the fixity of these terms, razes the wall that might keep them separated in the mind of the reader, removes their lack of cohabitation in something like a poem and poetry. While this sort of coalition and defamiliarization process isn't new—for instance, Amiri Baraka, Richard Wright, Nikki Giovanni, and Sonia Sanchez have all written works that confront the FBI and surveillance in poetry—what is particularly productive in "Drone" is the deployment of it. Sharif writes: "I say *Hello NSA* when I place a call." In this recounting of a speaker addressing the NSA while making a call to not-the-NSA, Sharif parrhesiastically loud-talks the surveillance state and the tradition.

Loud-talking is an African American signifying practice in which a speaker addresses an interlocutor while also intending to be overheard by another. The speaker shades or casts aspersions at the one over-hearing, making them more and more uncomfortable because they're being talked about directly but indirectly so. The goal of loud-talking is to make the one being shaded call themselves out in frustration, anger, or embarrassment. Another way of thinking about loud-talking is making a private critique public. In this performance of parrhesiastic loud-talking, Sharif subverts the secret of NSA surveillance through excess, the excess of direct acknowledgement. In other words, the speaker puts the NSA on notice, on blast, which renounces the blind or over-looked complicities most of us dwell in as citizens of a nation that exists in a state of exception, a state in which constitutional rights can be and have been disbanded at the wish of elected officials or appointed judges.

Putting the NSA on blast also wallows in the abjection of being surveilled while subverting it, thus resituating and exposing what is be-hind the screen. The voyeur is exposed, the surveillance revealed, and that revelation revises and potentially undermines the "information" the NSA is gathering. There is a simultaneous looking, a simultane-ous listening, which robs the voyeuristic NSA of its anonymity, of its power to gather information. All of the information divulged is done willingly and with knowledge that a conversation is being surveilled, thus subverting the efficacy of the surveillance. We might think of this loud-talking, this undermining as a type of ecstasy or an ecstatic ut-terance as well, an embodiment or inhabitation of freedom. *Hello NSA.*

This moment as a mock or indirect apostrophe—addressing the reader directly in the lyric or poem—also calls into question the very notion of what a poem can contain or what a poem is. The semantic and rhetorical gesturing renounces, interrogates, and through the in-terrogation (i.e., the writing of a poem) embraces and expands what it is to write a poem or what a poem is. The speaker's nod to the NSA (and concomitantly Sharif's nod to the NSA) is a rupture, an obliteration of form and even decorum, similar to the rabble of all these voices in "Drone" speaking at once and in chorus. Though an opaque multiplic-ity, an opaque droning, Sharif's poem destroys the notion of a singular speaker of the lyric, annotating the collectivity of the song, the poem, thus being fugitive in form, remonstrating and talking back or sidewise to the lyric tradition, a tradition that has cordoned off or sequestered "speaking" to that of the individual.

One might argue that T. S. Eliot performed a similar sort of amassing of "voices" in *The Waste Land*. And I would argue no, no, not quite. Sharif's gathering and renouncing do not corroborate a singular, broken consciousness of modernity that still seems quite whole, but rather Sharif implicitly argues that a lyric, a song, a drone is a simultaneous or collective utterance or enactment—a we, but not the *we* of "We the People," which is not a democracy or a democratic extension of voice but yawp of the elite and landed gentry masquerading as the collective sound of a country. The *we* that drones in Sharif's "Drone" is more closely aligned to Muriel Rukeyser's documentary poetry project, *The Book of the Dead*, a book of poetry that chronicles "the suffering of [coal] miners carelessly exposed to deadly silica dust." However, Sharif's "Drone" and *LOOK* depart from Rukeyser's chronicling in the obscuring of voice, the desubjectifcation of the other. In this process, we, the reader, are not allowed to find catharsis in affect or empathy, which interrupts and prevents the reader from narrowing the poem and book into a vessel for their "feelings," a fungible commodity that prioritizes the reader's emotional relationship to the material and thereby turns the subject of the material into an extension of the reader's affect and pleasure. Sharif does not allow us, the reader, to escape culpability through the easy and unaccountable residence of our feeling. Also, unlike Rukeyser, Sharif places victim next to victimizer, which troubles the reader's affective relationship to the collective. This collective singing is not without its own trouble and troubling. Nothing smooth, nothing easy, nothing without blood. What is resisted is a "proliferation of nostalgias," to call back to cultural theorist, novelist, and playwright Svetlana Boym. What is resisted is the empire—me and you.

"Drone" tells us what we must annihilate and who we must sing to. Or, more so, who we must bring out of the bomb shelter, and how untenable it is to have to sing a child inside one. "We have learned to sing a child calm in a bomb shelter," writes Sharif in the penultimate line of "Drone." We must eliminate the necessity of the bomb shelter, but are we willing to want a different America? Are we willing to tell the truth of the America we live in and what it costs to live here?

Intimate Freedoms, Intimate Futures

> The country begins with Indians but ends with Americans;
> there is no sense that they can coexist.
>
> —David Treuer, *The Heartbeat of Wounded Knee:*
> *Native America from 1890 to the Present*

> I am very much concerned that American Negroes achieve their
> freedom here in the United States. But I am also concerned
> for . . . the health of their souls, and must oppose any attempt that
> Negroes may make to do to others what has been done to them.
>   And I looked again at the young faces around the table, and
> looked back at Elijah, who was saying that no people in history
> had ever been respected who had not owned their land. And
> the table said, "Yes, that's right." I could not deny the truth of
> this statement.
>
> —James Baldwin, "Down at the Cross:
> Letter from the Region of my Mind"

We owned nothing. We sowed cotton. We harvested peanuts, some-times tobacco. We rode a horse named Dan, and when Dan was too old to ride, we gave him to the children to take out to the field to play with, the children often sidling Dan up to a tree and leaping down out of the low-hanging branches onto his back. The children, too, worked in the rows, in the fields pulling up peanuts.

For much of the history of my people in South Carolina, just forty miles south of Charlotte, we worked the land, first as enslaved people then as sharecroppers taking whatever the sandy fields yielded to the scales, to be counted, weighed, often cheated in the weighing. We lived and worked on land owned by White men and Black, reading Bibles in dirt-floor shacks with newspaper doubling as wallpaper and toilet tissue. When the land yielded only more discontent and starvation, some of us migrated north to New Jersey, worked as domestics cleaning houses for White folks in towns like Cherry Hill, Moorestown, and Medford Lakes. We saved money to bring north those who could not afford to come north in the late 1940s and early '50s. We squirreled away money to start restaurants, taxi cab companies, cleaning services, catering businesses. We bought houses in towns like Burlington, Willingboro, Pleasantville, Atlantic City, and Browns Mills, with little front yards and backyards.

When we could save enough money and had vacation time, we drove back south in ten-, sometimes fifteen-vehicle-long caravans, often starting in the blue hours of the morning, arriving in Black Creek in late afternoon. We bunked in the white clapboard, two-room schoolhouse we once learned to count and read in. The only textbook, a King James Version of the Bible. At night, we sat in front of fires and kettles of oil frying fish, telling stories of Old Dan or the doglike animal down by the well that would lick a child in the face if it got to close, that lick potentially deadly and disfiguring. We told stories of Uncle UF and working the land, the tincture of difficulty still there in our mouths like a bad tooth no one wanted to pull, the difficulty spoken of lightly, sometimes skirted altogether.

We still didn't own the land. We went back north to our jobs cleaning and cooking and driving and managing and rearing and cleaning and cooking some more. We saved some money. Then saved some more. We started to buy back the land we visited, we sharecropped and itinerantly farmed all those years ago, land that was once given to us by the slave master who was also the progenitor of some of our ancestors. Land taken by the county and the bank shortly after it was given to us because we didn't pay the taxes on it, as the story has been told. Parcel by parcel we bought back the land and anchored trailers, single- and double-wide, to the sand. I say "we" though I could say Aunt Annie, Uncle Vander, Uncle Ural, my own grandmother Elloree Lewis. When they tell these stories they say "we." "We left the South" or "we'd go and take cotton to the scales" or "we bought back the land." For them, the land, the "we" of it was most important, a "we" who had a place to go back to.

I've been thinking about this land in South Carolina and our future claim to it—land we cultivated, land we bled upon, slaved, cried, and created on; land that was stolen from the Cheraw, Edisto, Cherokee, among many, many other indigenous tribes. I have been thinking about the "we" of this land and who constitutes the "we." Have we considered all the various and diverse "we's" in thinking about our future on the land?

As an undergraduate who went south for college, I found myself in many Black progressive and radical spaces thinking about and discussing Black liberation and the pragmatic particularities of Black people's freedom in America. How could it be achieved, if it could be achieved? What was needed? Often, land—owning it, cultivating it, stewarding it, creating separatist communities upon it—became a sort of apotheosis. That in order for Black folks to gain the freedom we needed and searched for we needed more Black autonomous spaces. So owning, cultivating, and stewarding land was not only part of the conversation, but it was also understood as a political and spiritual practice. Collectives were started, money saved, land bought. In those discussions of buying land in rural Georgia and Texas, I don't remember us ever discussing where Native folks were in our buying back the land, starting communes, building Black autonomous spaces. How do we reconcile bunking and creating bonds of belonging on stolen land? Are we building our utopias on the foreheads and bones of the dead and dispossessed? How do we reconcile our overlapping, nonidentical, ongoing genocides? Not so much reconcile them as much as determine what room do we make for each other in our collective and separate desires for liberation, for autonomy and sovereignty? What is our future on this land? What is the future of this work of keeping us alive?

Might we need to think of our futures simultaneously—to think Blackly and Natively collectively without departicularizing each other's histories and collective strivings? We live—no, we are trapped in the same burning-down-house of America and are trying to survive it. Survive while the house is burning down all around us and survive after it has burnt down. I think that survival will necessitate a type of intimacy, an intimacy that might seem antithetical or outside of the political imagination of nation and blood relations. An intimacy built upon permission and consent, an intimacy that does not require recognition from colonizer, corporation, or State. An intimacy that makes each other and our futures possible.

An intimacy I've glimpsed in the speculative fiction of Toni Morrison. In *Beloved*, a novel many call historical fiction but also is quite speculative in its ability to reach beyond its historical setting,

Morrison created a character named Sixo, who appears in the narrative quite briefly but is as riotous and radical as the primary narrative of the novel: Sethe killing her child to prevent her from being reenslaved by her former master. Sixo is quite visionary and singular, one might say nonnormative or queer, in his predilections and living. Paul D, a friend of Sixo who's enslaved with him on a plantation called Sweet Home, reports that Sixo goes into the woods at night to commune with his bloodlines, with his ancestors. Sixo also stops speaking English, according to Paul D, because he sees no future in it. But what makes Sixo important and pertinent to the question of what is our future on the land is what he does when encountering a no-longer-used Native American sacred space.

In traveling to see his lover Patsy the Thirty-Mile Woman, enslaved on another plantation seventeen miles from Sweet Home, Sixo discovers "a deserted stone structure that Redmen used way back when they thought the land was theirs." This deserted stone structure is a third of the way from Patsy and would allow Sixo more time to visit with her rather than what normally happened when he had to walk the full seventeen miles between them—say good morning, turn back around, and begin the walk back to Sweet Home. These two long walks in less than twenty-four hours wore him down to nothing but a rag of a man who spends the day after these journeys sleeping beneath a tree called Brother. The other men on the plantation, the Pauls and Halle, cover for him, allow Sixo to spend Monday sleeping, his flame-red tongue hanging out of his mouth.

Wanting to minimize his exhaustion, Sixo asks Patsy the Thirty-Mile Woman to meet him at the stone structure he found. It takes two months, but he convinces Patsy to meet him there. However, before he invites Patsy to the lodge, he does something quite important and instructive for my own thinking about how to find a future, find liberation on stolen land. He asks for permission. "Sixo discovered it on one of his night creeps," writes Morrison, "and asked its permission to enter. Inside, *having felt what it felt like*, he asked the Redmen's Presence if he could bring his woman there. It said yes." Despite the permission granted and Sixo's plans, Patsy and Sixo never meet in the stone lodge. On the way, Patsy is confused, thinks she has been stood up or is going in the wrong direction, begins crying, and refuses to go on. When Sixo realizes Patsy hasn't made it to the stone lodge, he begins to frantically search for her, walking back in the direction she would have come from. Sixo stops, "[stands] in the wind," and asks for help. Morrison doesn't say who Sixo asks for help, but eventually he hears Patsy's muffled crying, finds his way to her, and they drop down there on the forest floor together and couple.

I've read this moment of Sixo's encounter with Patsy and the Redmen's Presence over and over again because it enacts the difficulty of navigating what it means for a stolen people to eke out brief and fleeting moments of intimacy, of a future on stolen land. This moment of permission and fugitivity also articulates a potential—how Black folks might acknowledge the difficulty of contending with Native American genocide and deracination while trying to subvert our own; how we might occupy the same land, the same space without competition or reifying the commodity-proprietorship nexus of land ownership—a model of ownership that is antithetical to the liberation we seek collectively and separately, one that has been foisted upon our people.

Sixo's asking for permission speculates darkly, disrupts the virtue signaling and flaccid efficacy that is the current practice of land acknowledgments, and allows for an allyship between Black and Indigenous political imaginaries that doesn't require a flattening or usurpation of one notion of sovereignty over another. Rather, a mutuality built upon difference instead of false equivalency. A mutuality built via affect and not some romantic, sentimentalized or banal form of political filiation. The affective relationship is one built upon conversation, one of consent and permission, one that requires constant maintenance.

Sixo's asking for permission and receiving that permission allows for two different desires, vulnerabilities, and precarities to exist alongside one another. This union also highlights the notion that Black folks' need for spaces of fugitivity that subvert the physical and social death brought about by slavery and its afterlife can acknowledge and be in community with Indigenous notions of sovereignty, land management, and stewardship. In other words, no one and nothing is violated. The usurpation of Native folks' land by non-Native folks and American slavery—these historical violations and their subsequent legacies end at the door of the stone lodge. When Sixo steps into its space after receiving permission from the Redmen's Presence, he consummates a new bond, a new sort of political and intimate filiation, one made inside the wound of history, one made out of emptiness.

In that moment of entering, Sixo also disrupts and defamiliarizes the notion that emptiness means unused, discarded, mismanaged, or derelict. Physically unoccupied does not mean outside of circulation or spiritually abandoned. The lodge's being unoccupied might be just for a season rather than forever. In the description of the emptiness of the lodge as "a deserted stone structure that Redmen used way back when they thought the land was theirs," Morrison opaquely points to the possibility that Native folks were driven from their land by pioneers and colonizers. That the Redmen's leaving was not of their own volition, and that they might, in fact, come back. In seeking approval to enter, Sixo confesses and honors the precarity of the meeting of these contiguous vulnerabilities and histories. To cross the threshold without asking is a potential violation, one more violation among many already suffered by Native folks. This potential for violation signals an opportunity for intimacy as well. Sixo seems to understand this situation and seeks this intimacy with the Redmen's Presence through feeling rather than through the traditional Western means of building relationships and intimacy—blood and legal contract. It is not an intimacy based upon sight and seeing but based upon a spiritual aurality, presence as enacted through feeling.

Sixo's feeling for permission contradicts and disrupts the settler-colonial practice of governments' deeming unoccupied land or land not in use as lacking proper management; therefore, in need of expropriating. The land made to labor under the supervision of the State. And those who were once stewards and keepers of the land must be put under the State's tutelage to learn how to properly administer it, as if they didn't have a diverse array of practices—culture, ethos, history, spirituality—that allowed them to successfully maintain and support various ecosystems of flora and fauna. This colonial perspective dismisses the notion of alternative visions or understanding of land use and care for natural resources. In Sixo's carefulness, in his centering of affect and intimacy, he highlights another possible political imaginary, another articulation of sovereignty and diplomacy. In seeking permission to enter the Native American sacred place, Sixo treats his "discovery" as possessing a history, as existing on a continuum, as already in motion, alive, possessed of itself rather than waiting for something or someone to animate it or possess it. The unoccupied stone structure is new to him, not new in and of itself, and does not require him to do anything with it. It's autonomous and treated as such.

This understanding of the stone lodge as autonomous corresponds with Indigenous practices of caring for what we in the West call non-human objects such as natural resources (i.e., land, stone, water, trees). Sixo does not seek to control or subjugate the lodge, only to occupy it long enough to fleetingly escape the hypersurveillance of slavery. The lodge becomes a sort of commons, a space for a type of refugeeism—a refuge from the terror of slavery. This refugeeism, this eking out of fleeting moments of freedom is beyond liberal multiculturalism and the banal conversations of empathy that normally follow. This moment is not a move toward integration, becoming a citizen through the alleged liberal largesse of the State. Instead, this moment is what theorist and poet Fred Moten terms invaginative; Sixo with the Redmen's Presence builds a nonsovereign, captureless autonomy that is outside of the colonial and plantation order while firmly inside it. It's not a beseeching to be grafted onto the civil, American body politic. This created intimacy, this refuge stands decidedly and purposely outside of America while yet being in it. Sixo turns away from his captors, turns away from asking them to take their boot from his neck. Instead, he turns to the other Others—Native folks—trapped in the burning-down-house of America and its nightmarish dream. Just as Sixo stops speaking English because there's no future in it, he understands his future, his peace and freedom requires him to speak with Indigenous folk. A speaking that exists metaphysically and spiritually, and that speaking must be ongoing.

Even after receiving permission to enter the lodge, Sixo does not treat his admittance as a given or an always and forever. His admittance must be constantly attended to, corroborated. This relationship between Sixo and the Redmen's Presence requires maintenance, study, work, a "figuring it out," but the work of figuring, maintaining, cultivating this intimacy, this relationship must be done in an affective tongue, embracing the metaphysics and opacity of feeling; that opacity acting as the presiding grammar and language between them. "Inside, having felt what it felt like," writes Morrison, "he asked the Redmen's Presence if he could bring his woman there." Sixo and the Redmen's presence improvise their communication through feeling. They wallow and "speak" in an errant and delinquent tongue. In their improvisation, they carve out new means of communicating desire, intimacy, the known and unknown world, and the politics of this world created in that moment, in their being out of order, which is within a newly arriving order.

I also think Morrison's narrative opacity is important in this moment because it refuses to offer up this moment of intimacy for our, the reader's, pleasure and spectatorship. Morrison does not shift into the "show, don't tell" model of contemporary storytelling, providing for the reader the details of the conversation between Sixo and the Redmen's Presence. Instead, she leaves it open and opaque, leaves it at "having felt what it felt like." In giving us only Sixo's feeling, Morrison disallows the reader to surveil the communications between the two. We, the reader, must imagine into what the feeling is that Sixo feels, imagine into what asking for permission sounds like or doesn't sound like, imagine into the feeling of receiving permission, thereby building the feeling, the permission. Does Sixo close his eyes, or does he keep them open? What does permission from the unseen but present feel like in the mouth, in the mind? What is the sensation along the skin? What did the trees do above him, or how might the underbrush have fluttered? Was the Redmen's Presence and conversation felt, its permission given in the underbrush, in the leaves, perhaps in the wind?

Morrison makes us work, makes us participate in the figuring, in the playing out of the plot. We must author the text alongside her, create a sort of ensemble, but she is the bandleader, has provided the sheet music, key changes, and melodic structure for our session. If we were ever looking for an example of the jazz aesthetic in fiction, particularly an improvisatory aesthetic or modality with all of its intended radicality, here it is. Morrison's retreat from overplaying, from writing exactly what we expect—expect to see—figures us in the work, in the study, in the act of reading, which is a political act of making. She refuses us a sort of aural or visual passivity. We must co-perform, create a social world, a sociality. We must create the refuge that Sixo seeks. And in making the refuge, we make something larger than a fictional world. We make, map, and begin to inhabit a politics, an otherwise that can be exported out of the text and into the world we occupy. We inhabit a radical imagination; we feel around the invisible. Sixo's desire for a nonsovereign future moves us into making one imaginatively, which makes it possible.

But Morrison's desire for us to imagine a nonsovereign future is not the only reason she refuses us the ease of spectatorship and conventional readerly pleasure. What it's all about is surveillance and subjugation, a refusal to subjugate her Black and Native characters, to the same prurient desires, to the same surveillance they would have suffered in their actual nineteenth-century lives. Morrison provides for her characters what many nineteenth-century Black and Native folks didn't have or had fleetingly—their own space, a space for intimacy and its negotiation. Withholding, a luxuriant withholding (to borrow from Stephano Harney and Fred Moten), enacts that possibility in the novel—a space for freedom, for intimacy. The chapter, the novel itself, becomes a stone lodge in which to hide, rest, and invent a future—not only for Sixo but for us, the reader, particularly the Black and Native readers who reside inside the burning-down-house of America.

Do you want to be an American? Why? What does it get you? I'm asking not only myself these questions but also an imaginary gaggle of Black folks gathered in a clearing in a forest, Black folks gathered by a stream running over limestone, Black folks fishing in a river, Black folks hunting deer in the Midwest and Oklahoma, Black folks gathered in pool halls, Black folks sitting in wooden-chaired auditoriums at Morehouse and Spelman College, Hampton University, and Bowie State, sitting beneath the deep bellow of pipe organs, Black folks rocking in pews in AME churches in Savannah and Atlanta and Los Angeles, Black folks on buses running up and down Western Avenue and Martin Luther King Boulevard in Chicago, the Black nurses gathered at the nurses station at UIC Medical. I am asking Black folks turning over slabs of meat beneath trees as relatives all wearing shirts that read "Bennett Family" or "The Johnsons" watch cousins, grandmothers, sisters, and uncles eat from Styrofoam plates heaped over with food—why do you want to be an American?

I'm asking us these questions after reading Nikole Hannah-Jones's preface to the 1619 Project in the *New York Times Magazine*, which "aims to reframe the country's history by placing the consequences of slavery and the contributions of black Americans at the very center of our national narrative." Through a series of essays, short stories, and poems, Black writers from across America interrogate, expose, challenge, offer, and resurrect histories, conversations, and critiques that examine the legacy of 1619, the year the *White Lion*, a slave ship, dropped anchor off the coast of Jamestown, Virginia, and unloaded its cargo, part of which were seventeen Africans who would become the first chattel slaves of the United States of America. And, for Hannah-Jones, this landing initiates the American project, American democracy. The 1619 Project sought to "bring slavery and the contributions of

Black Americans from the margins of the American story . . . by arguing that slavery and its legacy . . . shaped modern American life, even as that influence had been shrouded or discounted." The project was met with celebration and approbation. As Hannah-Jones herself notes in the preface, 1619 cookies were baked, hashtags started and proliferated all over social media, and "educators in all fifty states began teaching a curriculum based on the project." However, some historians sought to "discredit the project by challenging its historical interpretations and pointing to what they said were historical errors." Nevertheless, Hannah-Jones felt buoyed up by Black folks' reaction to the project, particularly Black students. "Black students," writes Hannah-Jones, "especially, told me that for the first time in their lives, they'd experienced a feeling usually reserved for white Americans: a sense of ownership of, belonging in, and influence over the American story." One student told a reporter from the *Chicago Sun-Times* that "the project helped her realize: We were the founding fathers." Pause.

I would like to ask that student: Is that what we want to be? Is that who we truly were and are, who our ancestors modeled themselves after—founding fathers, slave-owning, landed gentry? I want to hold in question this feeling that the project inspired in Black folks; I want to hold in question ownership and its erasures, the desire to belong to a country through an origin story, through centering. I want to hold in question the Project, not just the 1619 Project but the project of becoming American. It is not a piecemeal endeavor, one that only involves selecting the history we find most noble, most laudable, most favorable or casts us on the right side of history. Becoming American requires donning the bloody clothes of our genocides and dispossessions, our erasures.

I pause when I see the word *ownership* in such close proximity to discussions of slavery and no one batting an eye or calling into question what is meant when someone says that when encountering the 1619 Project they felt what White Americans feel about this country— a sense of ownership, of influence. Isn't ownership exactly the problem, how we got into this predicament of becoming American through chattel slavery, empire, Jim Crow segregation, the carceral state, deep economic disadvantage and inequality? We need to dismantle what it means to own and feel—to feel belonging through possession as opposed to permission. We must interrogate the easy commodification of our history, of Black history—both symbolic commodification through the marketplace of feelings and ideas and material commodification through the dispersal of our culture on wax, paper, sound wave, and internet superhighway. In the words of James Baldwin, "we create our history." We share our history. We tell it. We don't own it and wield it like a shovel or a barrel or a pair of shoes or a person for that matter.

Our history must be complicated through diffusion rather than centering, through a rhizomatic relationship to others and origins. In other words, leave us at our margins. Because, it is at the margins, in these zones of nowhere that we can imagine an otherwise, find the feeling that we have been meaning to come to, which is to say: the future. The center is too circumscribed, too invested in its centrality, in its order, in its borders and boundaries, in its scarcity. And because of this investment in exclusivity and scarcity, it could never produce anything like a future, a beyond. Whereas at the margins, in their borderlessness, in their ability to come all the way up to the center and sometimes pierce and even invaginate the center, there is abundance because everything is material and possible, even the knowledges of the center.

At the margins is where we figure IT out, where we have always figured IT out—whatever the "IT" is: our peace, our freedom, our love. Sixo, Patsy, and the Redmen's Presence in Morrison's *Beloved*, for instance, are examples of moving at the margins to improvise something like freedom. Sixo, Patsy, and the Redmen's Presence also contradict the notion that our story, our history can be told by centering it solely in a Black experience. Black life in America is always in conversation, in feeling, in intimacy and relation with Indigenous Presence. To uncouple these important historical bonds is to reinscribe the colonial enterprise of erasure. For instance, to center America's founding in 1619, in slavery, ironically, is to perform a type of US ethnocentrism that elides two ongoing histories in the Americas—that of Native folks and that of Black folks enslaved in the colonial Americas. The year 1619 is not the beginning. It is the middle—it is the middle of the Powhatan peoples and their history; it is the middle of colonization on the shores of North America.

Black folks had been running in and out of freedom in the southern parts of what would be the United States since the 1560s. We had taken up with the Apaches, the Edistos, the Caribs, the Seminoles. We had made lives with them in swamps and in brackish water. We were never a people that were solely alone . . .

I am not trying to swap one set of romanticizations for another. This history of coming together with Native folks is complicated—complicated by Native folks owning and participating in the slave trade, Native folks buying into and proliferating racism and anti-Blackness. Black folks participating in the genocidal Indian Wars in the Midwest during the 1860s and '70s as the vaunted and celebrated Buffalo Soldiers. The current struggle among certain Native nations about whether or not to recognize Black folks who also have Indigenous heritage. All are examples of the complicated and difficult relationship between Indigenous people and Black folks. This history must be deliberated and cried over, reckoned with, and told. And, it has. Scholars and writers like Tiya Miles, Tiffany Lethabo King, Caleb Gayle, and Kyle T. Mays have written about the intimate history of Black and Native folks in the United States of America. However, this history is relegated to one essay in the book form of the 1619 Project, and in the original project that appeared in the *New York Times Magazine*, Native Americans are conspicuously absent in the framing of the project.

This exclusion of Native folks in the project proliferates what writer David Treuer argues is part of the American project—that Nativeness and Indigeneity must be beautifully and romantically absent. "The country begins with Indians," writes Treuer, "but ends with Americans; there is no sense that they can coexist." In its reluctance to think about and consider the relationship between Indigenous peoples and Africans brought to America as chattel in the alleged origin story of the country, the 1619 Project commits itself to the same erasure. In the 1619 Project, the country, democracy, Americanness begin in slavery rather than with the founding fathers. And for Hannah-Jones, these contradictions—that slavery initiates democracy—can not only coexist but are the origins of the greatness of the country. Rather than trouble, challenge, or call into question the veracity of calling America a democracy, Hannah-Jones grafts the African American body onto the genocidal and disingenuous American mythologizing of its history. This act of inserting Black folks into the founding father framework reminds me of rap artist, record label owner, and entrepreneur Sean "P. Diddy" Combs descending into his infamous White Party in 2004 from a helicopter with the Declaration of Independence tucked beneath his arms. Just as Combs was putting in his application to become part of the founding mythology as capitalist scion, the 1619 Project hopes to trope our history of deracination and exclusion by the Democracy into democracy; a contradiction surely, and impossible.

The 1619 Project desperately wants to make us Americans though in fact we've never experienced *that* America—the America of milk and plenty, the bootstrapping America of Ellis Island and the Bank of Italy, an immigrant bank that was allowed to become more than a niche bank for Italians who had recently made their way to America in the early twentieth century, an immigrant bank allowed to become Bank of America, a bank of the nation, not just a bank for immigrants. As lawyer and legal scholar Mehrsa Baradaran notes in *The Color of Money: Black Banks and the Racial Wealth Gap*, Black Americans have been systematically ostracized and segregated from the mainstream economy of the country, ghettoized and disenfranchised through a series of policies that never allowed Black banks to establish credit and lending practices that could help Black Americans build wealth through homeownership and establishing businesses in our communities. We've never journeyed our way into acceptable Americanness, which is really Whiteness—nor should we want to nor have to. The hallmarks of the American empire we have experienced are those of colonization, dispossession, genocide, racism, and economic inequality.

The art, literature, culture, style, lives we've made out of that genocide, I would argue, do not belong to America. We've made beautiful things despite America. To give jazz, the blues, hip-hop over to America is akin to giving Frederick Douglass's master partial credit for writing Douglass's slave narratives and autobiographies. Yes, slavery created the predicament, but it did not teach Douglass to read nor did it provide him his pen. It only provided the gash in his feet that his pen could sit in. Everything else was Douglass.

So again I ask: Why do you want to be an American?

Or, in the words of W. E. B. Du Bois: *How does it feel to be a problem?*

Or, let's embrace being a problem, like Sixo, who stops speaking English because he sees no future in it, who goes into the woods at night to commune with his bloodlines, who would be hard to locate in something like a 1619 Project because he has refused to anchor himself to a master or mastering narrative, to anything like an origin. Because he's in league with what has been expelled and does not exist for America— the Indian. Sixo locates his possibility, his freedom diffusely, fugitively, creating bonds of belonging at the margins, with those who have been cast out and dispossessed. For Sixo, home is neither tethered to a redemptive narrative or mythology nor anchored in land. It is created, manifested in errantry, in exile, in affect, in what poet and philosopher Édouard Glissant would call the abyss. In locating home in this fashion, Sixo articulates and embodies a type of citizenship that does not receive its efficacy from its ability to exclude or include, from policing and maintaining boundaries and binaries, but a citizenship borne of flexibility, contingency, and expansiveness, one built upon improvisation and openness as opposed to rigidity and scarcity. What makes Sixo and Patsy's union in the woods possible, despite their not meeting in the stone lodge, is Sixo's seeking his future at the margins of plantation life, at the edges of language, at the edges of the imagination, at the edges of himself, which is at the edges of Native American life and dispossession. Might this need to be our new definition of home, of citizenship? Might this be how we might imagine the future and what it is to make a future—that it always must conspire with the edges and borders of another?

How might the permissions sought and wrought by Sixo counsel us today in light of Native Americans' still trying to regain sovereignty and autonomy of their land and lives and Black folks' resisting the bodily and social death of racism in America? How does a Black-Indigenous nexus shift our understanding of allyship, mutual aid, sovereignty, notions of home, and belonging? Might this intimacy of errantry, this nomadic belonging be the gift we've been meaning to give ourselves and each other?

Attempting to answer these questions, I might offer this—that the future we've been meaning to come to will require us to prioritize building bonds of belonging through affect, through intimacy, enacting and claiming our liberation now within the ongoing disaster of dispossession, racial terror, social death, and the threat of bodily death. In the building of these bonds, we offer alcoves, moments of rest and reprieve and, simultaneously, begin to construct alternative possibilities of sociality, family, community, and subsequently a politics and a world. The alcove becomes more than theoretical, becomes the study (in both senses of the word) and possibly steady. Here and now. Like Sixo and Patsy's dropping down onto the forest floor to couple or Sixo's asking and feeling for permission, we improvise our freedom, reifying it in thin air. Even if only for a moment. The momentariness, whether ended by something like the police or a patroller, creates an alternative history and possibility. It dents the dominant narrative and testifies even when the testament is torn into tatters, an archive of an absence made present. Ironically, the creation of intimacy, of this sometimes-fleeting archive, is not centered or grounded in shared or disparate traumas. Instead, the intimate bonding foregrounds the improvisation of a yet-to-be-known, a beyond, a freedom built of intimate study. This intimate study is centered upon the spiritual needs and political possibilities of the other.

As evidenced by Sixo, what is centered in the making of this new relationship is not the studying or prioritizing of the wound but what can be made inside it—what lives or intimacies are possible inside the stone lodge as a response to the dispossession of Native people and the rendering of Black life as merely flesh, commodity, labor, and social death by the nation. This improvisation, this intimacy is not an eschewing of the abjection of slavery or land dispossession and its afterlives. Rather, it is a complication and a refusal, a renouncing that is also a speculation about the future in the present, in the middle and muddle and muck of the ongoing catastrophe of racism and Native American deracination and disenfranchisement. This intimate study, this world-making inside the wound, rejects the fetishizing and commodification of our historical wounds. Rather than putting our disasters and wounds to work, to labor in the marketplace and political arenas of America, we turn toward each other and take back our time, our labor, our bodies. We also begin to imagine and enact possibilities that are not merely about making ourselves legible to the nation and our former captors. Instead, like Sixo, we create something beyond democracy, extending something like citizenship, but altogether different, to all the animals, to human and nonhuman, living and after and before.

In the turn toward the affective, to the intimate, Sixo teaches us to prioritize the knowledge of the body, of the metaphysical as a way of being in relation. It is a political act but one that does not traffic in the politics of representational governance or making oneself fit to go into the master's house and be recognized by the master's laws. The turn toward the affective is a small *p* politics, something more akin to the politics of friendship and improvisation of fostering or adoption.

I've been thinking of this moment of Native "presence" sheltering Sixo, providing for him a place to be fugitive and cared for, as a type of fostering, a fostering made through affect and spirit. The Redmen's

Presence provides a hedge of protection, a provisional care that reminds me of the practice in Black communities of taking in a brother's or sister's children, sometimes a cousin, sometimes a neighbor and raising them as one's own. It's a nonnormative notion of family, one that widens as needed. Something about this permission Sixo garners from the Redmen's Presence reminds me of this sort of flexible practice of folding in and making family. It is this folding in, this poetics of relation, that allows Sixo and Patsy to create, even if briefly, a union, a family built in fugitivity, of fugitivity. This adoption creates the possibility of a captureless future.

The future, then, is about troubling and complicating presence—the presence in absence, erasure, and genocide—presence despite genocide. Morrison's *Beloved*, once again, is instructive, particularly her choice of the term *presence* rather than *spirit* or *ghost*. Western notions of spirit or ghost traffic in the notion of a forever absence from the physical realm that would play into the romantic narrative of Indigenous extinction in order to have an American nation. Morrison's insistence on "presence" confirms that Native folks are still alive despite the emptiness of the lodge. The lodge, then, acts as a type of archive that testifies to both the erasure and genocide of Native Americans as well as testifies to their being unimpeached from the land. Morrison must deal with the historical fact of Native American land dispossession and death, but she also offers us another possibility in the middle of it—one that does not assume the teleology of the West, of Western notions of life and aliveness. That aliveness must always be visually corroborated (though it is opaquely via the stone house).

Sixo's using feeling as the mode of communication, as the grammar for convening conversation between him and a "presence," supposes a different way of making and inhabiting a world, one that does not rely on the supremacy and valorizing of sight as the best way of knowing something, of being. As Fred Moten notes in a short film made by the MacArthur Foundation, "The dominant philosophical tradition in which we operate is one that tends to valorize the visual over the oral." This dominant philosophical tradition Moten is speaking of is the Western European philosophical tradition that so much of our country is founded upon and rooted in. It is the philosophical tradition of social and legal contracts, the Enlightenment, the modern nation-state with its attendant discourses on citizenship, war, property, and conquest. Human and nonhuman. Empire and education. Colony and metropole. Dirty and clean. Barbarian and civilized. Worthy and unworthy. Us and them. And all of it based upon sight and the judgment that comes from it. Morrison through Sixo refuses these logics, orders, and supremacies because they produce the genocide that is America; it's how he gets to the plantation, it's why the stone lodge is empty. Sixo's turning toward feeling proposes that the world in which he would be free lies outside of the visual and can only be communicated with via feeling. He must lay down his sight, lay down seeing and listen and feel—feel for the world, feel for his freedom.

I'll admit it: I have been speaking of love this entire essay—what and how to love when there seems no room for it. Love as improvisation. As renouncement. As refusal. Love as fostering, bringing another into family. Love as permission. As nakedness. As negotiation. Love as political possibility, which is to say revolution. However, in striving to reckon with the ongoing genocides Black people and Native Americans face in this country, it seems almost sentimental, overly dramatic, inefficacious, and irresponsible to pitch love as a potential critique or combative element in the fight against our deaths and dispossessions. It would seem that we need more practical plans, more ideological apparatuses, more 1619 Projects or Inheritance Projects, more Deacons for Defense and Black Panthers and Brown Berets and Young Lords—not another writer telling of us of love.

But it is love that carries us off into the woods to seek shelter and lodging for our fugitive futures. It is love that sends us off to study and plan for these futures in the woods and undercommons. Love that gathers us in pews with guns ready to walk the neighborhood's streets at night to confront White mobs that seek to terrorize and destroy our people. It is love that sends us out to collect data on lynchings throughout the South despite the danger. It is love that suggests that every Black family should keep a Winchester in a corner of their house to protect themselves from the lynch mob and the Klan. It is love that sends us into the streets to march against the fire hose and tear gas. Love that causes someone to sit down and organize food campaigns for the poor, breakfast programs for Black children, newspapers that carry news of resistance, uprisings, and revolutionary causes in the far-flung jungles and steppes and crags of a world that seem divorced from our fields and struggle in Louisiana and Mississippi, our corner stores and bodegas in Los Angeles and New York City.

But this love is not some amorphous, facile love of romance or fatuous, sycophantic patriotism or abject nationalism. No, this love is the grit, pulp, belch, breath, funk, and countenance of possibility, of another thing, another way, a way of figuring IT out. This love requires risk, risking loss, risking the body for something like a future. The love I speak of is "a bondage which liberates you into something of the glory and the suffering of the world." This love carries you into the world because of its glory and suffering and wanting to do something about all of it—bring more glory, combat and end the suffering. And if ending suffering is not possible, at least delaying it, finding some tic of pleasure, some way to break or impair the suffering momentarily. For this is love—to refuse, to be free in whatever manner one can even if that freedom looks like exhaustion. Sixo, for instance, walking all day to see his lover, Patsy, and having no more than a moment to speak to her before he has to turn around and head back toward his plantation where he will fall down in exhaustion. Though it may seem that Sixo is suffering, he is not. He has authored his exhaustion. It belongs to him, Patsy, and his bloodlines. It is a testament to the world he's making, one that he refuses to express in his captor's language, a world made of feeling, of exhaustion. For this love is the foundation of action; it is what holds you up when the batons and tear gas tear you down. When you can do nothing but collapse in a heap after walking all night. This is the type of love that will send you to an empty stone lodge and speak with what cannot be seen but felt, which is to say the future.

I, too, have stood at the door of the stone lodge and asked for permission to enter more than once—out of love, out of the desire to forge friendship across the chasm of genocide and history. While giving a few readings from my first book of poems in the Pacific Northwest, G—, an Indigenous poet friend of mine, invited me to read and work with her at a Native American high school on the Quileute Reservation. G— and I had known each other about a year, meeting at various poetry conferences and readings, often sharing a side-eye at the foolishness that surrounds creative writing conferences. We had just experienced such foolishness on the longest, whitest, most opulent yacht in Seattle one can imagine, replete with tinkling champagne glasses, road, telecom, and internet barons, magnates, and wealthy wives. We understood that we were on this boat as the subdued, the captives who could speak the captor's language, but we were also, in every way we could, fucking that up as well, breaking the shovels and slipping the yoke much to the consternation of our handlers. We would disappear below deck or hang with the staff, away from the frail crystal and sharp, fragile smiles. When there was no avoiding the awkward question or the attempt at a joke that always slipped into some racist trope about Indigeneity or Blackness, we tried to interrupt or deflect on each other's behalf. There, we recognized something in each other—something quite hard to describe—maybe, a way of being, a way of knowing how to walk and move in a room full of knives and crystal and manners. Maybe, this recognition is why G— invited me to go with her to the Quileute Reservation to work with some high school students.

While sitting on the bumper of her car, slipping out of her dress boots and slipping back into some Chuck Taylors, G— mentioned the high school visit to me when we got back to shore. Would I like to come along? she asked. She would have to get permission from the elders, but it would be great to go out there together and work with the young folks. After the athletics of dipping, dodging, parrying these liberal good manners and intentions, I felt honored by the invitation. It was as if she saw me, saw that this shindig with its papery, gilded virtue was not me at all; that, in fact, I would rather be in a car, riding through a dense pine forest toward the coast where we might sit down and talk with students about poems and language and the difficulty of writing yourself and your world into being.

After receiving permission from the elders on the reservation, that's exactly where G— and I found ourselves, slipping through the mist and fog on some highway in the Pacific Northwest. We talked about gout, how folks on her reservation and in my neighborhood in southern New Jersey cut holes in the toes of a shoe to relieve the needling pains that prick them up and down their feet and calves. We laughed and laughed and laughed about the shoes, about being sent to the store to buy cigarettes for the old folks. "Newports, hard pack, not the soft pack. Don't bring that soft pack bullshit up in here," I said in the voice of one of the barbers I used to run errands for as a boy. On and on I went in the voice of the old people whom we loved and revered and who sometimes scared us, "Come here, boy . . ." On and on, we laughed driving through western Washington state. Now, ten years later, sitting in an air-conditioned library in Austin, Texas, where a colossal stone Olmec head faces the highway where white-trailered trucks transport onions and avocados from Mexico to all points north in America, I realize that there in the laughter, in the telling of stories, we had entered the stone lodge, had begun to feel, to make friendship, family across the chasm of our different histories. It was in our elders, in how we had come to know them, how they had influenced everything from our language to how we thought of forgiveness, and even love. Their prickliness, their guidance, their contradictions, their long looks, their sicknesses, their raw throats made rawer by the smoking of cigarettes, there was our language—a language that no longer carried only our historical subduing. Our elders were a wild language, a language unkempt at its corners. Irascible, utterly necessary, and radical without trying to be. They were how we had come into ourselves, and there in the car beneath the gunmetal gray sky, we wilded out, communing with our bloodlines and each other.

When we pulled up alongside Lake Crescent, the pines towering above us, we both went silent. The lake was immense. It astounded me, scared me really. I held the handle of the door as if the lake had some unseen volition and could snatch that very car door from its hinges and drag me into its waters. G— said something about the lake being created by a glacier, but that was it. For as long as we were in sight of the lake, we sat in silence. It was the type of sitting I had done as a boy whenever a lightning storm crashed through the sky during those summers in New Jersey. My grandmother would tell us to turn everything off—the television, the lights, the fans, even the air conditioner in the living room—"and let God have his way." And we did. We sat in darkness until the storm passed.

G— and I sat in that silence. It was as if we were asking each other to consider something—maybe the immenseness of the lake, our going to work with these young Native students—but it was also a moment of study and intimacy. I think one of the most difficult things for many people is to sit in silence—not have a radio or some music blaring, to have nothing but stillness. It is vulnerable and vulnerable-making to sit in quiet because in silence one must deal with oneself without distraction. And to do this with someone else, well, even more so. Personally, I love sitting in silence, but I know that not everyone does. But there, we sat, in whatever ease or discomfort we each felt, and it was peaceful, without any awkwardness. For me, this is absolutely necessary in friendship, in intimacy—the ability to be quiet together.

The conversations we began on that trip, the silences we cultivated have deepened and expanded, spooling out into discussions about the politics of land, ownership, who gets the oceans, whose people are of the desert, the territorialization of affect, autonomy, sovereignty, and desire. Long into nights where we stare at the same moon from different windows with cell phones in our hand, we've talked of our folk, our siblings, our language, the salt and tincture of our tears. Many times, the night has grown long and over our shoulders talking about the English language's inability to deal with the complexities of friendship and intimacy. Sometimes by a fire, sometimes over a cup of brown liquor, sometimes in taxis, sometimes from the bottom of love, where we did not want to be, after being scraped and bruised, we've spoken to each other at the frayed end, of ourselves about the frayed ends of ourselves. In the mountains, on ships splitting the cold water of a sound, we've taken to silence and allowed that silence to speak for us, staring out into waves and wakes of our past, of our future.

But it all began in La Push, on the road, in the high school, eating lunch in the classroom off of Styrofoam plates, the Pacific bursting up white and cold against the shore and the tall, hulking, tree-filled islets just beyond the shore. I had never seen islets before, but there they stood in the gray of the day, looking like stoop-shouldered giants who had been banished and now turn their backs to the land, refusing to watch what we, the humans, were doing.

While visiting the high school, I learned of the fishing practices of the Quileute and the dire consequences for an insufficient haul: banishment. With their potential expulsion resting at their feet, Quileute men paddled out into the ocean in red cedar canoes, sailing as far north as southeast Alaska and as far south as California armed with harpoons, but the hunt was not considered successful until they brought the whale to shore. The only way to keep the dead or dying whale from sinking was to sew up its lips. Sewing up the whale's lips required the men to dive into those rough waters and jab a harpoon-like needle and thread through its upper and lower lips over and over again, closing the whale's mouth, preventing it from taking on water. When I asked why such a heavy penalty, someone (was it G— or one of the elders there at La Push?) said that without that whale—its blubber, meat, skin, bones, everything—the tribe had nothing for the coming year—no food, shelter, clothing. All of life was there in getting a dead whale back to shore.

I trembled and became nervous at the thought of that: the young men trying to close up the whale, failing to do so, walking into exile, possibly through the forest we had driven through. Where had they gone? How had they survived, if they survived? Whom had they taken up with?

Once in the school, one of the administrators walked us into a classroom. Students hushed at our entrance, and that hush in the classroom remained for most of the visit, for the reading, for the questions we tried to ask of them. G— received this same silence as well. And why not—this silence? We were bringing a strange and unknown love to them. One of the most difficult sorts of love is to love someone who does not know or cannot ascertain how you have come to love them. This, the love of solidarity movements, of allyship, of political activism, of struggling for self-determination alongside another who's struggling for self-determination in a different community. It's as if you walk in somewhere and say: "You don't know me, but I want to struggle and think with you." That shit is hard—to accept that love, that intimacy, to believe the love is what you say it is. This is the difficulty of love borne of history, borne of collective and simultaneously divergent and disparate struggles. Your compatriot on the line with you may not realize you're on the same line, may not see you as a compatriot at all. In fact, they may not even know that there is a fight. Or, even worse, they may think it is *you* they need to fight rather than the country that is trying to kill them.

What type of stranger was I to those students that day? What did they make of me, of Black folks, of our history? Who was I to them—an interloper, some weird man with thick locs muttering about metaphor, a mentally ill sister, racism, and lynching? Had they thought of my history, how it might intersect with theirs? These questions, these chasms and abysses between them is what I groped and called across that day. This is what I felt I was up against in entering that classroom in that high school—love. I was up against love and who must die and who must live.

I was willing to stand in that awkward and discomfiting silence because I hoped that we might converse about the silence, the chasm between us, our people. Foolish, I know, to think I might get this sort of conversation from students I'd just met for the first time, but I was open to the possibility. I wanted to cultivate intimacy, one that continued the solidarity work and self-determination movement building of the Combahee River Collective and *This Bridge Called My Back: Writings by Radical Women of Color*. Continue the work of Black Power and Civil Rights activist Kwame Ture, who journeyed to Minnesota to support Dennis Banks and Russell Means in the Wounded Knee Trials in 1974.

These sorts of intimacies have been more than photo opportunities and junket tours; they have been truly transformative. So transformative that governments have assassinated and continue to try to assassinate leaders and community activists who have collectively struggled against land and cultural dispossession. A great example of this radical intimacy is that of the slain Indigenous Honduran activist Berta Cáceres and Black-Indigenous Honduran activist Miriam Miranda. Cáceres and Miranda refused the Honduran State–sponsored narrative of Indigenous folks as autochthonous to the land, a narrative that had no place for Black-descended Indigeneity. Instead, they united the Garifuna, Black-Indigenous Hondurans with those who were considered more traditional Indigenous Hondurans, such as the Lenca, Miskito, Maya-Chorti, and Xicaque, to resist the seizure of their lands by the Honduran government, agribusiness, and tourism projects. Their friendship and activism birthed such a powerful movement that the Honduran government assassinated Cáceres in her nightgown in her home. And the Honduran government is still pursuing Miranda, who continues her work of keeping her people free and on their land.

There, in that classroom, I sought to create this intimacy through what has brought me closest to myself and others—poetry. Poetry has brought me my closest friends and coconspirators.

Friendship is the most radical alliance one can make because it is one of the few things not organized and administered by the government—unlike marriage and family. Friendship requires no permits, licenses, or contracts. It is improvisational, contingent, errant, and opaque, and sits outside of large-scale legal apparatuses. In a documentary on the philosopher Éduoard Glissant, Glissant spoke about what to him was family; that it had nothing to do with blood relations but with politics, of a shared political striving. Family was the people whom he politically communed with. Glissant's notion of family emblematizes what I think of friendship—choice, intimacy, a collective striving that runs the full gamut of what it means to be alive.

I hoped in sharing with the students poems about my sister living and struggling with mental illness and my loving her through it; poems playing in the vernaculars of the South and hip-hop that I might cast my voice across the chasm of our difference; that they might hear care, love, the difficulty of growing up and living in a country where your captors keep reinventing the methods and linguistic traps of your captivity—sometimes calling your captivity freedom, citizenship, constitutional amendment, voting rights. I hoped the high school students could hear below the words, below the English, see something below my face. Yes, I was a stranger in the village, but, often, we have entertained angels and love unawares. I hoped to be that strange angel, not the saving kind, but one that they saw as asking for refuge, for a friend, one who comes for a visit and hopefully comes again.

I know friendship is not made in one visit, in one knocking at the door, but it does begin there. It begins in bearing that silence, in that potential rejection. So I knocked, and I continue to knock at the door of the stone lodge. Sometimes, I am permitted entrance, but, like Sixo, my admission requires constant maintenance, revision, checking-in. Sometimes, that entering will have limitations. I might be allowed only in the front room or in the yard, allowed in the kitchen but only to sit at a turquoise table, eat a meal then go home. Sometimes, that entering the lodge will be a call in the blue hour of the morning asking only my ear to become a house of refuge—nothing else. Not to be a speaking thing, a box of noise, but an empty house whose door is open. Sometimes, these visitations will be about bearing silence, the silence of someone sitting next to you, a silence that cannot be read, a presence marked by absence—like the students there at the high school. This, too, this, too.

When we left the silence of the classroom, I returned to the noise of the ocean breaking against the rocks and looked over to the islets, thinking of the young men trying to keep a dead whale from sinking. I stood there imagining them in their boats in the summer, throwing their harpoons into the side of the whale, then clambering over the sides of the canoe, swimming up to the dead creature, one young man piercing the lip of the whale with a harpoon that bore a rope and beginning to tie shut the mouth of the whale. Several men must have had to do this, go down under the water, shove the needle and rope through the bottom lip then pass the harpoon to someone else who continued puncturing and suturing closed the mouth of the whale. On and on they go under and pierce and pierce the tough mouth. Do they work in silence, or do they shout to each other? Had they felt anxious? Could they feel the whale sinking even as they tried to prevent it? How had they guided the large animal back to shore? Or, did they butcher it there in the ocean? What if they were unsuccessful? How had they left their people? Did their family mourn for them? Or, did they watch stoically as the young men left? Were those young men allowed to gather their things before they were exiled, or must they walk on, walk out into their apocalypse, into the dense pine forest?

The cold mist gathered around me like a coat. I stood there wondering about these young men all those years ago. Did anyone take them in? Did they make family somewhere else? What was their future upon the land? What is the future of this work of keeping us alive?

Notes on the Underground

He had to get away. I could not stop reading until Fred Daniels, the protagonist in Richard Wright's *The Man Who Lived Underground*, was ensconced in darkness in a sewer underneath the city, the water sluicing around his knees, a single beam of daylight falling through the manhole cover onto his face.

Despite my daughter and her five-year-old friend bouncing about the house, their bodies aimed toward razing the place to the very beams and caulking, I could not turn my attention away from Daniels and the police beating him, coercing him to confess to a murder he did not commit. I could not set the book down and pursue anything like a day until I knew he had escaped from the police, leaping from a hospital window to do so. Herein lies the seduction of Richard Wright's *The Man Who Lived Underground*: it's as if I'm watching someone write the recurring nightmare of the last twenty years of my life—that one day I will simply be walking out of a house, counting the money I've just earned for a day's work, and the police will decide I am an answer, their fantasy, an end to a problem.

I've had this nightmare off and on for twenty years. Sometimes just once a year. Sometimes every night for a week. The dreams began in Atlanta, while living in an eight-room, two-story boardinghouse just down the hill from Morehouse College, and continued as I moved to Texas, Brazil, Chicago, then back to Texas. The dream is the same with little variation. I'm accused of a crime that I did not commit. Interrogated. I profess my innocence to two detectives—both with brushy mustaches; one White, one Black, normally wearing blazers or sports coats. Their look: television cop detective drama fashion of the late 1980s. Somewhere between *Hill Street Blues* and *Miami Vice*. Blame my subconscious imagination's fashion on growing up in the '80s and watching too many cop dramas—*In the Heat of the Night,*

21 Jump Street, T. J. Hooker—either as reruns during early afternoon babysitting or at night with my grandmother dozing off after cleaning folks' houses all day in Cherry Hill, Medford Lakes, and Moorestown, the television light flickering against the lenses of her glasses, her eyes closed behind them.

In the dream, the officers, who are nameless, jab their knees into my ribs, grab the back of my neck and shove me toward the metal desk I am sitting at, handcuffed. Often, I feel as if I'm drowning or about to be submerged beneath water. No matter how much I profess my innocence, I wind up walking down a gray, cinder-block corridor. Jail cells line the hallway. Sometimes, the prisons they take me into are the Hollywood set-design cellblocks of the late '80s—steel bars, the clanging and slamming of cell doors, inmates' hands hanging out through the bars, the inmates' bodies, somehow, not there. Other times, the corridor is like the county facility in my hometown of Mount Holly, New Jersey, a facility I visited in high school as part of history class. No, no, it wasn't history class. It was a *Scared Straight* type of program, a program that took alleged at-risk and troubled youth into prisons to acquaint them with the soullessness of the place as a means of discouraging them from proceeding down paths of dereliction and crime. No, I was not deemed wanton or headed toward this sort of penitentiary life, but I was a young journalist in high school, saw myself as political and what we now call social justice oriented. I knew that the young men whom we would see in prison looked like me, came from the same places I came from, and so I wanted to write up something about them, about me, about how the world refuses to know us, to know what we love, and we are thrown behind these walls to be nothing more than a question the world refuses to answer, to be a fantasy.

So I hitched a ride on one of those death-trap yellow school buses and rode to several prisons and youth correctional facilities up and down the New Jersey Turnpike. Rahway. Burlington. Mount Holly. Those prisons were not like the Hollywood prisons of my imagination, of the '80s cop dramas. Their doors slid open from a central command. The buildings were rhombus-shaped, octagonal. Later in college I learned these shapes allowed panoptical observation of the inmates, allowed the incarcerated to feel observed at all points of the day. Punished. Some of the cells had televisions. Below the catwalks, a large, almost lunchroom-looking area complete with tables and benches bolted and anchored to the floor. The young men incarcerated were nothing like the actors incarcerated on television. They were young and Black like me. Fathers, some of them. They talked and talked about their families, getting out, going home, their mothers, their children.

The dream is nothing like this. In the dream, I am alone. Brutalized by officers before they place me in a cell. And there, once in a cell, this bereft feeling takes over. Nothing is coming for me, to take me out or away from there. My vision, the frame of the dream narrows, and blackness surrounds me in a long tunnel. The dream sounds cartoonish, I know, but for years it returns to me again and again and again. Sometimes, I'm running through the shopping center behind my grandmother's house, the police chasing me on foot. The plate glass windows of the bakery and the Chinese restaurant bounce my reflection back to me, my legs churning through the sloshy, concrete air of the dream.

Once, I did run like this from the police in my hometown except I was on a bike. Pedaling as fast as I could, I launched myself over the curb into the grass divide that separated the neighborhood from the back bays and parking lot that led out from the shopping center. I refused to turn and look behind me. The police car's tires loud in my ears. In my head, I thought of two twelve-year-old friends who were "mistaken" for grown men by the police. This mistake allowed the police to toss them against a police car, beat them, and carry them off to an adjoining neighborhood where two Black men had allegedly just robbed a house. When the police pulled the boys from their car and made them stand in front of the woman whose house was robbed, she pointed out that my friends were, in fact, boys, children, and not men. It was men who had robbed her house, she said. The officers left my friends there in this strange neighborhood, lips swollen, crying.

So I ran when the police car pulled alongside me outside the shopping center. I ran before the officer could roll down his window or summon me over to him or tell me not to ride my bike on the narrow sidewalk in front of the bakery, the Chinese restaurant, the Acme. Not to ride out back behind the shops where the trucks docked and slid their long trailers into the cavernous ports and driveways that descended into darkness. They wanted us nowhere in the parking lot so I ran . . .

I run in the dream, in the dreams that are not dreams because they were and are too much like the facts of my childhood in southern New Jersey. So what is it that I am experiencing at night over the last twenty years? Reality, of course. Not a dream but the ongoing catastrophe of trauma. What it means to survive your captor, America, while yet having to live in its capture. There's nothing profound or extraordinary about this insight or my life. It is the banal abjection of being Black in America. Change the region, the clouds and sky, the temperature, the decade, the neighborhood, the legislature, the police car's color and the color of the officers' hands, and nothing changes but a few particularities of my dream. Of reality. The largest question is, Did you survive?

If the answer is yes, then the question after that is, And now what? What does it mean to survive the dream, survive in America under these murderous conditions, conditions that can and will revisit you the day, week, or year after you survived the last visitation by the police, by terror? Or, maybe, some perverse sense of luck or grace befalls you, and you never experience it again. But there it is now: that worry, that remembrance, the exhaustion, the feeling of your breath in your ear as you run, trying to evade your capture or potential death. It's as if they—the police, the State—have built a prison, a captor inside you, one that prepares you for your eventual capture. In his poem "An Agony. As Now," Amiri Baraka writes there's a man who looks out from behind his eyes and hates him in his flesh. I hear in this admission by Baraka a prison guard, a captor.

And what is it to hold a potential prison, replete with guards and panopticon, inside you, awaiting you at every thought and dream? It reminds me of state governments and the federal government building prisons on rural tracts of land across this vast country in anticipation of prisoners, crimes yet to be committed, their penitentiary remuneration dreamt of in the large, sleeping head of the nation. Those empty prisons a type of forecasting, wishing, blood alchemy. They've begun building those sorts of prisons inside us, inside me, inside you. And like Fred Daniels in Wright's *The Man Who Lived Underground*, the police are waiting to take you out—out of the world—and put you in the dream of yourself, which is really a fantasy they've been cultivating inside you since you were a child.

To be alive merely as fantasy, as the desired prop of a nation, to be anticipated as that which needs correction, to live this sort of life might devastate someone, plunge them into a lifelong despair, malaise, depression, terror if it were not for our communities—our mothers, brothers, aunts, uncles, fathers, barbers, beauticians, poets, godmothers—teaching us, showing us the opposite, providing us with an underground, another way of holding ourselves, shaking our dungeons, slipping dynamite into the crevices of the fortresses where they would damn up our souls and keep them from the light. This damning of our souls, this shackling of our bodies, is the relationship this nation would want us to have with ourselves—that of the imprisoned. And not just the Black *us*, but the All of *us*.

A friend of mine, who spent several years in prison, said something similar to me while driving from the airport. On an overbright autumn morning, construction dust kicked up and coated the windshield of my truck, turning the morning into a golden haze. We both slipped into conversation about the reason he came to Austin, a conference at the University of Texas Law School, to explore poetry and its efficacy in advancing prison abolition. We crawled through airport and morning traffic in Austin, our conversation moving rapidly until he hesitated and said something like, "I've been thinking about the omnipresence of prisons." Maybe he didn't use the word *omnipresence*, but he was talking about prisons being at the very center of culture, of our social world. He said (and I'm paraphrasing and very well could be making this up) that we tend to think of prisons as aberrations, as something far away from us—community, culture, life. In this way, prisons are marginal, something exceptional, an exceptional state of being. But in actuality, prisons are not on the margins. They are the very center of life in America. Prison is the beating heart of America. That last sentence is me, not him.

I'll never forget the day, the highway, the swirls of construction dust rising and surrounding us. The sun bright and leaning its heat against my hand. It was one of the most profound things I had heard. That prison is not out there in the dark, in the unterritorialized ether of America, but it's in the well-lit center of us darkly. I wanted to turn to him, to somehow physicalize for him how profoundly his comment landed, but, of course, I was driving. I could only nod and say something like, "That's right, that's absolutely right." We are all in some relationship with prison.

While driving through the autumn afternoon with my friend, I hadn't thought about the years and years of my prison dream and how my dream life corroborated this insight of his. It wasn't until reading Wright's *The Man Who Lived Underground* that I thought of the ongoing anthology of my dreams for those many years, waking fitfully in beds from Atlanta to Rio de Janeiro, glad to have passed through the itinerant veil of the dream, glad to be disturbed on this side of it. And not in prison.

There's a timelessness to Wright's *The Man Who Lived Underground* that has little do with some surreptitious notion of universality or some ephemeral and inexact artistic ideal. Its timelessness lies in its ability to articulate the stone, water, blood, and darkness of what it means to live between and during hostilities, hostilities thrust on a people by a nation. The novel articulates what it means to live one's life as a dream, as that which must be held on to and simultaneously discarded. Wright vocalizes and reifies terror and its temporary, itinerant assuagements.

The character of Fred Daniels embodies the utter terror of being a Black American—that at any time your life can be snatched from you. Controlling one's life belongs to someone or something else. The French philosopher Michel Foucault calls it the biopolitical. The Cameroonian historian and political theorist Achille Mbembe takes this notion a step further and calls it the necropolitical—the State having the ability to kill at will. The State deciding who dies. It is a predicament of utter, omnipresent terror. Terror that is sometimes submerged so deeply that one cannot do something as simple as walk by a police officer at the entrance of a grocery store and not feel as if one's death is ceremoniously waiting for you there next to the watermelon where the officer stands. Not allowing oneself to drift off into the terror of what if—what if the officer mistakes me pulling my cell phone from my pocket as—I stop there. I try not to lynch myself or others over and over again in my subconscious, giving America the imaginative real estate and tree that it would deny it wants though doesn't mind idly standing by, and if I put in the effort of imagining myself there going up a tree, why not, why not tug on the rope, raise my body like a dark sun into the sky?

What becomes scarier is when our White compatriots in America deploy and enact this racist imagining and State terror in our communities. In July of 2021, near my hometown of Mount Holly, New Jersey, a White man decided to verbally and physically terrorize his Black neighbors, mocking and goading them, relishing the fact that he could bait and harass them and nothing would be done about it because he was White and they occupied the pitiable position of being

Black. And nothing would be done to him because the police are, in fact, on his side. He declares this impunity while being videoed, unfazed, unashamed, and unbothered that he's being recorded, that he's providing the sentence and rope for his trial.

And why should he be bothered? The video of the incident corroborates his assertion—that the police are on his side. When a Mount Laurel police officer shows up to mediate—and I use the word *mediate* lightly and sarcastically—the dispute, which is not a dispute but an assault, the officer treats the screaming man with deference and respect. The officer doesn't upbraid the White man or demand he cease his tirade. The officer does not choke him, tase him, or shoot him when he curses and continues to verbally assault his neighbors. Instead, the officer calls the assailant by his name, Edward, and tells the man to get back, allowing the assailant to calm himself at his leisure. Eventually, the White man calms himself, finally taking the admonishment of the officer, but he also points out to his victims that the police are with him. They are his ally, and the police, for that matter, point to this fact—that they are on the assailant's side—by calling him by his name, by their show of familiarity, by their willingness to allow the assailant to stop his verbal haranguing when he felt good and ready.

These everyday practices of annihilation are not unfamiliar to Black folks or our fellow Americans. A list of names that are testament to this violence could be inserted here. Or a list of infamous moments. The killing of Medgar Evers in Mississippi by Byron De La Beckwith for championing voting and Civil Rights in 1963. The assassination of Martin Luther King in 1968. Ahmaud Arbery chased and killed by White vigilantes because he was taking a jog in his community in 2020. These incidents are pornographically and absurdly known. Timeless. This tradition, unfortunately, has become a pastime and preface to several American summers, which leads to the fashioning of the same book, the same story to follow. After the killing, protestors overwhelm the streets to express their discontent and anger; then, hand-wringing by politicians who hang their heads or kneel in contrition beneath gold-domed statehouses; then sloganeering by businesses that have under-employed and underserved Black communities and benefited from this negligence; then nothing. No, not nothing but a backsliding into the tumult of gilded and empty American morality. A cooling-off period. A muting of pain. The graffiti—Fuck the Police! Black Lives Matter! once vigorously scrawled on the highway, on sidewalks, on police station walls, on statues of Confederate generals—melts into the edifice it once gleamed against, its shouting, spray-painted colors of red and blue and white a little less bright after a few weeks of rain and sun and summer heat. And when the protests dissipate to nostalgia and memory and the mealymouthed correction made by liberal politicians is lost to the newest scandal on the news, the newest American tragedy, out of that diminished flame rises another incident—some "good" White folks harassing and harming "good" Black folks (if you let the liquor and conservative politician tell it). And the police showing up and nothing being done until there is some absurd, over-the-top video evidence of the killing of another Black person who was casually going about their day—reading, jogging, bird-watching, selling loose cigarettes.

I wonder what type of social world am I being invited into? What type of ensemble, band, country are we making here in America? It is nothing short of an apocalypse—a war. There's only so long before folks come down out of the lynching trees and refuse to go back up again. And, I'm not saying that those captured and lynched willingly and passively capitulated to their captors. We know they did not. What I'm thinking about here is what would happen if we collectively refused, collectively went underground like Fred Daniels. Or what if the underground began to be our prevailing political and social position to America? What if we brought the underground above? It is violence without violence. It would be nothing short of a revolution. Freedom.

In *The Fire Next Time*, James Baldwin cajoles his nephew not to be driven from his home, his home being America. "Great men have done great things here," writes Baldwin, "and will again, and we can make America what America must become." When I arrive at this moment in the letter, I always feel let down, as if my uncle who said he was going to come by and pick me up to toss a ball around never showed, and I'm waiting at the door, the descending night just beyond the screen mocking me. Baldwin's turn to "make America what America must become" feels as if Baldwin, himself, doesn't realize that he is trapped in history, trapped in a rhetoric of liberalism, of exceptionality, trapped in American optimism, which is a blind arrogance based upon the superiority of our alleged wit and muscle. A superiority that eschews reality, history, and experience. It is this superiority, this willful blindness, that has led to our people being billed as monstrous in the American movie playing in the streets and schools of our local communities.

Baldwin's turn at the end of the letter to love—loving our White brothers who have sought to subdue us at every turn—refuses to acknowledge America's outright, multigenerational project of homogeneity through various genocides—Native, Black, queer, women, poor folks—and how difficult it might be to trust let alone love my brother. Baldwin doubles down and writes that "great men have done great things here." Baldwin's turn toward unnamed "great men" feels a bit suspicious to me because it reminds me of the pedagogy of fourth-grade social studies—the sycophancy and making hagiography of the founding fathers, explorers, and "pioneers" who literally rampaged and ravaged the people and land to extract and cultivate this "great" America. This turn to greatness reminds me of our present mythologizing of not only American excellence (former President Trump and the far right's cry to "Make America Great Again") but also Black excellence as a counternarrative and counterargument to the historical preoccupation with Black folks' alleged inferiority and underachievement. #BlackExcellence has become a sort of superficial tag, a gimmick, that is supposed to interrupt and differently narrate the living history of Black folks enduring and succeeding within the chaos and destruction of White supremacy, but it always does so on the terms of our captors—merit, wealth production, winning, individualism. What is mostly celebrated with #BlackExcellence is how we got or are getting "the bag." But what isn't always acknowledged is who is being exploited while we're "getting the bag"—that exploitation occurring in other countries, in foreign wars, on sweatshop floors, in kitchens and bedrooms whose curtains we cannot imagine.

This ballyhooing our alleged American greatness belies the woundedness, nay, the absence of it. The turn to greatness by Baldwin is a romanticization, a move toward sentimentality, that I'm surprised to see him gesture toward especially after his trouncing of the sentimental tradition and Harriet Beecher Stowe's *Uncle Tom's Cabin* in his essay "Everybody's Protest Novel." I'm not here to slay fathers, monsters, dragons, or uncles. Baldwin's written and oral work is crucial in the thinking about where, what, and who Black people are in America, to America. In fact, there would be no Roger Reeves as a poet, essayist, playwright, or fiction writer without James Baldwin. But as a native son and a great-grandnephew of Baldwin, Wright, Malcolm X, *and* Georgia Gilmore, Fannie Lou Hamer, Ella Baker, and Queen Mother Moore, I have to ask: what is this preoccupation, this capitulation to this dream deferred, to this magic America that constantly eludes the grasp of Black folks, to these "great men"? The end of Baldwin's letter feels as if Baldwin is dangling this future liberation in front of us—his nephews, his sons and daughters—and as we grasp for it, strive for it, beseech, march, and protest for it, yet it drifts further and further from our grasp. It's as if Baldwin, unwittingly, is trapping us inside a history of striving, of progress borne upon what looks like faith but is in actuality what the late scholar Lauren Berlant would call a "cruel optimism."

And why, why would we want to continue to partake in this cruel, American optimism? America has refused us our making, cajoling, beseeching. America has refused us our very lives. Why wouldn't we go underground? Why not seek refuge in nowhere? Because the truth of the matter is our freedom resides in this nowhere, in this invisibility. Our freedom is invisible—not because it doesn't exist but because it has yet to be achieved. We must go underground not merely to escape our deaths (or at least delay them) but to figure out who we are, what we want, and what we mean to each other. Therein is our freedom, our liberation.

And who do I mean by *we*? "We who believe in freedom," says Ella Baker. We who have been blackened, raced, othered, and extracted from in order to make the American empire rise out the swamps and hollows and plantations and graves. I'm not here to elide the particularities of historical struggles. The struggle of Native Americans inside, outside, and against the American empire is not the struggle of Arab Americans inside, outside, and against the American empire. The struggle of Arab Americans inside, outside, and against the American empire is not the struggle of Black Americans inside, outside, and against the American empire. However, we are kin and comrades in our struggles against our annihilation, against our respective colonizations, racisms, and exploitations, in our struggles for self-determination here in America. As scholar Ussama Makdisi suggests, the question is "how to imagine, articulate, and enact—and to commemorate—this solidarity without privileging one discourse and experience of oppression over the other."

I'd humbly offer that the space to imagine this solidarity is underground, away from the swarming of American optimism and the fetishizing of freedom. Where we can talk among ourselves. Where we can *be* with each other. This is what I mean when I say we must know what we mean to each other. We must also be honest about what we have meant to each other, how we have harmed each other, used each other, at times, in our acquiescence to American optimism and American notions of success.

In the underground, value—what America values—submits to the distortion of darkness and darkness's defamiliarization. Careerism, wealth, nationalism, patriotism lose their hold on our imaginations because they can no longer supply the fiction of stability or safety. We must grope in the dark for what truly makes us, keeps us *US*. In the underground, our American vision is useless because it cannot rely on a veneer, a history of fraudulent illumination, a corrupt and lied-about hagiography. I'm not quite sure I'm making sense. What I might be calling toward, summoning, might feel like the ephemeral matter of a poem, of feeling. And, it might be that, too. But I assure you that even in its ephemerality it is real. It was what Fred Daniels realizes when he's underground. Money and riches become literal ornamentation—useless, nothing—because what is at stake for Daniels is his life, rescuing it from his captors, the police. When Daniels swipes a bunch of cash during one of his adventures into the belowground rooms that connect to the sewer, rather than come aboveground to use it, he lines the walls of his underground lair with it. Money no longer carries for him the allure, the seduction it once did aboveground. In the underground where what is at stake is his life, money becomes mere paper. It loses its coin because it is outside of circulation; thus, it must bear the obscenity, violence, and waifish-ness of its fiction.

The underground also allows for Daniels to hear the multidirectional, often contradictory nature of desire. I might say that he actually hears below desire—he hears desire's desire. Desire unmanicured. Desire unadorned. Desire that is truly vulnerable to itself. Which might be one of the most useful aspects of being underground—your desire, my desire only ambiguously tethered (maybe even slightly untethered) to the past, to expectation, to the nation. In order to for you to understand what I mean there's this moment that I have to describe to you from the book. Stay with me. I know we prefer our hot takes and think pieces without literary allusion or criticism, but I'll try to make this move against decorum and the zeitgeist worth it. So check it.

Daniels is in the sewer, enshrouded in darkness. The floor he's been walking on falls off precipitously. With a pole that he's been using to test the depth of the water sluicing about him, he slides down into the little room below him. He hears a voice. It's singing, a singing that's both "strange" and "familiar." A singing suffused with longing that causes Daniels to run toward it, causes him to listen closely, to listen beyond the words, beyond the notes to where urge and striving and want reside. The singing is coming from a Black church, and when Daniels slides his eye into a crevice, he sees Black men and women holding raggedy hymnals, their mouths upturned, singing about wanting Jesus to take them to heaven and wrap them in the love of his bosom. No longer in the world of the aboveground, of the Black church, he hears their singing differently. "His life had somehow snapped in two," writes Wright:

> When he had sung and prayed with his brothers and sisters
> in church, he had always felt what they felt; but here in
> the underground, distantly sundered from them, he saw a
> defenseless nakedness in their lives that made him disown
> them. A physical distance had come between them and had
> conferred upon him a terrifying knowledge. He felt that these
> people should stand silent, unrepentant, with simple manly
> pride, and yield no quarter in whimpering. He wanted them
> to assume a heroic attitude though *he himself* had run away
> from *his* tormentors, even though he had begged *his* accusers
> to believe in *his* innocence.

In this moment, Daniels resides in bewilderment—a very useful bewilderment. It is the unclean, impure, raggedy bewilderment of escape and fugitivity, which is both the front and back door to freedom. In the singing in the Black church, Daniels recognizes the need for and the enactment of a type of escape—Black folks trying to get outside of their subjection through the will of the voice, the will of the body. However, this lyric form of fugitivity bears irony and contradiction because of the singers' supplication, because of their "physical distance" from actual escape and freedom. Daniels, who has enacted a different commitment to his freedom by escaping from his captors and going underground, feels terrorized by the inadequacy of their singing, by their beseeching of an unseen God to rescue those he has seemed to ignore. Daniels would have them assume a "heroic attitude" and "stand silent, unrepentant, with simple manly pride," though "*he himself* had run away from *his* tormentors," the same tormentors "he had begged . . . to believe in *his* innocence."

Daniels himself is also sitting in the seat of irony—he himself a contradiction. This sort of contradiction is nothing but the blues, the epistemological scaffolding of Black American aesthetics. Some folks might even call it a Black surrealism, and if I were trying to write an aesthetic treatise I might go there. But, that's not where we are. We are underground and must stay there for a while—in darkness, the water sluicing about our knees. But we are not alone; we are with each other in this blackness that is also blue.

We must reside in this ironic sensibility, this swank swerving into the broken because this breaking is what it's all about. In the essay "Memories of My Grandmother," which Wright wrote as a sort of account of the personal, aesthetic, and historical ideas that influenced and conducted the writing of *The Man Who Lived Underground*, he describes this sort of breaking but in terms of characters. "This breaking, in my opinion, represents a point in life where the past falls away and the character must, in order to go on living, fling himself upon the face of the formless night and create a world, a *new* world, in which to live." Fred Daniels has flung himself into the darkness, resides in the void, in the nowhere that is the underground. The past falls away, and he must confront the contradiction that is the beginning of the freedom—the contradiction of the past as well as the contradiction of the present—that in order to create the world he desires to live in he must embrace nowhere. Nowhere is the somewhere he wants to be—where he must be. Like Daniels, we must embrace the formlessness of nowhere if we mean to come to who we want to be. We might not stay there long, but we must run away from the somewhere of our prisons.

Instructions for the Underground

: Sleep.

: Sleep some more.

: If you've made it here, wherever here is, you are probably tired and in need of rest, so rest.

: In the underground, we steal from those not in the underground.

: We try to appear as if we're not in the underground. There are people who and entities that do not want you to be here and will do anything they can to take you out of here and away from us.

: In the underground, eat well.

: Laugh.

: Dance.

: Play spades.

: Read books.

: Bake cakes.

: Fuss, fight, fuck, and carry on.

: Make mistakes.

: Forgive.

: Open the underground to others.

: Close the underground to others.

: Be here uncomfortable and be comfortable in it.

: In the underground, we afflict and comfort.

: Afflict and comfort.

: Do not require the aboveground to be the underground.

: Do not require the underground to be anything like the aboveground.

: Grace—have it, be with it.

: Don't die—then, sometimes, do.

: Be quiet when you want to.

: Your money is no good. if we decide to make money good, then we will need an underground beneath, above, or to the side of this underground.

: What will we make for each other in the dark, in the heat, in the cold, in the silence?

: Will we bring with us the songs from before?

: What will we do with the old Gods?

: The old Gods are not required to love us here.

: No God is required for entry.

: Be careful, the underground may not, in fact, be under.

: Never mistake what it is for what it ain't.

: You can hum here if you want.

: Come on, come on, come on now, don't you want to go?

: You can leave when you want, but you may not be able to get back in.

: Everything here is on the one.

: The underground moves at will—sometimes against its will, sometimes at our will.

: There is no safety here.

: Remember to sleep.

: Sleep some more.

: Eat well.

: Remember what you couldn't out there.

: There's so much not to know down here.

: Do nothing.

: Listen for what you could not hear before.

: You may already be in it—the underground.

: Some of us may never get there.

: Allow the children.

: Teach the children to forage and hunt.

: Travel only at night.

: be as definitionless as possible.

: Be.

: Wilderness.

: Reenchant failure.

: Love what you couldn't love out there.

: Come on, come on, come on now, don't you want to go?

: Build new granaries, new storehouses, new paths.

: Map none of this.

: Be as ancient as you want to be.

: Being here does not exonerate you from suffering.

: Be formless.

: Be ready to move.

: Move.

: Open the underground to others.

: Do none of this.

: Do none of this.

Something Good

1

It's the silent abandon by which they kiss, as if they are aware of someone striding toward them, this someone's finger wagging, telling them, "No, no, not here, stop that now, or I'll be forced to separate you, you profligate negroes." But before this imagined censor can reach them, they pull each other close and kiss again, their mouths disappearing into each other's, their mouths taking the shape of their longing. They touch each other as if they had just been released from something, as if their license to touch is short, stolen, or forged. In *Something Good*, the first known cinematic kiss by a Black couple filmed in 1898, it appears as if the two actors, a peach pit–toned Black man wearing a bowtie and jacket and a peach skin–toned Black woman wearing a ruffled collared dress belted at the waist, are touching each other after a long period of denial, as if they have forgotten what the other's mouth and hands and neck felt like and were now voraciously reacquainting themselves with each other. The pit of the peach swaddled by its flesh, becoming whole there on the limb of the day. Voraciously seeking itself, making itself happen—be. No, not quite voraciously, but without caution or care for who's watching, though they are both aware, and we, too, are aware that someone is watching their performance.

They do whatever they like, their arms swinging back and forth between forays of kissing, as if they are going to a carnival down by the railroad tracks or have suddenly come out of a clearing, the man having drunk water from a stream, the sky all in it and when he looked up, there she was this peach-skinned woman. The man's mouth moves as if he were remembering the taste of water, and the woman moves about him as water and what he could not predict, which is the sky and the shore that makes the water possible. In less than twenty seconds, they move together as earth moves with water, unpredictably, their kissing meeting and coming apart without a preordained or announced rhythm. Earth and water. Peach swelling into its flesh and pit on the limb of the day.

2

This was love unjailed, loose like corn silk, loose and free and scattered. This kiss, this something-good could not be accounted for, measured, borrowed against, traded for, short sold, chained, marched from port to pesthouse, coffled, rented out, quartered, sliced, enclosed, leveraged, loaned out, compounded, bought, reduced, spoiled, shuttered, stunted, remanded to the margins, exploited, extracted from, "mortgaged, won, stolen, or seized," mined or dynamited into oblivion. This kiss, this something good, could not be killed, punished, burned, Jim Crowed, couped, circumvented, forced to sit in the balcony, hung from a telephone pole, hung from a bridge because it whistled at a White woman, hung from a tree in the middle of a town square for demanding wages earned for working in some White man's field. This kiss was without tradition, therefore inaugurates tradition. Pleasure that was once remanded to the dark of cabins and cornfields, to forest floors and swamps, is now lit in the center of a movie camera's frame. Ecstasy without interruption or intervention. Freedom without the harness of propriety. Pleasure not yet yoked to spectacle.

Somehow, this kiss escaped the eye-bucking and over-exaggeration of minstrelsy, escaped the potential for it to become yet another manifestation of the White imagination circumscribing and speculating about Black life, escaped the pessimism and destruction of race in America at the precipice of the twentieth century. This kiss was love in the Nadir, in the Dark Ages of Black Freedom. The year of *Something Good*, the year of this kiss, 1898, is also the year of the Wilmington massacre. In North Carolina's largest city at the time, a city where Black people made up the majority of the population, a mob of about two thousand White supremacists not only burned their way through the Black part of town, destroying a Black-owned newspaper and killing more than three hundred people but also overthrew the local Fusionist biracial government, deposing both White and Black elected officials in the only successful coup in the history of the United States. This mob installed public officials who would inaugurate a brutal regime of exclusion that we would come to know as Jim Crow. The phenomena of White mobs burning and lynching their way through Black enclaves occurred all over the South during the Black Nadir. In the middle of such horrors, in a movie studio in Chicago, two Black actors, Saint Suttle and Gertie Brown, kissed, and it was recorded on celluloid.

Their silent kissing offers a symbolic counterbalance to the loud terror of the mob. And not just the mobs of post-Reconstruction America but also the paterollers and slave masters and senators that upheld slavery from the country's founding. Suttle and Brown kiss in the middle of ongoing catastrophe, in the middle of our American eyes. They embrace a transparency that's disarming in its vibrancy and clarity. It feels—no, it is revolutionary in its unabashed intimacy, an intimacy to be worn and borne publicly, an intimacy that seems to burst forth from its hiding place. During slavery, intimacy was fraught because slavery erected not only a barrier between the self and another, but it also threw up barriers within oneself. What is intimacy when it and the feelings that come from it can be claimed by another; when another, someone who calls himself master, can claim the body that feeling runs through?

In *Something Good*, it's as if Suttle and Brown refuse the barriers and walls of slavery, refuse the surveillance and apartheid of post-Reconstruction America, as if they were the grandchildren reared on their parents and grandparents stories of having to eke out moments of pleasure during the spectacle and banality of slavery, heard stories of sprigs of lavender and mint placed in a doorway or in a handle of an iron to sweeten the sweat and labor of cleaning and cooking and tending and mending in a White woman's kitchen, heard stories of going to bodies of water to hush the sound of study and meeting a lover one was forbidden to meet; it's as if Suttle and Brown mixed in these stories with their own desire and kissed and kissed and kissed. Loose, free, and scattered.

3

Why is their kissing so loud? I hear it, hear them despite the kiss occurring in the black-and-white silence of the film. Maybe this inexplicable and unlocated loudness is the "something" of the title. "Something" about a kiss. "Something" about the way it opens a man's face into a bright noise. After each kiss, Suttle pulls back from Brown and his face bursts into an explosion of satisfaction and ecstasy. You can almost hear him say, "Ahhh, now that's it—that's it." His face in its ecstatic glee, the sound of it, reminds me of the dark brown faces and voices of older men that I have loved in my life—sometimes very difficult men who died very difficult deaths and lived difficult lives before those difficult deaths. One, for instance, dragged down a road when his pant leg was caught in the door of a car, his body eventually thrown across a field, his body coming to rest only when a fence post impaled his head. The scar of it, the post's impaling, he carried with him in and out the barbershop he worked in, carried it with him when leaning back against one of the walls in the barbershop, a curtain of smoke falling about him as he puffed and grinned into a Newport. He carried the scar with him to his death, which occurred less than ten years after the incident. The scar, his cratered and forever-dented head all because a woman saw her husband coming down the road and sped off before this man could exit the car properly. Despite these difficulties, I have glimpsed moments of this sort of ecstasy, this sort of satisfaction that creases Suttle's face, this "something good" in the faces of these difficult men, these men thrown down by both life and unwise decisions, thrown down upon the road and dragged to their deaths. I have heard this joy, this bright noise in their faces despite their difficult lives, sometimes because someone or something beautiful crossed their paths or because a trumpet's plaintive wail made its way out of a radio speaker and touched something deep down in them, and you hear them shout, "you ought to be more careful."

"You ought to be more careful," my grandfather would shout and shake his head when I made him laugh, delighting him while standing on the shore of some creek or river in the early morning, a fishing pole in my hand, the leaves overhead scattering their shadows on the surface of the water. My grandfather, too, was a difficult man who died a difficult death—a heart attack while in the hospital being treated for emphysema. The man gasping for breath, his heart, unable to take the stress of his laboring, gave out. The beginning of his life—orphan, having to steal in order to feed himself—as difficult as his end. Yet, the man loved to cut up and laugh, his thin, brown face often becoming nothing but a large grin and cheeks.

In the bursts of joy that flood Suttle's face, I hear a shout, I hear my grandfather's "you ought to be more careful," an announcement of a surplus of satisfaction—"a something good" that cannot be controlled, cannot be measured. It is an outburst that lacks self-consciousness. Not one stitch of embarrassment wrinkles Suttle's brow or scatters across his face. There's no worry of what we, the viewer, might think. There's only the woman in front of him. Although he is an actor and therefore laboring, there's nothing in his face that suggest fatigue or exhaustion, the laboriousness of work. Nothing feels contrived or says, "I can't wait until this is over." There, in Suttle's face, is a territory of possibility. His face conveys the joy of asking to be in joy and enjoyed. Could you imagine—being directed to be in a state of pleasure not for others but for oneself? It appears as if Suttle directs himself toward pleasure, finds something beyond the direction to kiss, finds something good.

4

Gertie Brown finds something so good that she can do nothing but shake her head at it, shake her head at the man on the other side of her who dips his head down and kisses her. In the writing, I typed "sips" instead of "dips." Maybe that's what Brown is shaking her head at— that she becomes what is on the other side of his thirst. And that he is on the other side of her—her thirst, her pleasure, her playing with pleasure in front of this new technology called a movie camera. I want to stay with her shaking her head for a moment. Maybe her bashfully shaking her head "no, no" is again another manifestation of a surplus of satisfaction and the irony of being all in it, being in the middle of something that overwhelms you with its goodness. So overwhelmed, in fact, that she must turn her head away from his as if in removing him from her sight she staunches the feelings that convulse and breach the banks inside her.

In the turning of her head away from Suttle, Brown reminds me of my grandmother refusing to look at my grandfather at his funeral. Yes, this the orphaned grandfather of the difficult life, the grandfather who left my grandmother in her late thirties for another woman just two towns, a cornfield, and cow pasture over. My grandmother turned her head like Brown when she walked up to the casket to look at my grandfather one last time before the eulogy. I remember it well. Someone prodded her to go look at my grandfather because she had refused to do so throughout the service. Not even during the viewing of the body before the service did she cast her gaze toward my grandfather laying in a tan suit in the casket, a tan suit with a chocolate stain on the lapel. My grandmother sat, turned away from him in the small, warm chapel of the funeral parlor, the polished wood panels gleaming on that overcast afternoon. My grandmother kept her body tilted on the seat as if she were trying to overhear something my grandfather might say but without looking at him, her ear cast over her shoulder. It appeared as if she expected to hear an apology or acknowledgment of the life they shared since she was a teen. Finally, when none came, because the dead cannot offer in death what they would not offer in life, someone cajoled her, nudging her, then pulling her gently up by the elbow, escorting her to edge of the casket to witness what death and the mortician had done to my grandfather. It might have been my mother, her daughter, who escorted her to the edge of the casket and prodded her to look, to look down at her former husband. In fact, I think it was my mother who took my grandmother by the elbow and stood with her until she could no longer look at him.

My mother was also my first example of loving, abiding, and being with difficulty, which I have yet to master. How could she love this man who left her mother in a house with one apple tree in the backyard, a falling down shed, and bats in the basement? Perhaps, my mother's love for her father was because despite the breakup between he and her mother, he never stopped loving and caring for her and her mother. When a bat that had taken up residence in a dark corner of the basement decided to fly about the house sending us all to hide in the television room, it was my grandfather who came over with a net, trapped the bat, and brought his size seven brogans down on its head (his words not mine). And, it was my grandfather with his eighth grade understanding of mathematics who came over and built a new shed from scratch, all be it with his own sense of measurements which meant that he would have to re-hang the door several times because he didn't build the shed according to the specifications that came with it. It was also my grandfather who would sometimes watch my sister and I when my mother or grandmother had to work overtime.

But this is about my grandmother, her walking up to the casket, peering over the side of it, and when she was sure it was my grandfather, she turned from him, shaking her head as if to say, "yes, that's him, and he's dead." It was the same sort of head shake that Gertie Brown offers us and Saint Suttle—surplus, being in the middle of something and being in disbelief, which is a form of belief. My grandmother's head shake of "yes" also bore a bit of "no," as in "no, I can't believe it ended this way." I can't be sure, but I believe I heard her say such—that she couldn't imagine my grandfather dying like he had—fearful, choking, then a heart attack. Sometimes, I see my grandmother standing on the plush burgundy carpet in the funeral parlor looking down at my grandfather. I hold her where she refused to stay, her head shaking at this love that was now dead in a casket wearing her grandson's suit that no longer fit him, a stain on the lapel.

5

We are suspicious of beauty because of its shifting, opaque, and often diffuse definition. Depending upon who holds or manipulates beauty, utters something about it, there tends to be in that utterance, in that holding or manipulating, power—a wresting and hoarding of it. Beauty becomes the weather—the sun and rain—by which all the people beneath it must ask or pray for mercy, for grace, for a kind visitation, for it not to bruise their heads with too much heat or flood their fields or houses with too much water. To be found outside beauty or without beauty is often to be found sitting in the seat of the scornful—unlucky, condemned, graceless, and unfavored. Beauty becomes tied to success, goodness, truth, divinity, and moral rectitude. A bean to be counted, to be measured and weighed against, beauty is a chit and so can become a weapon, a means of exploitation, a fungible commodity, a gimmick. And, in the transaction, those who possess and manipulate beauty hold and wield a power they should have never been given or taken. We are right to be suspicious of beauty. So when I say *Something Good* is beautiful, I am aware that I am wading into this fraught territory of exclusion, power, and marginalization. But dammit, their kissing, their frolicking in and with each other inside the frame of that film is beautiful because it lacks what exclusion, power, and marginalization do not— domination. When Suttle pulls Brown toward him or Brown turns her face from Suttle, nothing about their pulling or tugging upon each other is about a struggle for power. They revel in the pulling, in the tugging— being drawn to each other. They hold hands and swing their arms back and forth as if cradling and nurturing beauty between them—the beauty born there in the moment of them coming together.

There is also something else there, something I can't name, but I know it's participating in me calling them, calling this film, beautiful. Something ineffable and simultaneously delightful. It's actually more than delight, more than pleasure, more than justice and permission. Maybe it's freedom. It's as if in this cinematic moment between Brown and Suttle, we've been released from something, as if we've closed our eyes and now can see what we could not see before, feel what we could not feel before. Maybe its beauty. Maybe that's what beauty truly is— sensing something beyond sight but requiring both a corroboration and subversion of what we think we know of seeing, feeling. Maybe it's moving beyond or below noise. Maybe that something is silence—that silence makes a thing—makes a life—beautiful. Beauty not in noise but in what is without. Beauty as that which takes away, and in the taking away makes life more abundant. Maybe that—sound without sound. Eyes closed and seeing. Maybe what Brown and Suttle offer for twenty seconds is paradise but without borders, dread, exclusions, a nemesis, or a need to keep out the other. Paradise without a gimmick or an angel at its gates with a flaming sword. Maybe they offer us an invitation to our own beauty, an invitation to feel without the previous harnesses and gates thrown up in front of us. And it is all done silently. Silently. Not because their love is without sound but because absence of sound offers us more possibility, makes manifest what we couldn't feel before.

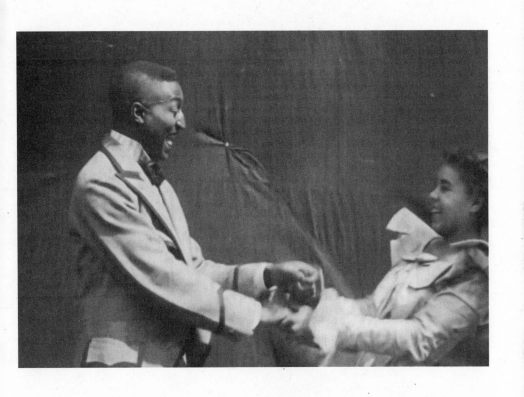

Selected Bibliography

Agamben, Giorgio. *What Is an Apparatus? and Other Essays.* David Kishik and Stefan Pedatella, trans. Stanford, CA: Stanford UP, 2009.

Baldwin, James. *Collected Essays.* Toni Morrison, ed. New York: Library of America, 1998.

Baradaran, Mehrsa. *The Color of Money: Black Banks and the Racial Wealth Gap.* Cambridge, MA: Belknap Press of Harvard UP, 2017.

Brown, Jericho. *Please.* Kalamazoo, MI: New Issues Poetry and Prose, 2008.

Borges, Jorge Luis. *Selected Poems.* New York: Penguin, 1999.

Douglass, Frederick. *Narrative of the Life of Frederick Douglass, an American Slave, Written by Himself.* David W. Blight, ed. Boston: Bedford/St. Martin's, 2002.

Eady, Cornelius. *Hardheaded Weather: New and Selected Poems.* New York: Penguin, 2008.

Eliot, T. S. *Four Quartets.* New York: Harcourt, 1943.

Edwards, Brent Hayes. *Epistrophies: Jazz and the Literary Imagination.* Cambridge, MA: Harvard UP, 2017.

Erskine, Noel Leo. *Plantation Church: How African American Religion Was Born in Caribbean Slavery.* New York: Oxford UP, 2014.

Foucault, Michel. *Fearless Speech.* Joseph Pearson, ed. Los Angeles: Semiotext(e), 2001.

Gilbert, Christopher. *Across the Mutual Landscape.* Port Townsend, WA: Graywolf, 1984.

Hannah-Jones, Nikole, Caitlin Roper, Ilena Silverman, and Jake Silverstein, eds. *The 1619 Project: A New Origin Story.* New York: One World, 2021.

Hartman, Saidiya. *Scenes of Subjection: Terror, Slavery, and Self-Making in Nineteenth-Century America.* New York: Oxford UP, 1997.

Harvey, Paul. *Through the Storm, Through the Night: A History of African American Christianity.* Lanham, MD: Rowman and Littlefield, 2001.

Hurston, Zora Neale. "Drenched in Light." *The Portable Harlem Renaissance Reader*. David Levering Lewis, ed. New York: Penguin, 1994.

King, Tiffany Lethabo. *The Black Shoals: Offshore Formations of Black and Native Studies*. Durham, NC: Duke UP, 2019.

Makdisi, Ussama. "Racism and Sectarianism." Translation and the Afterlives of Anglophone Theory (https://tif.ssrc.org/2021/07/21/racism-and-sectarianism/), July 21, 2021.

Mayes, Kyle T. *An Afro-Indigenous History of the United States*. Boston: Beacon Press, 2021.

Mbembe, Achille. *Critique of Black Reason*. Laurent DuBois, trans. Durham, NC: Duke UP, 2017.

Miles, Tiya. *Ties That Bind: The Story of an Afro-Cherokee Family in Slavery and Freedom* (2nd ed.). Oakland: University of California Press, 2015.

Morrison, Toni. *Beloved*. New York: Random House, 1987.

Moten, Fred. *In the Break: The Aesthetics of the Black Radical Tradition*. Minneapolis: University of Minnesota Press, 2003.

Raboteau, Albert J. *Slave Religion: The "Invisible Institution" in the Antebellum South*. New York: Oxford UP, 1978.

Robinson, Cedric. *Black Marxism: The Making of the Black Radical Tradition*. Chapel Hill: University of North Carolina Press, 1983.

Sharif, Solmaz. *LOOK*. Minneapolis: Graywolf, 2016.

Treuer, David. *The Heartbeat of Wounded Knee: Native America from 1890 to the Present*. New York: Penguin Random House, 2019.

Wall, Cheryl A. *On Freedom and the Will to Adorn: The Art of the American Essay*. Chapel Hill: University of North Carolina Press, 2018.

Wright, Richard. *The Man Who Lived Underground*. New York: Library of America, 2021.

Acknowledgments

Versions of these essays have appeared in the following journals: *Granta, The Sewanee Review, NACLA Report, The Dirty South: Contemporary Art, Material Culture, and the Sonic Impulse, The Yale Review, Harriet* (the blog for *Poetry* magazine), *Virginia Quarterly Review.*

The photograph that accompanies "The Angel of History" was taken by Julio Jimenez.

I would also like to acknowledge the people who have helped my thinking along the way (in no particular order): Monica Jimenez, Claudette Reeves, Elloree Lewis, Daniel Black, Melvin Rahming, Meta DuEwa Jones, Matt Richardson, Natalie Diaz, Solmaz Sharif, Malachi Black, Meghan O'Rourke, Eric Smith, Randi Gill-Sadler, Chris Loperena, Courtney Morris, Martin Perna, Naima Jimenez-Reeves, Ana Schwartz, Jenny Kelly, Marisol LeBrón, Ashley Farmer, Pavithra Vasudevan, Nicole Burrowes, Minkah Makalani, Edmund T. Gordon, Terrance Hayes, Tracy K. Smith, Jericho Brown, Natasha Trethewey, Kyle Churney, Jenisha Watts, W. Ralph Eubanks.

I would also like to thank Jeff Shotts for his exacting, compassionate, and intelligent pen, Casey O'Neil and Ill Nippashi for their belief in this book, Katie Dublinski for her precise editorial eye, Chantz Erolin for the conversations and permission, Carmen Giménez for her championing the book, and everyone at Graywolf who works on behalf of bringing writers' ideas out of our caves and into the world.

I would also like to thank Eric Simonoff for shepherding some of these essays to the better states and for the guidance. And for long conversation about jazz.

Roger Reeves is the author of two poetry collections, *King Me* and *Best Barbarian*, which was a finalist for the National Book Award and winner of the Kingsley Tufts Poetry Award, and was named a *New York Times* Notable Book. His essays and poems have appeared in *Poetry*, the *New Yorker*, *Granta*, the *Yale Review*, and elsewhere. He is a recipient of a National Endowment for the Arts fellowship, a Ruth Lilly and Dorothy Sargent Rosenberg Fellowship from the Poetry Foundation, a 2015 Whiting Award, and a Radcliffe Fellowship from Harvard University. He teaches at the University of Texas at Austin.

The text of *Dark Days* is set in Warnock Pro. Book design by Ann Sudmeier. Composition by Bookmobile Design & Digital Publisher Services, Minneapolis, Minnesota. Manufactured by Friesens on acid-free, 100 percent postconsumer wastepaper.